The New Puritan
Generation

edited by

José Francisco Fernández

Gylphi

The New Puritan
Generation

A *Gylphi Limited* Book

First published in Great Britain in 2013
by Gylphi Limited

Copyright © Gylphi Limited, 2013

A CIP catalogue record for this book is available from the British Library.

ISBN 978-1-78024-015-2 (pbk)
ISBN 978-1-78024-016-9 (Kindle)
ISBN 978-1-78024-017-6 (EPUB)

Design and typesetting by Gylphi Limited. Printed in the UK by imprintdigital. com, Exeter.

Gylphi Limited
PO Box 993
Canterbury CT1 9EP, UK

Contents

Acknowledgements

I would like to thank all the contributors for their enthusiasm, energy and dedication to the project. I am most grateful to Nicholas Blincoe and Matt Thorne for kindly answering my questions on the New Puritans. Paul March-Russell provided continuous support. My sincere thanks also go to Leo Hollis, Richard Beard, Ignacio Padilla and Vladimir Arsenijević for their help. On a personal level, I would like to dedicate the present collection of essays to my kids, Jose and Blanca, who have happily delayed the completion of this book. This one is for you, guys, with boundless affection.

The editor

Notes on Contributors

Miriam Borham-Puyal completed her BA in English Philology at the University of Salamanca, where she currently teaches English language and literature. Her fields of interest are women writers and the presence of Cervantes' *Don Quixote* in British literature. She has written an entry on satirical Quixotes for the *Gran Enciclopedia Cervantina*, as well as papers and articles on female quixotism.

José Francisco Fernández is Senior Lecturer in English Literature at the University of Almería, Spain. He has published widely on the contemporary British short story, including articles in journals such as *Journal of the Short Story in English, ZAA, AUMLA* and *Irish Studies in Europe*. He is co-editor of *Contemporary Debates on the Short Story* (Peter Lang, 2007) and he has recently edited *A Day in the Life of a Smiling Woman. The Collected Stories*, by Margaret Drabble (Penguin, 2011).

David James teaches modern and contemporary literature in the School of English and Drama at Queen Mary, University of London. He is author of *Contemporary British Fiction and the Artistry of Space* (2008), and, most recently, of *Modernist Futures* (Cambridge University Press, 2012). He has edited a number of collections, including *The Legacies of Modernism: Historicizing Postwar and Contemporary Fiction* (Cambridge University Press, 2011), and has guest-edited with Andrzej Gasiorek a special issue of *Contemporary Literature* on 'Fiction since 2000: Post-Millennial Commitments'. With Matthew Hart and Rebecca L. Walkowitz, he edits the book series *Literature Now* for Columbia University Press. He is currently editing *The Cambridge Companion to British Fiction since 1945* (forthcoming 2015).

Bianca Leggett is a final year PhD candidate at Birkbeck, University of London, who has recently submitted her thesis, *Englishness Elsewhere: Negotiating English Identity in the Contemporary Travel Novel*. She has published articles on backpacker fiction and Black British travel narratives and has reviewed for *Textual Practice, Contemporary Literature* and *Twentieth Century Literature*. She was the co-covener of the conference *Twenty-First Century British Fiction* in May 2012.

Paul March-Russell teaches Comparative Literature at the University of Kent, Canterbury. He is the author of *The Short Story: An Introduction* (Edinburgh University Press, 2009) and, with Carmen Casaliggi, co-editor of *Ruskin in Perspective* (Cambridge Scholars Publishing, 2007) and *Legacies of Romanticism* (Routledge, 2012). *The Postcolonial Short Story*, co-edited with Maggie Awadalla, is forthcoming from Palgrave. He is currently writing *Modernism and Science Fiction* also for publication with Palgrave.

Sara Martín is a Senior Lecturer in English Literature and Cultural Studies at the Universitat Autònoma de Barcelona, Spain; she also teaches at the online Universitat Oberta de Catalunya. Dr. Martín specialises in Gender Studies, particularly Masculinity Studies, which she applies to the study of popular fictions in English, with an emphasis on science fiction and horror. She has published extensively on Gender Studies, popular fictions and film adaptations. Among her books are *Monstruos al final del milenio* (2002), *Expediente X: En honor a la verdad* (2006), *Recycling Cultures* (ed., 2006), *La literatura* (2008) and *Desafíos a la heterosexualidad obligatoria* (2011).

Laura Monrós-Gaspar is university lecturer and researcher at the Universitat de València. Among her recent publications are *Cassandra the Fortune-Teller: Prophets, Gipsies and Victorian Burlesque* (Levante Editori, 2011) and *Persiguiendo a Safo: Escritoras victorianas y mitología clásica* (JPM, 2012). In 2004 she became member of GRATUV (Grup de Recerca i Acció Teatral de la Universitat de València) where she is now a research fellow. At present she is Honorary Research Associate at the Archive of Performances of Greek and Roman Drama at the University of Oxford.

David Owen lectures in English Literature at Universitat Autònoma de Barcelona (UAB). A graduate of the University of Edinburgh, he wrote his PhD at the UAB on the early stylistic development of Jane Austen. His research and publications focus principally on Austen's literary beginnings, the history of the English Novel and epistolarity. In 2010, he published the first ever monographic study on Austen's *Lady Susan* (*Rethinking Jane Austen's Lady Susan*, Edwin Mellen) and is currently preparing a critical edition of Anna Maria Porter's *Walsh Colville*, due to be published in 2013.

Sonia Villegas-López is Associate Professor of English Literature at the University of Huelva, Spain. She has done research on Gender Studies and contemporary women's writing in English. She is the author of two monographs on Anglophone women's fiction of the late twentieth-century and feminist theology (*Mujer y religión en la narrativa anglófona contemporánea*, 1999; *El sexo olvidado: Introducción a la teología feminista*, 2005). Lately, she has co-authored *Transnational Poetics: Asian Canadian Women's Fiction of the 1990s* (2011).

Chapter 1

Introduction

José Francisco Fernández

1. The birth of a new sensibility

Reading the assessments on British fiction that were regularly published in the 1990s a certain sense of complacency can be gleaned, as if the novel published in Britain at the time had reached its prime, having left behind previous accusations of provincialism, introspection and lack of adventure.

There were reasons to be satisfied. The writers who had emerged in the late 1960s and in the 1970s flourished in the following decade, producing some of their finest pieces by placing themselves outside outdated modes of narration (Fay Weldon, Beryl Bainbridge, Martin Amis, Ian McEwan, Salman Rushdie, Angela Carter, Rose Tremain...). The new writers of the 1980s had added vigour and freshness to this scenario, contributing with unusually rich forms of invention (Jeanette Winterson, Hanif Kureishi, Ben Okri, Alan Hollinghurst, Kazuo Ishiguro...). It seemed, then, that a healthy and modern form had at last become consolidated. The British novel had somehow come full circle starting with the brilliance of Modernism in the first decades of the twentieth century and ending in the 1990s with a fresh surge of creativity. In the words of Malcolm Bradbury, writing in the first issue of *New Writing*:

> Aesthetically, it [British fiction] is equally plural, ranging freely from one genre to another, from the detective story to science fiction, the historical novel to the post-modern pastiche, reviving forms of writing from the past while experimenting with the often media-based forms of the future. (Bradbury, 1992: 9)

Things had been done properly, a dignified status had finally been achieved and the reward was justly earned, and consequently Bradbury (1992: 8) spoke about new writing characterized by 'its variety and pluralism, its multiplicity of expression, its breadth of voices'.

Three years later, in the same publication (*New Writing 4*), A. S. Byatt (1995: 439) shared Bradbury's views on the good quality of British fiction in the early 1990s and the excellent prospects for the novel in the years to follow: 'I do think the British novel at the moment is full of truly inventive writing – new forms are being discovered, old forms are being subtly altered, there is a sense that anything is possible and, moreover, anything has a chance of being taken seriously'. Critics and scholars were basking in the glow of the roaring fire fed by a variety of fiction: writers from the Celtic fringe of Britain were producing outstanding works, women's writing had never been such a prominent part of the mainstream as it was then, 'new voices' from countries which had once belonged to the Empire had undoubtedly enriched and energized British fiction. Even repulsion and abjection in sexual matters, including descriptions of physical violence by the boldest of novelists was perfectly admitted, and playing with history was a readers' favourite.

However, one cannot help noticing that there was a residual sense of belletrism in the critics' assessment of fiction published at that time in the British Isles. A. S. Byatt (1995: 441) celebrated the 'excitingly *mongrel* nature' (emphasis in original) in the finalists for the 'Twenty Best of Young British Novelists (1993)' for which she was a member of the panel. It was good to be hybrid as long as it was framed in a good novel.

Malcolm Bradbury himself could not help feeling the ennui that sometimes accompanies the feeling of having been well nurtured and satiated. I had the opportunity to interview him in the mid-1990s and he told me that the established writers of the day were very much living on the surge of energy of the previous decade, when powerful ideas had triggered the writers' imagination. For him, the world had changed radically after the collapse of Communism, but British authors were continuing with old forms, unaware of the fact that the approaching end of the millennium demanded a new literary conscience: 'The world has changed far more than writing has and we haven't yet generated the new writing' (cited in Fernández, 1998: 225). What he was looking for, he said, was someone who could

> describe the world that follows this [the fall of the Berlin Wall], and describe it not just in terms of its habits, and not some commonplace facts, but a story that was really about that great sense of difference, and who could actually articulate this as the writers of the Romantic Movement did after the French Revolution. (cited in Fernández, 1998: 225)

Bradbury did not complain about the absence of good writers. There were plenty of gifted artists: that was not the point. What he found missing was the 'magician' of the moment, someone to grasp the spirit of the confusing, heady times they were living at the end of the century.

It is fanciful to imagine a new Milan Kundera or an updated version of Václav Havel disregarded by critics and unknown by the general public, but let us imagine that the new writer had not just been released from prison in Eastern Europe, or that he/she had not secretly been writing their big novel in some miserable bedsit while working part-time in an obscure administrative job. Perhaps the new writing, the literature that encapsulated the hollow excitement of the times had not one but multiple faces and could be found just round the corner, in the shopping centres, the disco-clubs and in the streets of suburban neighbourhoods. Perhaps in the 1990s no coherent concept of culture could be encapsulated anymore by just one single style or an encompassing worldview, because:

> Everything had gone all slippery, like spilt mercury; and when the tweezers of criticism tried to pick up a trend or a product or an event it seemed to split up into cunning little sub-sections of itself, scattering hither and thither with a wanton disregard for any singularity of purpose – any one meaning. (Bracewell, 2002: 2)

Times had changed indeed and they did not have the shape anyone would have predicted for a grand finale as befitted the end of the millennium. There was a sense of provisionality in all spheres of life, and the new urbanscape was neither downtown Manhattan nor a semi-detached house of the professional middle-classes in Chelsea, Hampstead or St John's Wood, but places like the Old Pier in Weston-Super-Mare, the epitome of English tackiness, where the protagonist of Matt Thorne's novel, *Tourist* (1998), dresses up as a cabaret artist in an attempt to revive the fortunes of a seedy music hall venue. Sarah Patton, the protagonist of Thorne's first incursion into long narratives, was more a representative of the cultural atmosphere of the 1990s than any frustrated over-intellectualized fictive writer going through a self-destructive middle age crisis. 'I'm twenty-seven years old and I don't know who I am' (Thorne, 2001: 231), says Sarah reflecting upon her own life. She earns her living in a low-paid job, searches for meaning in a number of personal relationships finding sex instead, goes out to pubs or clubs ending up in other people's houses and is as devoid of cultural referents as the rest of her friends, with video-games and bowling alleys as the main highlights in her daily drudgery.

My point is that a new kind of fiction which never reached the bestseller lists was lurking in the shadows of mainstream publishing in the last decade of the twentieth century and that it contained the seeds for the narrative of the new millennium. The literary novel, understood as an artistically ambitious work of fiction, more than 30,000 words long, not commercial and not genre (Jack, 2003: 11) was seen as an outmoded form by a new generation of writers who thrived on sub-standard literature and who lived in a consumerist world. Tony White put it succinctly when, thinking on the motivation for putting together his anthology of alternative writing *britpulp!* (1999), he said:

Just developing the idea about the writers who were emerging in the mid-nineties, who seemed to be ignoring any orthodox 'literary' canon, and taking some kind of cue from popular fiction of the sixties and seventies. The ones who were any good, that is. It felt like an important moment that no one was picking up on. (cited in Marshall, 2002)

Most of the new writers who did not fit into the prevailing pattern of high literary standards did not go to the lengths of Tony White in his first novel, *Road Rage!* (1997) when he imposed himself the rules of not spending more than two weeks on its composition, not doing any research and not forgetting to include at least one scene of sex or violence in every chapter (cited in Marshall, 2002), but it is nevertheless true that they wrote against the canon, or rather, they did not care about following the tradition of their elders, which was already showing signs of jadedness.

The dominant literary novel, different voices complained, was more concerned with plunging into the past, following the classic 'what went wrong' theme, trying to make sense of a country dealing with decline as a worrying yet comfortable topic. Speaking in 1994, J. G. Ballard compared English writers with the regular customer at a restaurant, going back again and again to the same flavours: 'What happened twenty years ago, or thirty years ago, or even half an hour ago tends to be the subject matter of most English fiction; it is profoundly retrospective' (cited in Self, 2006: 28), he said. Similarly, Ian Jack complained of the stress on self-examination so characteristic of English novels of the mid-1990s. They were not necessarily historic fictions, but they all dealt 'with the country and people that seemed to be there a minute ago, before we blinked and turned away' (Jack, 1996: 8).

Whatever its merits, or lack of them, the fiction that could not find an outlet in established printing presses was furiously located in the present time, proudly wearing the badge of modernity as teenagers flaunted the names of fashion designers on the elastic bands of their underwear. It was simply the arrival of a new concept of writing that was gradually expanding among younger authors, a fresh approach to literature by youths who were not ashamed of their long hours in front of the TV or of the time they spent playing with their Nintendo. The house of literature was treated as one treats any other house, not as the sacrosanctum of their forefathers. That was the new spirit that was being adopted by a then unknown generation of writers. It is significant that, at the beginning of his apprenticeship as a writer, Toby Litt counted among his guiding principles: 'Most particularly, to trust to the contemporary. Not to hedge. Not to try and write something that looks like literature, smells like literature, etc.' (cited in Mahoney, 2000). For many, like literary agent Jonny Geller, this meant 'a scaling down of ambition', the English novel being turned into a 'kind of contemporary sitcom' (cited in Cowley, 1999: 13). At the other end of the spectrum, an editor of alternative short stories like Sarah Champion (1997: xiv) believed that the porous quality of the new fiction was something natural; fiction could receive the influence of disco music just as the Beat generation in the 1950s had been affected by jazz.

The new attitude in young British fiction was not of course something that appeared overnight. There were forerunners, signs that predicted a change in literary perceptions, early flashes of a changing mode in the way literature could be understood. Since the 1980s some American writers had been using a style characterized by its complete immersion in consumer society. What was generally termed as 'blank fiction' featured a set of motives that now sound familiar when examining radical British fiction of the 1990s: furiously contemporary texts in which the young, idle scions of an affluent middle class showed more than simple curiosity in gratuitous violence, repulsive scenes and sexual perversions. The narrators were normally the youths themselves, casting a morally empty glance at what surrounded them, their own world clearly defined by television programmes, cult movies and video games. Bret Easton Ellis appears as the high priest of the neutral school of writing, with his characteristic ambivalence between high and low culture, his interest in shallowness and his metafictional devices. Ellis, too, represents an oblique form of social criticism that has frequently been overlooked:

> Blank fiction writers have an exceptionally sophisticated apprehension of the excesses of our culture and show them from within, posing a criticism which is not directly voiced through a narrator but through the textual implications and the excesses that are satirized in their blank writings. (Baelo-Allué, 2011: 35)

Ellis' debut novel, *Less than Zero* (1985), and particularly his third novel *American Psycho* (1991), set the course for a whole generation of budding writers to follow. Douglas Coupland was not far behind; his novel *Generation X. Tales for an Accelerated Culture* (1991) brought into prominence the lives of underemployed, highly educated youths with few perspectives for a promising future.

Back in Britain, the novels and short stories of Irvine Welsh showed that powerful narratives could be built out of the lives of underprivileged characters, and furthermore, that the use of expletives and slang would be an integral part of them. *Trainspotting* (1993) was more than a referent for the generation that would start publishing at the end of the decade. Welsh's fluency and apparent carelessness in matters of style, his unashamed breaking down of genre barriers and his refusal to be dragged down by boredom or complacency created a powerful impact on younger artists: anything was possible, anyone could write, any story was valid. If Martin Amis complained at the time of literature having turned into 'the great garden that is always there and is open to everyone twenty-four hours a day' (Amis, 2002: xiv), the young writers were squatters in that carefully maintained garden, having jumped the fence and peed in the hedges.

2. An elusive literary generation

This, in broad terms, is the breeding ground that favoured the publication of the anthology of short stories, *All Hail the New Puritans* (2000), edited by Nicholas Blincoe and Matt Thorne, chosen here as the representative collection of a whole style of writing and a particular moment in English literature. The act of defining a generation is fraught with perils, particularly in this case when all of those who took part in it characteristically disavowed the whole enterprise somehow or other. When asked about the collection years after its publication, most of the writers dismissed their contribution to it, denying being part of a group and playing down its importance as something episodic, circumstantial and inconsequential:

> I think the general consensus on the *New Puritans* is that we were all a load of wankers with an over-inflated sense of what we were doing. If I hadn't been part of it, perhaps I would have thought that too – after all, I'm not sure we put across what we were trying to do in the most diplomatic way. But I can't resist a manifesto, and it was a good idea ... But being referred to as 'New Puritan, Scarlett Thomas' does wind me up. As they say, you shag one sheep ... Anyway, it was years ago and it was an experiment. (Scarlett Thomas cited in Purbright, 2005)

Curiously enough, their transitory gathering together for the book made them typical of the prevalent attitude of the times; their indifferent, casual approach to the whole affair was what marked them as members of a contradictory, ephemeral but nevertheless distinguishable literary movement. Four women and eleven men, most of them born in England, contributed to the collection: Scarlett Thomas, Alex Garland, Ben Richards, Nicholas Blincoe, Candida Clark, Daren King, Geoff Dyer, Matt Thorne, Anna Davis, Bo Fowler, Matthew Branton, Simon Lewis, Tony White, Toby Litt and Rebbecca Ray. At the time of the publication of the book, they were in their late 20s and early 30s, and had already published a couple of novels. Geoff Dyer was the eldest, 42, and the most experienced writer of the group – his first novel, *The Colour of Memory*, went back to 1989.

The claim for the participants in *All Hail the New Puritans* to be grouped as a literary generation needs further consideration. They certainly shared some of the aforementioned attitudes common to anti-establishment writers: they were commercially focused, colloquial-language adepts, furiously contemporary and, above all, willing to take part in a playful and stimulating adventure like writing a story for a book with a manifesto stated from the outset. In any case, a generous amount of artistic licence can be taken if one belongs to the vanguard of a literary movement, and tools like a manifesto can later be disowned if need be. The manifesto, furthermore, can be interpreted both as a question of nailing their colours and as a gesture in itself, a mark of their existence.

When the book was launched, they were met with a storm of criticism and the problem of the harsh antagonism that they found was that the critics took the initiative at face value, not realizing that it was in part a strategic move by two intelligent editors in order to find an outlet for a good idea: they had wrapped themselves up in a movement to accompany the publication of a book of short stories. Among their many contrasting features, it must be said that the movement was very much a virtual one; no press conference was announced to issue a declaration, no final document was passed around for the participants to sign, but it is nevertheless true that the contributors enjoyed doing what they were asked to do. Their atypical features can be best exemplified if the concept of a founder is applied here: any literary movement has a leader, someone who clearly imagines the future and designs its ideology. But the symbol of a founding figure is not perhaps appropriate in a group of people who belonged to the same cultural milieu and drew on the same temper. Besides, editors Nicholas Blincoe and Matt Thorne were also contributors to the volume with one story each. Like the writers whose stories they commissioned, they were at the beginning of their literary careers too. Apart from that, the spirit of the experiment was very much equalitarian: 'Fifteen writers; ten rules' (Blincoe and Thorne, 2001: vii).

If the New Puritans can be compared with a canonical literary generation, that is, any of the families of the poetic avant-garde in the first decades of the twentieth century, there are grounds to claim their belonging to a group, diffuse though it may be, diffuse as all groups are. As radical young writers, they considered themselves at the forefront of literary experimentation and as a demonstrative gesture that they had arrived, a ten-point declaration was boldly printed on the first page of the book. This would count as the birth of any movement in classical terms: 'In the case of groups that intend to be considered avant-garde, this process often involves a joint declaration of purpose or manifesto that identifies members and enemies' (Strong, 1997: 7).

The New Puritan manifesto, later to be discussed in detail, was not the product of a joint discussion of the participants in the collection of short stories; it was solely conceived and written by the two editors of the collection, Nicholas Blincoe and Matt Thorne. But then all the writers they had approached sensed that it meant something new and not distant from their creative interests. Besides, they surely understood that it provided them with a trampoline for public recognition. As Beret E. Strong (1997: 8) argues, 'participation in a group empowers poets most when they are trying to make a name for themselves', and he adds: 'As a tool that helps recently launched writers become known, the avant-garde group is useful for a limited time only and is then often dismantled as systematically as it was created'. According to this authoritative opinion, the New Puritans could be considered a literary movement even if their members had only gathered for this particular occasion and if the movement had later to be disowned.

The writers of the collection had been chosen because for the editors they shared certain 'modern' requirements. They were the representatives in British fiction of 'an international turn away from a baroque literary sensibility to something cooler and essentially prose- and narrative-driven' (Blincoe, 2011). Nicholas Blincoe and Matt Thorne perceived that there was a new style struggling for recognition; recent experiments in alternative fiction (*Children of Albion Rovers*, 1996; *Disco Biscuits*, 1997; *britpulp!*, 1999) had proved successful. Blincoe and Thorne were part of that environment and they were well-connected. They simply presented in one bold move what was already there in a dispersed way: fiction that addressed the quotidian in a prosaic way, as if following a call to arms by the captain of disaffected suburban youth, Morrissey, when he had sung a few years before that the music played by the DJ no longer had the power to express the sense of his reality. They felt that a new vocabulary had to be invented.

3. The making of the book

The actual process of edition of the book was as follows: early in 1999 Nicholas Blincoe came up with the idea of translating into fiction what had been successfully made on film by Danish director Lars Von

Trier and his *Dogme 95* project. Von Trier had envisaged a new kind of film production in which all unnecessary elements were reduced to a minimum. The basic idea was to record the work of actors set in the present and in real locations, without recourse to special effects, additional lightning or music. In 1995, he and his colleague Thomas Vinterberg developed the ten rules of what they termed 'The Vow of Chastity', or the foundation of the new movement. All of these rules reinforced the idea of austerity in film making and by the end of the decade several productions, including the much acclaimed *Festen*, Jury Prize in Cannes Film Festival in 1998, were made following the trend initiated by Von Trier.

Nicholas Blincoe talked to his friend Matt Thorne about the project and they decided to go ahead with it. The title for the book was Blincoe's idea, taking the cue from a ballet by Michael Clark he had recently seen: *Hail the New Puritan* had been a collaboration of Clark with post-punk group The Fall, and Blincoe liked it for its iconoclastic attitude. The starting point was the writing of the manifesto itself. There was something imposing, continental, authentic, reminiscent of the surrealist movements of the 1920s and 1930s in the drafting of a manifesto. In the case of Blincoe and Thorne's, it was meant to be not only prescriptive, but also encouraging, that is, it was meant to promote the kind of narrative that they admired: 'The initial concept was to come up with a list of restrictions (*à la* Dogme Vow of Chastity), but as we thought about it, we decided that the list would be a combination of qualities we recognized in the fiction we liked by contemporary writers and deliberate restrictions' (Thorne, 2011).

The editors then drafted a list of anti-formalist rules that fulfilled different functions: they set the standard for the stories in the anthology, they expressed their reaction against the previous generation of 'literary' writers (in the subsequent discussion after the manifesto, *Time's Arrow* by Martin Amis and *Midnight's Children* by Salman Rushdie, were mentioned as the kind of literature they reacted against) and by this set of rules they announced to the world the official birth of the new sensibility:

THE NEW PURITAN MANIFESTO

1.- Primary story-tellers, we are dedicated to the narrative form.

2.- We are prose writers and recognise that prose is the dominant form of expression. For this reason we shun poetry and poetic licence in all its forms.

3.- While acknowledging the value of genre fiction, whether classical or modern, we will always move towards new openings, rupturing existing genre expectations.

4.- We believe in textual simplicity and vow to avoid all devices of voice: rhetoric, authorial asides.

5.- In the name of clarity, we recognise the importance of temporal linearity and eschew flashbacks, dual temporal narratives and fore-shadowing.

6.- We believe in grammatical purity and avoid any elaborate punc-tuation.

7.- We recognise that published works are also historical documents. As fragments of our time, all our texts are dated and set in the pres-ent day. All products, places, artists and objects named are real.

8.- As faithful representations of the present, our texts will avoid all improbable or unknowable speculation about the past or the future.

9.- We are moralists, so all texts feature a recognisable ethical reality.

10.- Nevertheless, our aim is integrity of expression, above and beyond any commitment to form.

The spirit of the whole enterprise was both serious (some rules had to be obeyed) but also playful (it was fun to experiment with writing, to play the game). The ten rules certainly curtailed the writers' freedom of choice, but it was liberating at the same time to tell a story pure and simple. In any case, it was obvious that the participants would take the manifesto as a guide, not as an inflexible set of commandments:

The manifesto was the point but should never be taken too serious. It could be interpreted on a number of levels – as a literary clarion call, as well as a very strong publicity bomb to throw amongst the critics. It raised some interesting ideas about fiction; it was also interesting to parallel fiction with the DOGME film discipline. But in the end, none of the writers took it particularly seriously and broke the rules at will. (Hollis, 2011)

When the book was published in September 2000, one of the most remarked-upon features of the anthology was that the stories covered more ground than was initially outlined: 'Even at the time' novelist Richard Beard remembered 'I felt the manifesto didn't match the contents of the book. The stories in the book are far more varied in style than the manifesto declares so stridently they ought to be' (Beard, 2011).

But going back to the initial stages of the book, once the manifesto was written and revised (a technical restriction, for instance, urging contributors to write two rough drafts and a polish, was dropped), the idea for the book was sent to different publishing companies. It was actually very well received, with seven major publishers bidding on the rights. Blincoe and Thorne finally accepted the offer of Fourth Estate. The idea of the manifesto was thought to be good for advertising, it was timely and at the publishing house they found that the collection would enhance British fiction in their catalogue, which they felt was underrepresented. Surely the benefits in terms of cohesion provided by the initial ten rules did not go unnoticed to the publishers, as Paul March-Russell (2009: 63) states: 'The manifesto, then, overtly demonstrates how anthologies attempt to bind individual short stories to an overall purpose and identity'.

Here the name of Leo Hollis enters the stage. A young and dynamic editor at Fourth Estate, he already knew Blincoe and Thorne and reacted favourably to the list of potential contributors that accompanied the manifesto. Of the initial twelve names, two of them, Douglas Coupland and Haruki Murakami, declined the invitation (Murakami had originally sent a story that would have not been accepted anyway, because it broke some of the rules), and new names, this time all British, were added to the list as both of them, Blincoe and Thorne, read more work from recent young authors. Leo Hollis supervised the process but did not intervene until the end, when all the stories had gone through Blincoe and Thorne, and he did a general edit of the whole collection. He worked with the book as with any other publication, without taking into account the rules of the manifesto. Only a limited amount of editing was done on the stories, normally by the editors in collaboration with the writers themselves so that they fitted the set of rules. For Blincoe, it was important to bring to life intelligent, beautiful stories without excessive intervention. For Leo Hollis (2011) this was a point he disagreed with: 'I felt that the stories could have been worked on far harder than they were in the end'.

Finally, Blincoe and Thorne wrote the introduction to the collection, which took the form of a dialogue of the editors although, as Nicholas Blincoe admitted to me, the dialogue form with two voices was 'slightly artificial. There was a process of joint editorship so nothing that is said, could be attributed to either one or the other with one hundred percent certainty' (Blincoe, 2011).

The fictitious conversation between Blincoe and Thorne is full of enthusiasm for the new trend and makes a strong case for pure storytelling as the *raison d'être* of the anthology. The editors made sweeping statements that relegated all other forms of writing to the paper bin: 'without narrative the most attractive constellations of words or the most carefully poised sentences are nothing but make-up on a corpse' (Blincoe and Thorne, 2001: viii). But of course they had to be provocative, bold, embattled, as befits the crusading spirit of the leaders of a cultural revolution. Other examples of this attitude, which did not really match what was on offer, included:

'Today, fiction should be focusing on the dominance of visual culture...' (ix)

'Poetry is so different to prose, it has nothing to offer or to teach the prose writer.' (x)

'It is impossible to write verse without turning life into artifice.' (x)

'Flashbacks are a cheap trick.' (xiii)

But the introduction also offered fresh, thought-provoking and exciting ideas, particularly for young writers:

> 'Narrative is essentially flexible, it is flexible at its very core. In the end, stories resist any attempt to categorise them.' (xi)

> 'The truth is not that fiction can be escapist, but that fiction embodies a desire for freedom.' (xi)

> 'The bond between writer and reader is one of contemporaries, of peers, not master and initiate.' (xvi)

> '[F]iction writers should at least be the ones who legislate what is and what is not fine writing.' (xvii)

The introduction to the book is savvy and smart, and maybe it played its part by generating such an angry response in some quarters. Statements like 'British fiction is currently among the most exciting in the world' (vii) or the anthology being 'a chance to blow the dinosaurs out of the water' (vii) sound too ambitious for just a collection of short stories, and it was bound to meet a negative reaction. As Nicholas Blincoe admitted many years later: 'We tend to pontificate and also to leap off from each rule to make wider social comments. Maybe we could have focused more on the key idea: what is prose fiction? Why does it work? And what makes it beautiful?' (Blincoe, 2011).

4. The reception of the New Puritans

The critical response to the anthology once it was published was in many cases fairly negative, even outrageous. One cannot help thinking, when reading the reviews, that Blincoe and Thorne gave many hostages to fortune when they drafted the manifesto and particularly when they wrote the dialogic comments on their common venture.

Criticism was not directed against the stories themselves, which in general were praised as interesting instances of narrative. There was general agreement on the remarkable poignancy of some of the pieces, particularly on the stories written by Anna Davis ('Facing the Music'), Geoff Dyer ('Skunk'), Alex Garland ('Monaco'), Nicholas

Blincoe ('Short Guide to Game Theory') and Toby Litt ('The Puritans'). It was also agreed that first-class standards were approached when 'the writers were not at work with a photocopied manifesto tacked up above their desks' (Clark, 2000: 29), that is, when the rules of the manifesto were overstepped. It was also generally admitted that the collection as a whole was not very different from similar anthologies published at the time (March-Russell, 2009: 64).

The first line of attack on *All Hail the New Puritans* is the direct result of their being fairly good stories, but that there were no grounds to announce that this was the ultimate collection that the editors proclaimed it to be. Alex Clark, for instance, insisted on the average quality of the stories of the anthology: 'It is, however, difficult, verging on the impossible, to see any of them as the beginning of a new wave … this project seems to favour clubbability rather than iconoclasm, and chin-jutting adolescent defiance rather than an engagement with form or content' (Clark, 2000: 28). Sean O'Brien took the argument further claiming that the poverty of the approach made the editors' enthusiasm difficult to share: 'The arid here-and-now of much of the material admits no sense of context. History, politics, economics, race and class are loudly absent; the result is banal and reactionary – an accurate snapshot of contemporary Britain, perhaps, but one which is imaginatively dead' (O'Brien, 2000: 8).

The second line of attack focused on what was termed as the making a virtue out of necessity: the emphasis that the editors placed on reducing the literary language to a minimum, the avoidance of all elements that departed from an austere conception of style in favour of a story simply told, in fact, revealed that they could not work with the language the way accomplished writers could. The New Puritan's explicit rejection of tradition and also their ambition to make their narratives resemble film or TV did nothing but reinforce this feeling: 'It flourishes the possibility of a new kind of fiction, but in fact it represents a kind of hidden shame about literature, and an embarrassment that fiction is not more like film. It is really a manifesto for the New Philistinism' (Wood, 2000).

A third line of attack consisted of denouncing the blatant use of the manifesto and 'The Pledge', as the introduction was called, as a marketing ploy, a gimmick to sell more books and enhance the literary careers of the participants in the experiment. For fiction writer Richard Beard the commercial motives were uppermost on the list of priorities of the New Puritans, thus explaining their leaning towards economically profitable forms of writing, like screenplays:

> But if the book says anything about the general panorama of British fiction at the time, it announces a growing cynicism about what writing is. For some writers, it was less about the writing than the marketing, and New Puritans was a bold self-promotional vehicle rather than a project of genuine literary value. (Beard, 2011)

James Wood continued in this vein at the time of the publication, remarking that what the New Puritans really craved for was the success obtained by movies, and what posed as an artistic declaration was in fact a commercial strategy (Wood, 2000). Similarly, Alex Clark condemned the publicity that had surrounded the anthology even before its publication, being a book 'whose very existence was devised to elicit maximum coverage at the same time as furthering its editors' and contributors' careers' (Clark, 2000: 29). Less harshly, Boyd Tonkin took the question of publicity lightly as a logical side-effect of the book publication; theirs was simply the latest instalment of a recurrent call in literature for an unobtrusive approach to any subject matter: 'But why bother to take a gang of publicity-hungry young contenders at face-value? ... the media-friendly New Puritan postures will, inevitably, go the way of all flash. But they testify to a perennial – and fundamentally healthy – desire to clear the clutter out of culture' (Tonkin, 2000).

Negative criticism on the book had, among other consequences, that of the book being talked about and creating a stir and, subsequently, the opening of a debate about the kind of fiction people wanted to read and the state of British fiction at the time, and it helped to shake off the complacency that had surrounded English letters for more than a decade: 'But why is it that the roster of British literary heavyweights has not changed for 20 years? Have no new stars emerged to challenge the gilded quartet of Amis, Barnes, McEwan and Rushdie – or do we lack the curiosity to find them?' (Moss, 2001: 2). The author of this opinion was journalist Stephen Moss who, in a two-page article published in the *Guardian* a year after the publication of *All Hail the New Puritans* tackled the question of the jaded state of mainstream literature in Britain. Basically what he put forward in his analysis was that the group of established writers mentioned earlier had made of the literary novel their stronghold, blocking the entrance of new talent. Consequently, young writers were turning to genre fiction or the middle-market. The new writers were explicitly anti-canonical, 'wearing their ignorance of literature as a badge of honour, more interested in Limp Bizkit than lit crit' (Moss, 2001: 3).

The existence of an undercurrent of change in English Literature had been registered, and *All Hail the New Puritans* was heralded as the most relevant offspring of that restlessness. In the article by Moss, Matt Thorne was quoted as saying: 'It is not a fight for writers or readers. The anthology was a way of democratising writing, an attack on the inflated self-worth of writers, a war on egoism' (cited in Moss, 2001: 3). A few years later Suzanne Keen placed the book edited by Blincoe and Thorne in a current which rejected the past and embraced 'the contemporary as a proper subject' (Keen, 2006: 181), implying its being at the spearhead of a change of direction in English fiction.

5. Assessing the impact of the New Puritans

The forces of democratization in literature, to use Martin Amis' term, were pushing hard. New collections of short stories emerged in the following years which clearly shared the minimalist aesthetics of *All Hail the New Puritans*. The influence of Blincoe and Thorne's book, for instance, can be clearly seen in books like *Piece of Flesh* (2001), a collection of pornographic short stories edited by Zadie Smith, in which she counted on the work of four New Puritans: Daren King, Toby Litt, Rebecca Ray and Matt Thorne. In her introduction there is something reminiscent of the matey, straight-forward attitude of 'The Pledge' that Blincoe and Thorne had shown:

> Hello. So here I am editing a book of five pornographic stories. Well, when I say *editing*, I mean that at the suggestion of the ICA I invited

five bright, young writers with a healthy clutch of novels between them, all more or less friends of mine, to write stories of a pornographic nature for which they would receive £250 each. In effect, I paid my friends to write about sex for me. (Smith, 2001b: 7)

The same nonchalant, casual tone can be detected in another collection also edited by Zadie Smith that same year, *May Anthologies*. The contributors were Oxbridge gradutates chosen by Smith herself and in her introduction, again, the example of *All Hail the New Puritans* is clearly at work, particularly in Smith's recommendations to would-be writers on the need to focus on simple prose, a distinguishable plot line and a neat description of things: 'let's try walking before we start running' (Smith, 2001a: 7). In 2007, Smith edited a new collection of short stories, *The Book of Other People*, and echoes of Blincoe and Thorne's project were still appreciable. Not only were the stories commissioned with an explicit request (in this case to invent a character and to name the story after them), but in her introduction Smith also stressed the joys of 'simply writing', reminiscent of the return to pure fiction advocated in 'The Pledge':

> It is liberating to write a piece that has no connection to anything else you write, that needn't be squished into a novel, or styled to fit the taste of a certain magazine, or designed in such a way as to please the kind of people who pay your rent. (Smith, 2007: ix)

Even in a collection like *Comma* (2002), edited by Ra Page, in which the efforts of Blincoe and Thorne were rebuked for being 'regressive' and for not making any explicit reference to the short story in their manifesto, the compiler made a plea for making literature accessible to the public and for letting the world get inside the stories, instead of shutting it out. Ra Page emphasized the aspect of the short story writer's work that connected it to the public: 'Not garret-bound or graveyard-seated, nor ivory towered or arcane, but common' (Page, 2002: x), which chimes with the New Puritans' interest in reflecting the contemporary as a mark of modernity.

Those involved in *All Hail the New Puritans* went their separate ways after the publication of the anthology. There were still some half-hearted attempts towards a continuation of the experiment that they had initiated in the book, but with no ambition of making it last much longer. A group story, 'Bangkok Hilton', by Nicholas Blincoe, Scarlett Thomas, Tony White, Matt Thorne and Anna Davis was published in the New York magazine *Black Book* in the Fall issue of 2001, and that was the only other time when some of the New Puritans wrote under the same name, in this case 'The Players'. It was a choose-your-own-adventure style story and the playful nature of the whole thing was clear from the start.

Nicholas Blincoe's novel *White Mice* (2002), set in the fashion industry, was the only long narration written following the rules of the manifesto. But that was it. The New Puritans project, however, continued appearing in surprising venues outside Britain. The New Puritans have often been linked to international movements by young writers who shared the same iconoclastic attitude, notably the *Crack* group in Mexico. While this literary movement, formed by writers Ignacio Padilla, Jorge Volpi, Eloy Urroz, Pedro Ángel Palou, Ricardo Chávez Castañeda and Vicente Herrasti, shared with the New Puritans a rebellious attitude toward their immediate predecessors, they also differed in many respects. For a start, their own manifesto was published four years earlier, in 1996, and their reaction was against the poor, indulgent and commercial literature that had followed the glorious Latin-American 'Boom' of the 1960s and 1970s. Their ambition was to go back to their pantheon of classic writers (Carlos Fuentes, Julio Cortázar, Jorge Luis Borges, Gabriel García Márquez...) and they favoured a kind of cultivated, learned and complex literature in which linguistic experiments were not shunned, very much the opposite of 'the lineal, direct, almost Hellenic narrative' (Padilla, 2007: 35–6; my translation) promoted by the New Puritans.

Both groups met at an event organized by the ICA in London on 26 November 2002 with Ignacio Padilla and Pedro Ángel Palou, on one side, and Matt Thorne and Ben Richards (the member of the British team who was best acquainted with Latin American literature), on the other, and had a pleasant public discussion, as Ignacio Padilla remembers:

Everything was very correct and civilised, cleverly incensed but within a sober atmosphere, appropriate for university students fed up with their bohemian predecessors and perhaps wearied also by our own comings and goings around the world, tired of our own manifestos, blatantly playful as they were, certainly contradictory and not as immobilized as everyone else thought them to be. (Padilla, 2012; my translation)

The continuation of the New Puritan project came from old Europe, from a country which had just come out of a war and was experiencing a thirst for culture. Croatia was one of the countries where the translation of *All Hail the New Puritans* was first produced, a few months after the book was published in English. Some of the contributors to the book were invited to a Croatian festival of alternative literature (FAK) by one of the organizers, writer Borivoj Radaković, who had in fact coordinated the translation of *All Hail the New Puritans*. In the FAK gatherings writers from all over the former Yugoslavia came together to give public readings of their work to an enraptured audience. These readings did not take place in institutionalized places of culture, but in pubs or clubs, and the young British authors felt enthusiastic about the energy and high spirits of these events and were frequent guests at them.

For Nicholas Blincoe, the two groups shared the same views on literature, but they approached the matter from different perspectives. If the New Puritans reacted against historical and poetic writing for aesthetic reasons, Croatian writers had more profound motives to supersede old forms. On the one hand, they needed time to digest the recent war in the Balkans and were not prepared to look back to the immediate past, preferring instead to focus on the contemporary. On the other hand, an inclination to poetic language would imply a continuation of the bardic tradition, which has a strong nationalistic bias in Croatia, and they wanted to avoid that at all costs. Perhaps for these reasons the link that existed between the New Puritans and the FAK writers was somehow based on a 'slight misunderstanding' (Blincoe, 2005).

As a consequence of the collaboration between young writers from such different parts of Europe, a volume of short stories, *Croa-*

tian Nights, was published in 2005, edited by Borivoj Radaković, Matt Thorne and Tony White. The anthology included stories by six New Puritans (including Thorne and White) among its 18 contributors, nine of them British and nine from Serbia and Croatia.

The stories in *Croatian Nights* do not follow the rules of the New Puritan manifesto, although they share a direct style and an interest in the present. All but one are set in Croatia. Serbian writer Vladimir Arsenijević, one of the contributors, explained in this way the affinities of the Serbian and Croatian writers with the New Puritans:

> The thing is, we discovered that just like us they rebelled against the previous generations of writers and the baroque pomposity of the then prevailing literary style and wanted to craft something which was much more simple, sharp and in tune with the times and our own general sensibility which was formed as much through music, movies, youth subcultures as through direct touch with literature. However, while our writing in the region of former Yugoslavia was by far more politically charged and anti-war at that … they tended to be more inclined to pop culture and cultural references as well as boldly redefining elements of genre, etc. But we were both strongly drawn to return to basic storytelling and saw ourselves as something like literary punk rock as opposed to deadly boring prog-rock of the symphonic, overtly complex and self-absorbed writings of the previous generation. So, you could say that we were quite alike but we also differed greatly at the same time and I think that this was the element which made us connect so well. (Arsenijević, 2011)

Gradually the impact of the New Puritans began to ebb away and the idea that the movement involved a close-knit generation of writers, had it ever existed, disappeared completely. In 2004, Nicholas Blincoe even published a historical novel, *Burning Paris*, the very genre they despised at the time of their seminal anthology. He had become, he said, a Renegade Puritan: 'I really strongly believe now that if you destroy everything and blow all the bits up into the air, you've got no control over the way they fall' (cited in Guest, 2004).

The kind of writing that *All Hail the New Puritans* promoted was also suffering the effects of wear and tear and it was in many ways turning into a mannerism. Blincoe, reflecting on what they had achieved, believed that their focus on the present had led to 'a curious affectless, almost autistic tone which can now be seen everywhere – in TV and films as well as contemporary fiction. I would characterize it as a semi-dazed aesthetic, appropriate to our times' (Blincoe, 2011). Blincoe's complaint about a style that was getting old strongly echoes Toby Litt and Ali Smith's comments in their introduction to *New Writing 13*, published in 2005. Having read a large amount of fiction that was submitted for the anthology, Litt and Smith lamented the profusion of unadventurous, bland and dull writing among the typescripts: 'we began to believe that somewhere out there is a strange, pseudo-English country called Short-Story-Land where all day long, peculiarly short-story-like things happen. We began to dread starting a story only to find we were once again in Short-Story-Land' (Litt and Smith, 2005).

What is left of the New Puritans, then? Why a collection of essays on this evanescent literary group? Those whom we have given the name of the New Puritan generation were a few more than a dozen writers who just got together for a short while on a common project and then carried on with their careers in their own particular way. But for a brief period they managed to suspend time and, like a mosquito trapped in an amber drop, produced a handful of stories which reveal an untainted, empty and media-orientated commercial age locked with its own obsessions, unaware of the horrors that would shortly begin. The extreme reactions provoked by that particular collection of stories initiated a debate on the future of the new literature whose implications are still resonant.

6. The present study

The purpose of this book is to study the impact made by the New Puritans on British literature and to examine the evolution of some of the most relevant members of the group. A number of academics from Britain and Spain have elaborated scholarly essays with the aim of providing varied and stimulating insights into this current of writing. The chapters collected here are assembled thematically, offering general characteristics of the group in the first half and studies of individual authors in the second.

Paul March-Russell looks into the careers of the New Puritans in the decade that followed the publication of the book. He examines the ideological environment of the day and assesses the importance of the movement and its different outcomes, providing guidelines to understand the whole generation of writers. David Owen's polemical essay casts a dispassionate glance at Blincoe and Thorne's rules of composition in *All Hail the New Puritans*. He explains the grounds on which the editors of the collection based their rupture from the past and finds in their prologue shallow motives to disregard a previous tradition. Sonia Villegas-López reads the stories of the four women writers in the collection from a genre perspective, using the notion of 'trace' as a critical tool. In her article, issues such as family dynamics, love, place, mourning and loss are analysed in the light of Feminist narratology. José Francisco Fernández traces the connections between the New Puritan movement and the dominant political project of the period, New Labour, finding that the stories in the anthology reacted dubiously as regards the model of society promoted by Tony Blair. Bianca Leggett pays attention to the two most cosmopolitan authors of the collection, Geoff Dyer and Alex Garland, and takes their forays abroad as the starting point for a disquisition on their Englishness as well as other issues, including the blurring boundaries between travel writing and travel fiction. Sara Martín reviews the irregular and fascinating career of Alex Garland, once the rising star of a literary generation, and explores the author's search for self-expression through screen writing, graphic novels and computer games. Miriam Borham-Puyal studies the features that have made Scarlett Thomas' writing so distinctive, including her transgression of genres, her penchant for riddles and puzzles and her recreation of (and reaction to) a consumerist culture. The need to understand Toby Litt's deconstruction of contemporary Englishness informs the essay by Laura Monrós-Gaspar. England, Gaspar argues, appears in Litt's novels both as a perfectly recognizable and an utterly distorted entity, as befits a country in a moment of transitional identity. Finally, in his Afterword, David James considers the legacy of the New Puritans within the wide context of contemporary literature, revealing their inner tensions and contradictions as well as the relevance of their pronouncements.

As a final remark, the anthology that has given rise to the present project should be considered as a prism that refracts a number of critical debates on contemporary fiction, which is in fact one of the aims that Nicholas Blincoe and Matt Thorne had in mind when they published their book. As it is being considered from different perspectives, quotes from the anthology are occasionally repeated in different chapters. This is not an oversight on the editor's part, rather it reflects the impact that the prologue and the stories of *All Hail the New Puritans* were able to generate.

Works Cited

Amis, M. (2002[2001]) 'Foreword', in M. Amis *The War Against Cliché*, pp. xi–xv. London: Vintage.

Arsenijević, V. (2011) Answers to questionnaire on the New Puritans, e-mail message, 29 September.

Baelo-Allué, S. (2011) *Bret Easton Ellis's Controversial Fiction*. London and New York: Continuum.

Beard, R. (2011) e-mail message, 8 December.

Blincoe, N. (2011) Answers to questionnaire on the New Puritans, e-mail message, 7 July.

Blincoe, N. (2005) Readings and debate on *Croatian Nights* at the University of Warwick, *Writers at Warwick Archive*, 18 May, http://www2.warwick. ac.UK/fac/arts/English/writingprog/archive/writers/blincoenicholas/ croatian (consulted September 2011).

Blincoe, N. and M. Thorne (2001[2000]) 'Introduction: The Pledge', in N. Blincoe and M. Thorne (eds) *All Hail the New Puritans*, pp. vii–xvii. London: Fourth Estate.

Bracewell, M. (2002) *The Nineties. When Surface Was Depth*. London: Flamingo.

Bradbury, M. (1992) 'Introduction', in M. Bradbury and J. Cooke (eds) *New Writing*, pp. 1–10. London: Minerva and the British Council.

Byatt, A. S. (1995) 'A New Body of Writing: Darwin and Recent British Fiction', in A. S. Byatt and A. Hollinghurst (eds) *New Writing 4*, pp. 439–48. London: Vintage and the British Council.

Champion, S. (1997) 'Introduction', in S. Champion (ed.) *Disco Biscuits*, pp. xiii–xvi. London: Sceptre.

Clark, A. (2000) 'No Dancing, No Music', *London Review of Books* (2 November): 28–9.

Coupland, D. (1998[1991]) *Generation X: Tales for an Accelerated Culture*. London: Abacus.

Cowley, J. (1999) 'Searching for England', *Waterstone's Magazine* (Summer/ Autumn): 3–14.

Fernández, J. F. (1998) 'Waiting for the New Writer: An Interview with Malcolm Bradbury', *BELLS* 9: 217–26.

Guest, K. (2004) 'A Passionate Puritan', *Independent*, 16 July, http://findarticles.com/p/articles/mi_qn4158/is_20040716/ai_n12803495/print (consulted October 2007).

Hollis, L. (2011) Answers to questionnaire on the New Puritans, e-mail message, 14 February.

Jack, I. (1996) 'Editorial', *Granta* 56 (Winter): 7–8.

Jack, I. (2003) 'Introduction', *Granta* 81 (Spring): 9–14.

Keen, S. (2006) 'The Historical Turn in British Fiction', in J. F. English (ed.) *A Concise Companion to Contemporary British Fiction*, pp. 167–87. Oxford: Blackwell.

Litt, T. and A. Smith (2005) 'Introduction', in T. Litt and A. Smith (eds) *New Writing 13*. London: Picador, http://www.tobylitt.com/newwriting13introduction.html (consulted February 2007).

Mahoney, K. P. (2000) 'Toby Litt Interview', *Authortrek* (Summer), http:// www.authortrek.com/toby_litt_interview.html (consulted November 2011).

March-Russell, P. (2009) *The Short Story: An Introduction*. Edinburgh: Edinburgh University Press.

Marshall, R. (2002) 'The White Stuff: An Interview with Tony White', *3:AM Magazine*, 12 April, http://www.3ammagazine.com/3am/the-white-stuff.an-interview-with-tony-white (consulted March 2011).

Moss, S. (2001) 'The Old Guard', *Guardian*, G2 (6 August):1–3.

O'Brien, S. (2000) 'This Blessed Plot, This England', *TLS* (1 September): 8.

Padilla, I. (2007) *Si hace crack es boom*. Barcelona: Urano.

Padilla, I. (2012) e-mail message, 4 January.

Page, R. (2002) 'Introduction', in R. Page (ed.) *Comma*, pp. vii–xii. Manchester: Comma Press.

Purbright, J. (2005) 'Scarlett Fever' *3:AM Magazine*, www.3ammagazine. com/litarchives/2005/jun/interview_Scarlett_thomas.html (consulted November 2011).

Self, W. (2006) 'A Conversation with J. G. Ballard', in W. Self *Junk Mail*, pp. 23–40. New York: Black Cat.

Smith, Z. (2001a) 'Introduction', in Z. Smith (ed.) *May Anthologies*, pp. 7–9. Cambridge: Varsity.

Smith, Z. (2001b) 'Piece of Flesh: Introduction to this Book', in Z. Smith (ed.) *Piece of Flesh*, pp. 6–14. London: ICA.

Smith, Z. (2007) 'Introduction', in Z. Smith (ed.) *The Book of Other People*, pp. vii–ix. London: Penguin.

Strong, B. E. (1997) *The Poetic Avant-Garde. The Groups of Borges, Auden, and Breton*. Evanston, IL: Northwestern University Press.

Thorne, M. (2001[1998]) *Tourist*. London: Phoenix.

Thorne, M. (2011) Answers to questionnaire on the New Puritans, e-mail message, 6 July.

Tonkin, B. 2000. 'Back to Basics (Yet Again)', *Independent*, 2 February, http://www.independent.co.uk/arts-entertainment/books/news/back-to-basics-yet-again-638112.html (consulted February 2007).

Wood, J. (2000) 'Celluloid Junkies', *Guardian*, 16 September, http://www.guardian.co.uk/books/2000/sep/16/fiction.reviews1 (consulted January 2011).

Chapter 2

The Jilted Generation?
The New Puritans A Decade On

Paul March-Russell

The name, 'New Puritan', was taken from a 1982 song-title by the alternative rock band, The Fall. In retrospect, a contemporaneous album title, The Prodigy's *Music for the Jilted Generation* (1994), might serve as a better descriptor. The album, released in the wake of the Criminal Justice Act, which effectively outlawed the free party scene and heralded the transition of rave music into commercially regulated, inner-city venues, positions its listenership as outcast.

The disenfranchisement of the outcast is constituted through the legal structure of the polis – the construction of the 'jilted generation' is actively produced through the passing of the Criminal Justice Act – just as The Prodigy's naming of their audience in turn constructs their own status as an authentic dissident voice. In other words, the separatist dream of rebellion does not occur: dissidence can only happen through the already mediated space of public discourse. Individuals can assume (or be made to assume) the status of the outcast, not that of the outlaw, and this process is inherent to the New Puritan aesthetic.

At once identified as 'jilted' but also being jilted from any kind of collective consciousness that might become subversive, the New Puritan writer is always mediating the crowded space of his/her culture; a self-reflexivity that connects them generationally to other members of the polis while at the same time undermining the potential radicalism of the group or generational identity. The New Puritans are significant for calling into question how literary history is periodized through the use of group identities: a critical tool that retroactively masks the extent to which these identities are dispersed by the underlying effects of economic, social, legal and political dependence. If group identities are meant to acquire a critical mass for the individuals concerned – critical and commercial success often being more easily achieved as part of a group rather than as a solitary artist – then the fate of the lesser-known members is, in many ways, more telling than those who are celebrated.

Ten years ago, Matthew Branton was a successful and popular novelist. On the strength of his first three novels, *The Love Parade* (1997), *The House of Whacks* (1999) and *Coast* (2000), he was an ideal candidate for inclusion in the New Puritan anthology. The first novel that he published describes a pop musician's doomed attempt to turn the tables upon the music industry; the second is a crime novel set in 1950s Chicago where the participants of a disastrous heist are all victims of the illusory 'American Dream'; and, the third is a coming-of-age novel in which the teenage protagonists are abandoned by their parents to brew their own supply of crystal meth, much to the anger of the local drug baron. Youth, crime, sex, drugs, pop culture – all themes that are immediately recognizable from the pages of *All Hail the New Puritans* (2000) and written in the same, familiar, taut prose.

The key motif in Branton's fiction is that of the victim. His protagonists, even the assassin of his fourth novel, *The Hired Gun* (2001), are all victims of social, economic and organizational structures – whether they are work, family or leisure-related – which they vainly attempt to subvert. In *Coast*, for example, the casual use of sex and drugs by Bay and his adolescent friends merely replicates the 'drop-out' culture of his mother, who has deserted Bay to follow the hippy trail – in unconsciously clichéd fashion – to India. Branton's characters rehearse social and economic roles that turn them into caricatures of human behaviour: the very flatness of their thoughts and descriptions rendering their loss of autonomous identity. His contribution to the New Puritan collection, 'Monkey See', distils this process through its first-person narrator and his absorption into local sex parties where he feels compelled to perform what he believes to be the appropriate sex acts with his wife. The title's allusion to the monkey who sees no evil comments upon the narrator's metaphorical blindness: his inability to see his behaviour as a mechanical process that liquefies his own individuality. Although the flat prose style of the New Puritans is nothing 'new' (it echoes the minimalist fictions of American writers such as Raymond Carver, Richard Ford and Tobias Wolff whose work had long been popularized in the UK by magazines such as *Granta*), Branton's linking of depthless style to a social flattening of individual personality by the economic forces that underwrite work and leisure can be seen as integral to the New Puritan aesthetic.

While I am arguing for the centrality of Branton's fiction to an understanding of the New Puritan legacy (if there is one), then all of the above is very strange since Branton is now largely unknown. And, just to make it stranger still, each of Branton's first four novels received average advances of £50,000 and each was optioned for a film (none of which have transpired). In 2000, he cut his ties with the world of London publishing by moving to a self-sufficient existence in Hawaii and, in 2003, committed commercial suicide by offering his fifth novel, *The Tie and the Crest*, as free to download from his personal website. In an emailed conversation with the journalist, Miranda Sawyer, Branton wrote:

> I don't want their stupid money until the industry is less stupid ... Culture is important; it affects how people think of themselves, the world, their place in it, and the publishing industry in this country is now a joke that's gone too far. (cited in Sawyer, 2003: 17)

As Samuel Johnson once observed, 'no man but a blockhead ever wrote, except for money' (Boswell, 1791: 241), Branton's solitary protest against commercial publishing was doomed to failure. Yet, it is too easy to dismiss Branton, as William Leith does, by suggesting that 'things ... got too much for him' and he 'finally cracked' (Leith 2003: 16). His rationale, if not his response, is worth exploration:

> The culture industry in Britain since the early Nineties has come to consist almost entirely of consumer capitalist propaganda dressed up as 'better living': young people are made to feel that living some kind of cross between *Sex and the City* and *Cold Feet* with a swindling mortgage and a swindling pension and a house stuffed full of cheap tasteful shit manufactured for sub-breadline wages in China is the best you can hope for in this life. (cited in Sawyer, 2003: 17)

As Branton's use of the phrase 'culture industry' implies, a generalized version of Theodor Adorno's critique of ersatz culture underlines what Leith discounts as a 'rant' (Leith, 2003: 16). Although Branton's logic is hardly systematic, there is a vein of thought which is clearly identifiable from the left-wing theorists of mass culture and from anarchic documents of counter-cultural thinking such as Valerie Solanas' *SCUM Manifesto* (1967), namely, that the sheer dullness of interchangeable, mass-produced cultural products conditions the populace to become politically apathetic. As Branton summarizes:

> It's because of this dumbing down, and our collusion in it, our acceptance of it, thinking that watching soaps every day is somehow authentic, thinking that buying chick-lit and lad-lit and Harry bloody Potter is okay because it's a meaningless holiday read ... I believe that it's directly and at least partly responsible for our participation in this filthy enterprise in the Middle East. (cited in Leith, 2003: 16)

Branton's recent disavowal of these comments – that 'he disappeared up his own fundament' – and acknowledgement of 'a particularly crunchy breakdown' (Branton, 2010) as well as the diagnosis of Dissociative Identity Disorder should not obscure the relevance of his outburst for an understanding of the New Puritans. The cultural logic of mass production permeates the anthology, in stories like Nicholas Blincoe's 'Short Guide to Game Theory', while the immersion of the fictional protagonists in commodity culture had already been signalled in the title to Litt's debut collection, *Adventures in Capitalism* (1996).

Branton's solution that 'we just need some kind of place where people who are getting fed up with the way things are going ... can come together' is politically naive and, in any event, its romantic utopianism had already been satirized in Alex Garland's *The Beach* (1996). However, it expresses 'a kind of mourning that things are not as we know they should be' (cited in Sawyer, 2003: 17), a pathos that, due to the brevity of the short stories and their preference for anti-climactic endings, runs through the New Puritan anthology. This sense of mourning, which Branton associates with the collective grief at the death of Princess Diana in 1997, was very much a part of academic writing within the Humanities following the publication of Jacques Derrida's *Specters of Marx* (1994), which related deconstructive practice to the traditions of Karl Marx and G. W. F. Hegel and, thence, to the Romantic legacy of melancholic imagination: a link that had previously been made by a number of other deconstructionists, most notably, Paul de Man in *Blindness and Insight* (1971). Although, the academic manifestation of mourning in the 1990s, with its associated tropes of haunting, possession and trauma, took on a political aspect by foregrounding feelings such as loss, absence and dislocation in contrast to the vindication of Western capitalism in such texts as Francis Fukuyama's *The End of History* (1992).

For Gillian Rose, unconvinced by this political transformation in deconstruction which she brackets with postmodernism as a symptom of 'despairing rationalism without reason' (Rose, 1996: 7), mourning nevertheless becomes the counterpart to an over-rationalized, patriarchal legal system. This relation she portrays in terms of the polis. Beyond 'the boundary wall of the city of Athens', Rose (1996: 35) writes, 'we find mourning women': Antigone, her sister Ismene and the wife of Phocion. Instead of identifying mourning as an act of transgression, Rose associates these women with politically re-energizing the polis:

> Mourning draws on transcendent but representable justice, which makes the suffering of immediate experience visible and speakable. When completed, mourning returns the soul to the city, renewed and reinvigorated for participation, ready to take on the difficulties and

injustices of the existing city. The mourner returns to negotiate and challenge the changing inner and outer boundaries of the soul and of the city; she returns to their perennial anxiety. (Rose, 1996: 36)

Rose's position is quite different from those of postmodernism and deconstruction where the keynotes are upon pathos (as a symptom of Jean-François Lyotard's emphasis upon the unrepresentable) and melancholy (as in Emmanuel Levinas' passive abdication of the self to the Other). Instead, following Sigmund Freud, Rose distinguishes mourning from melancholy by regarding the former as successful grief-work, an active and self-willed process of healing that returns the individual to the polis and is of potential social benefit. Although nowhere near as well defined as Rose's thinking, Branton's use of mourning nevertheless suggests something similar: the need to reintegrate the individual with the polis and to actively change the polis by the process of reintegration. The failure to achieve the latter, for example in Tony Blair's co-opting of national grief via his idealization of Diana as 'the People's Princess', returns the individual to a potential state of melancholy.

Mourning has also played a central role in Toby Litt's fiction. As Leigh Wilson (Litt's partner) notes, his writing 'has been possessed by the experience and dynamics of possession' (Wilson, 2006: 105), most notably, in the composite novel *Ghost Story* (2004). Through her reading of the traumatic experiences that underline this work, Wilson demonstrates how Litt's fiction distances itself from both Derrida's notion of 'hauntology' and postmodern play upon language and representation via a commitment to plot, genre and the readerly pleasures to be found within narrative. Wilson's fine – even brave – reading finds correspondence with the argument being advanced here. Mourning can only be successfully completed through the workings-through of plot and linear narrative (two New Puritan tenets) that Wilson summarizes as the 'classical plot', borrowing the term from the classicist N. J. Lowe (Wilson, 2006: 106). This summary immediately connects with Rose's use of classical tragedy as a template for mourning and the rejuvenation of the polis. The reader is encouraged to immerse him/herself in the fiction not only through the subject-matter, which might on the contrary be too painful to read, but also through Litt's wholesale borrowings of genre conventions and reader-ly expectations. These generic markers, rather than being catalysts for self-reflexive play, enable the reader to plumb the emotional depths of his/her own responses to what s/he is reading and to resurface at the narrative's closure. During the time spent with the story, however, the reader has been effectively possessed by the narrative – what Litt describes elsewhere as an 'enraptured reading' (Litt, 2003: 56) – so that the reader resurfaces but is not quite restored to him/herself. In Freudian terms, we would describe this experience of reading as un-canny (*das Unheimlich*): the reader is no longer at home with him/herself; the security of home is an illusion; there is no such thing as a safe reading. In this sense, then, the Aristotelian goal of catharsis is substituted, and with it the possibility of self-satisfied sympathy that, in effect, disavows the needs of the other, for a more modern outcome in which the narrative tensions that bind the reader as s/he reads are exchanged for ethical tensions that entangle the reader and thread him/her to the demands of the polis. As Litt acknowledges, he is a political writer by attempting 'to understand the relationship between individuals and groups, and groups that dominate societies' (cited in Tolan, 2008: 80).

Ghost Story was widely seen as signalling Litt's maturity as a writer and it is perhaps to the annoyance of his critics that he continues to '[play] with form' rather than 'just telling a story' (Weston, 2010: 11), but viewing *Ghost Story* as marking a watershed in Litt's fiction glosses the endurance of the New Puritan aesthetic and the trope of possession that has persisted from his early short stories to the novels published either side of the New Puritan anthology, *Corpsing* (2000) and *deadkidsongs* (2001), through to his most recent fiction.

The charge of postmodern self-consciousness is used, as in Gabriel Weston's review of the Gothic thriller *King Death* (2010), to under-cut Litt's technical acumen as a writer even though, as already argued, self-reflexive play is not Litt's primary objective. The inability of at least some critics to engage with Litt's fiction may also describe an ir-ritation that he has (so far) refused the mantle of becoming a literary figurehead like his predecessors, Martin Amis and Ian McEwan, those writers that (at least notionally) New Puritanism was designed to oppose. With Litt's refusal to accept such a role, and with the disappearance of Alex Garland as a fiction writer, critics have turned instead to another member of the group as a potential substitute: Scarlett Thomas.

Thomas was principally a crime writer before the New Puritan anthology and her apprenticeship in plotting serves her well in her most celebrated novel, *The End of Mr Y* (2006), while her most conspicuously New Puritan novel is *Going Out* (2002), a picaresque tale of twenty-somethings who have effectively opted out of mainstream society. Although reviews were mixed at the time, in retrospect *Going Out* points to a narrative trope in Thomas' writing between the mundane and the marvellous. The novel takes Frank L. Baum's *The Wonderful Wizard of Oz* (1900) as its template with a mysterious faith healer replacing Baum's fake magician. This fairy-tale framework buttresses the otherwise banal events surrounding the two protagonists; the housebound Luke and the social drop-out Julie. Thomas effectively uses the same embedding technique in *The End of Mr Y* and *Our Tragic Universe* (2010), where the mundane details of, respectively, academia and journalism are framed by the cosmological significance of, first, the Troposphere (a Kantian ideal where entire universes can be re-shaped by subjective consciousness) and, then, the Omega Point, which implies that our current universe is only a virtual construct. Whereas *The End of Mr Y* is, despite its fanciful content, tightly plotted, *Our Tragic Universe* is (like *Going Out*) fundamentally a picaresque: its meandering narrative formally dramatizing Thomas' theme that life, unlike fiction, is plot-less. This message duplicates Luke's storyline in *Going Out* where, following his incarceration at home, he now confuses television drama with reality and expects life to have neat, predictable outcomes. Both *Going Out* and its successor, *PopCo* (2004), ironically collude in their characters' (and possibly readers') fantasies of wish-fulfilment by supplying just such an ending, while *The End of Mr Y* knowingly plays upon the science fiction cliché of the 'Shaggy God Story'. *Our Tragic Universe*, by contrast, resists such a romantic closure since it would run contrary to the theme of indirection. In so doing, the reader is left uncertain as to whether

Meg's mundane story, and the many other stories that filter through the narrative, are to be read in terms of the cosmological framework or should be regarded as separate: that the Omega Point is really only one story among many and that perhaps, after all, life might just have a plot. Although Thomas has received serious critical attention due to the layers of intellectual thought that embed her narratives, ultimately these can be read as framing devices for the mundane content that constitute her characters' lives. In this sense, Thomas has refined rather than broken with the New Puritan aesthetic that was present in *Going Out* while, at the same time, offering a humanistic appeal that offsets not only the rationalism of institutional forces – capitalism, education, mass media – but also that of her own novels' intellectual frameworks.

Humanism is also at the forefront of Matt Thorne's fiction. As one of the editors of the New Puritan anthology, he drafted point nine that proclaims 'We are moralists, so all texts feature a recognisable ethical reality' (Blincoe and Thorne, 2000: xvi). It is a point he has restated in interview, arguing that writers must 'have a strong moral sense in their fiction' and that the dominant theme of his work is 'how contemporary society can make people ... sociopathic' (cited in Tew, 2008: 149, 151). In what Thorne has acknowledged as a triptych of New Puritan novels, *Dreaming of Strangers* (2000), *Pictures of You* (2001) and *Child Star* (2003), he details how three examples of popular culture – respectively, cinema, lifestyle magazines and television – warp and transform his protagonists' perception of reality. As Philip Tew (2008: 157) writes, 'desire is reduced to archetypes ... image displaces ontological urges and identities lacking a sense of affect predominate'. Like Branton, Thorne regards his characters as victims of the culture industries, whose object is to manipulate and diminish individual subjectivity, but unlike Branton, Thorne is not romantically naive. For example, like Litt's *deadkidsongs*, Thorne discredits the romantic nostalgia that surrounds childhood: the former child performers of *Child Star* have each been abused, abandoned or manipulated by adults. Nevertheless, in each of these novels, Thorne tentatively suggests some form of development on the part of his characters: a partial self-realization that is horrifically denied in the male sexual fantasy of *Cherry* (2004), a novel that can be read (at least for now) as the culmination of Thorne's New Puritan aesthetic. Since the murderous outcome of *Cherry*, Thorne has published no new adult novels although he has written for children and continues to review and promote the work of his contemporaries. For Thorne, New Puritanism represents more than a tag-line: it is a vital group identity, embodying principles of moral and artistic integrity, which he has sought to bind and hold together.

It is significant though that Steve, the (possibly) psychotic hero of *Cherry*, cites 1987, when rave music crossed from Ibiza to the UK on a public scale, as his perfect year. The year becomes for Steve a pre-lapsarian moment before the fall into a rationalized, homogenous urban existence, where Steve continually fears for his personal safety and lack of human contact. Although Thorne skilfully dramatizes the pathological process by which Steve's paean for a lost idyll becomes an *idée fixe*, an overwhelming passion to return to this illusory utopia that takes physical form in Cherry, the mysterious object of sexual desire, he nevertheless hints at the melancholia that permeates the New Puritan aesthetic and other like-minded anthologies such as Sarah Champion's *Disco Biscuits* (1997). Daren King's novels, which veer between fantasy and realism, child-like naivety and physical and verbal grotesquerie, embody this tendency. The drug-addicted lovers of *Boxy an Star* (1999), the ghost title-character of *Jim Giraffe* (2004) and the hedonistic urbanites of *Manual* (2008) are all alienated figures, in search of something that would make sense of their existence, but condemned to live out linguistic, sexual and social games. King's surreal worlds are fundamentally melancholic: effective mourning cannot take place in such dislocated environments where the characters are so adrift from anything like the polis.

For Alex Garland, the most celebrated but also the most reluctant of the writers, a melancholic unease has bedevilled his relationships with the publishing industry: 'I often find writing a kind of irritating way to spend my one shot at life. I never felt short of things to write about. It was more to do with the will to write' (cited in Adams, 2004: 17). The son of Nicholas Garland, the political cartoonist, he has always seemed to miss the visual arts as his true vocation. *The Beach*, his unexpected best-selling debut novel, began as a comic book and Garland later collaborated with his father on *The Coma* (2004), a novella suffused with dream imagery and the imperceptible layers between sleep and consciousness. Garland compared his approach to writing with that of his father's woodcuts: 'The way he does woodcuts and linocuts very much influenced the way I write prose. I mean the heavy emphasis on craft with the aim of making things simple, hopefully deceptively so' (cited in Adams, 2004: 17). The insistence upon craft, while indicating an almost Flaubertian approach to fiction, also suggests a visual aspect: of seeing the finished result before it is done and of moving quickly towards that end. Kazuo Ishiguro, whose novel *Never Let Me Go* (2005) was adapted to film by Garland, has spoken of his astonishment at Garland's speed: 'I thought: it's unfilmable. And then Alex comes and turns it into a movie in three days! It's a bit dispiriting. I was trying to make it really, really literary!' (cited in Macdonald, 2010). Garland's incisive adaptation, foregrounding the love interest within a more explicitly dystopian, science fictional context, emphasizes that in the visuality of screenwriting he has found his metier. The screenplay of *28 Days Later* (2003) began with its John Wyndham-inspired image of a lone individual walking the streets of a deserted city while *Sunshine* (2007), although scientifically dubious, has several memorable images. The collaborative nature of film-making has also been an important allure for Garland in contradistinction to the melancholic image of the solitary writer:

> If you were asking were there times when I thought, 'Fuck this, I've had enough of writing, I don't like the book world … I don't like sitting on my own in a room for hours on end,' then yes, there were loads of times like that. (cited in Adams, 2004: 17)

While there have been commentators who have lamented Garland's departure from literary fiction, he has effectively supplanted one group – the New Puritans – for a host of others within the film industry.

The desire for collaboration seems more than an economic opportunity for the New Puritans. The anthology was initially a joint affair between Blincoe and Thorne, and both have continued to collaborate with others: Blincoe as part of the International Solidarity Movement, which campaigns on behalf of Palestine and Thorne as co-editor, with Boro Radaković and Tony White, of the fiction anthology, *Croatian Nights* (2005). These collaborations were driven by the moral imperative that, for Blincoe and Thorne, underwrote the New Puritan aesthetic but they are uncharacteristic of other collaborations pursued by former members. White, for example, continues to work as literary editor of *The Idler*, a yearly magazine founded in 1993 which, as something of an in-joke, can only be indirectly related to the international Slow Movement and its resistance to the speed of mass consumerist society. More convincingly, Rebbecca Ray has re-emphasized the links between rave and New Puritanism by co-organizing the Newfoundland Secret Summer Gatherings in 2007 and 2009. Thomas' *PopCo*, despite criticizing global corporations and the fabrication of reality by mass advertising, evades overt political commitment while at the same time seeking a happy ending for its principal characters. Both Litt and Thomas have found collaborations of a sort through their academic affiliations, but in 2011, Litt returned to the territory of *Ghost Story* for *Life Cycle*, a sequence of songs chronicling the conception and birth of a child and the onset of motherhood, written with the composer Emily Hall. This collaboration, in particular, conveys the New Puritan needs for communality between artists and for the inspiration of different media so as to free personal expression. More than moral or political allegiances, collaboration has involved a search for a social infrastructure of like-minded individuals, in place of the Romantic cliché of the struggling artist, and a series of friendships that might further the writer's artistic development. In so doing, the former members of the New Puritan group have broken away from their original associations.

The desire for collaboration operates all the while in social, economic and political contexts that, from the New Puritan perspective, have devalued the significance of subjective and interpersonal relations. These contexts also underwrite the organization and marketing of the original anthology and shape the fragility of the group identity. For though I have attempted to outline a core aesthetic that might define New Puritanism, I have also indicated that it was symptomatic of social and economic changes that were in the process of dissolving such communal identities – with the rave scene acting as a lost ideal of what such communality might represent. It is impossible to speak of a generation, in terms of years as opposed to attitude, when the most critically respected member of the group (Geoff Dyer) is twenty-one years older than the youngest (Ray). Dyer's inclusion, which was partially due to his accounts of sex, drugs and tourism in his novel, *Paris Trance* (1998), offered a literary figurehead for the anthology, even though the collection's commercial potential would turn upon its inclusion of trendier writers, most notably Garland. It is notable then that, even as the editors sought 'to blow the dinosaurs out of the water' (Blincoe and Thorne, 2000: vii), they still needed to include someone of an older generation, whom they admired, and would confer artistic gravitas to their project.

Even from the outset, there were peripheral figures whose inclusion seemed to be at odds with what might be taken as the core beliefs of New Puritanism. Candida Clark, for instance, was included on the basis of two well-received novels, *The Last Look* (1998) and *The Constant Eye* (2000), both of which as their titles indicate, play with notions of perspective and point of view. Clark has cited modernists, such as Joseph Conrad, E.M. Forster, Henry James and Virginia Woolf as influences – 'Woolfian' is an epithet that has been applied to her work – but, whereas Litt cites James 'as almost "postmodernist before the fact"' (in Tolan, 2008: 73), Clark is less concerned with modernist techniques that provoke fragmentation as those that create an impression, in James' terms, of organic form. This effect can be partially attributed to Clark's description of Britain as 'an island of fishermen and farmers' (Clark, 2006), a very different view from those of Thorne's metropolitan novels or the brand-laden fictions of Thomas, with *The Mariner's Star* (2002) set at sea and three further novels set in the countryside. The most recent, *The Chase* (2006), was inspired by the ban on fox hunting but the political context is submerged within the affairs, both domestic and sexual, of the country house.

Anna Davis, too, seems to have had only temporary affinities with the New Puritans. Her debut novel, *The Dinner* (1999), is a contemporary satire that takes Petronius' *Satyricon* as its classical template.

Her most New Puritan-styled novels are *Melting* (2000), a picaresque tale of con-artists, and *Cheet* (2001), which focuses upon Kathryn Cheet and the night-time cab ride she takes between the lovers who compensate for her own sense of anomie. Since then, Davis has written two novels set in the 1920s, *The Shoe Queen* (2007) and *The Jewel Box* (2009), both of which can be read as attempts to equate her own period with that of the mythical 'Lost Generation' from the years after 1918. However, if we read them in this way, the results are mixed since Davis forces too many historical references into what are otherwise conventional romance narratives, while in any event the analogy – if it is there at all – depends upon the myth of the Lost Generation for its effect. Both Clark and Davis, by breaking with the urban contemporaneity of the New Puritan manifesto, can be regarded, at best, as fellow travellers.

What, though, is to be made of the case of Bo Fowler? He had published two novels, *Scepticism Inc.* (1998) and *The Astrological Diary of God* (1999), prior to the New Puritan anthology as part of a £140,000 advance from his publisher, but nothing else has appeared since. Like Clark and Davis, Fowler added to the kudos of the anthology but his reputation came chiefly from the absurd sum that his publisher had advanced him: one of many such absurdities within the publishing industry of the late 1990s and which Branton targets in his criticism of contemporary culture. Fowler is the embodiment – whatever the merits of his fiction – of the hype that critics of the New Puritan anthology regard as definitive. And, to some extent, this criticism is justified since to, first, sell the idea of the collection to a potential publisher, and second, to have it succeed commercially Blincoe and Thorne had to use all the techniques of modern marketing (however much they might be satirized in Blincoe's own contribution to the anthology). Following the collapse of the systems of patronage that effectively bankrolled modernism (Rainey, 1999: 33–69), writers have had to work through either the major systems of publishing or small independent presses. Only the most puritanical of readers would accuse of Blincoe and Thorne of selling out, but in labelling themselves and their contributors as New Puritans and in appealing to authenticity as their central aim, they inevitably compromise themselves.[1]

Compromise – call it complicity in a commercial structure that the New Puritan otherwise abhors – shatters the putative aesthetic even while its name, like Douglas Coupland's popularization of 'Generation X' before it, soon caught on and became a cliché among literary reviewers. Nevertheless, the stories are in print and their collective influence has been considerable outside of the Anglophone world, especially in Hispanic-speaking countries, such as Mexico and Spain, in France and Italy, and in Eastern Europe. The New Puritans, like other groupings that were randomly assembled, like the pre-1914 Georgian Poets, lacked a coherent group identity and have not left behind them a school of thought. Their identity has been formed at the point of reception. In the UK, this response was mixed: some writers, such as Dyer, were already of such standing that they could escape untarnished; others like Litt and Thomas were given a boost; others still like Branton and Garland were fatally or near-fatally holed. Overseas, the New Puritan project has received a more approving reception and the work has helped to inform local artistic activities. It is the international reach of the New Puritans which is, perhaps, the most unexpected aspect for the work of mourning is accomplished elsewhere: art returns to nation-states where, perhaps, it is felt that art is more urgently wanted than in the UK. For, in Britain, the economic, political and cultural tensions that both shaped and sundered the New Puritan identity are, if anything, even more present than at the end of the 1990s as public arts funding is slashed, civic space diminishes and social control becomes more intense as government finances are squeezed. Generational voices become harder to find, harder still to be heard, and so the New Puritan project has to be seen in concert with the emergence of literary figures (A. L. Kennedy and Ali Smith are examples) who do not speak for a generation but whose voices are nevertheless distinct. In this respect, the ultimate edifice of New Puritanism may well be Ray's *Newfoundland* (2005), a thousand-page novel that describes in microscopic detail the life of a small, benighted Welsh village. It is no longer in print but those interested can download it to the e-reader of their choice. Ray's third novel, *The Answer*, remains unpublished in any format.

Note

1 It has to be remembered that the writers were only given the ten points of the manifesto before writing their fictions. The comments of Blincoe and Thorne were added later to form the introduction and were not agreed by the writers. The ironies that bedevil New Puritanism were not lost on Thomas as she wrote *PopCo*.

Works Cited

Adams, T. (2004) 'Coma chameleon', *Observer* [reviews] (27 June): 17.

Blincoe, N. and Thorne, M. (eds) (2000) *All Hail the New Puritans*. London: Fourth Estate.

Boswell, J. (1791) *The Life of Samuel Johnson*. London: Dent.

Branton, M. (2010) 'New Blog on DID by Prominent Author', *DIDIVA*, http://didiva.com/2010/03/new-blog-on-did-by-prominent-author/ (consulted December 2011).

Clark, C. (2006) 'Q & A with Candida Clark', *Reading Circle*, http://www.readingcircle.co.uk/thechase2.html (consulted December 2011).

Leith, W. (2003) 'Matthew Branton: Publishing is for wimps', *The Independent* [arts] (13 April): 16.

Litt, T. (2003) 'Reading', *Poetry Review* 93(2): 56–9.

Macdonald, M. (2010) 'Novelist Kazuo Ishiguro on the film adaptation of *Never Let Me Go*', *Seattle Times*, http://seattletimes.com/html/movies/2013030613_ishiguro03.html (consulted August 2011)

Rainey, L. (1999) 'The Cultural Economy of Modernism', in M. Levenson (ed.) *The Cambridge Companion to Modernism*, pp. 33–69. Cambridge: Cambridge University Press.

Rose, G. (1996) *Mourning Becomes the Law*. Cambridge: Cambridge University Press.

Sawyer, M. (2003) 'Matthew and Sun', *Observer* [reviews] (13 April): 17.

Tew, P. (2008) 'Matt Thorne', in P. Tew, F. Tolan and L. Wilson (eds) *Writers Talk: Conversations with Contemporary British Novelists*, pp. 142–61. London: Continuum.

Tolan, F. (2008) 'Toby Litt', in P. Tew, F. Tolan and L. Wilson (eds), *Writers Talk: Conversations with Contemporary British Novelists*, pp. 72–87. London: Continuum.

Weston, G. (2010) 'Scalpel, Please: *King Death* by Toby Litt', *Guardian* [reviews] (5 June): 11.

Wilson, L. (2006) 'Possessing Toby Litt's *Ghost Story*', in P. Tew and R. Mengham (eds) *British Fiction Today*, pp. 105–16. London: Continuum.

CHAPTER 3

WRITING BY NUMBERS
DISAVOWING LITERARY TRADITION IN
ALL HAIL THE NEW PURITANS

David Owen

Publishing a manifesto is a bothersome affair; it is the literary equivalent of parading up and down a crowded high street wearing the very
latest fashion in hats, or boots, or outrageous ties. It probably seemed
to be quite the statement at the time, but the danger of course is that
you can soon look foolishly outmoded, usually by the middle of the
following week. And if the basis of a collection that aims so openly
to disavow much of English literary tradition is actually articulated
through a manifesto, the danger is then two-fold: in the harsh light of
a newer day, the ideas may subsequently appear rather shaky; and the
works based on these ideas may then fail to make the cut.

The purpose of this discussion is to assess Thorne and Blincoe's
rules of composition in *All Hail the New Puritans*, to consider their
feasibility and worth, and then to see the manner in which the two
editors – now in their guise as authors – follow their own indications,
and the results that they achieve. Beyond this, I will also briefly be
referring to texts by other writers in this collection as a further means
of putting the editors' rules to the test.

For at some point or other, any discussion of *All Hail the New Puritans* needs to tackle the way in which these rules frame the texts themselves (and in case we might lose sight of this, 'The New Puritan Manifesto' is printed out on the very first page of the book, before any other editorial matter, like some latter-day Ten Commandments). Indeed, not only is the manifesto a series of guidelines by which the writers – in this collection at least – were expected to live, it also implicitly aims at instructing its readers on how to critically approach these stories and, perhaps, how therefore to appreciate 'worthwhile' literature in general.

So there are deeper concerns in all this. One considerable question is whether the English literary 'tradition' (however we define this complex notion, which is no easy undertaking) is now an exhausted vein of writing, as Thorne and Blincoe would appear to have us believe; and whether, by setting us on a new course in these tales, if that is what they have done, the editors were successful – both in the collection and in the writing that came after this work – in their attempt 'to blow the dinosaurs out of the water' (Blincoe and Thorne, 2001: vii).

It might be objected at this point that this entire Manifesto ought surely to be taken with rather less seriousness than my aim in this discussion requires; that the literary *credo* expressed in these New Puritan ideas are somewhat tongue-in-cheek and that to engage over-intensely with all this would be to miss the irony of the whole undertaking. That may be so, but my feeling is that it is not: the introduction seems to me to take itself fully at its own word, and so it is perfectly coherent to follow the editors' lead in this and to trace the validity of that word. And I also feel that the ideas of Thorne and Blincoe – as with any literary manifesto – ought to be given the critical respect of being taken entirely in earnest.

Naturally, it befits a group of young writers trying to clear a space for themselves on the literary scene to reject established contemporary authors (such as Martin Amis or Rushdie, whose *Time's Arrow* and *Midnight's Children*, respectively, are taken to task on p. xiii), and to take a sideswipe at canonical figures; it also behoves them in this undertaking to disparage established stylistic techniques and consolidated genres. As a pose, as an aesthetic stance, this is perfectly understandable. Yet, as readers in these current times, we are vastly removed from those who would have first encountered Wordsworth's truly revolutionary literary manifesto, to give the obvious example of an earlier model of a literary *mission statement*. Those people, I imagine, must surely have felt a visceral shifting of tectonic plates as the staid and ornate edifice of Enlightenment rhetoric began to crumble and give way to the language used 'by men'. To such readers, Wordsworth's 'Preface' to the *Lyrical Ballads* was something genuinely new, something previously unseen: a writer speaking directly of his craft, justifying his artistic decisions and trying to mark out new directions. (I might also add my own view on this, for what it's worth, which is that the *Lyrical* Wordsworth – for the young poet himself, for the moment in which he was writing, for his extraordinary work, for the depth of its legacy – encapsulated a more truly revolutionary form of literary expression than the whole New Puritan group will ever be able to muster in their entire careers.) In the twenty-first century, things are rather different. From politics through to pop, we have been inundated with manifestoes that faltered and floundered almost before the ink was dry on their pages. For us, the model we might bear in mind is not so much William Wordsworth as Pete Townsend. Though he may loudly have protested about decline and old age, though he may truly have hoped to die before he got old, he is still here – still playing his guitar, still banking the profits – as his eighth decade draws nearer. So much for the posturing … Let us return, however, to the question in hand: does this manifesto pass muster? Is the result that we see in this collection a better kind of writing in any strict or meaningful sense?

As a way of approaching these issues, a reasonable starting point is to ask ourselves just what Thorne and Blincoe were setting themselves against. They tell us, in Rule 1, that 'we aren't using history as a justification. Story-telling does not need the validation of tradition' (Blincoe and Thorne, 2001: viii). Defining the real meaning of that nebulous word 'tradition' is a thankless task, as I have already suggested. Is it, perhaps, the Great Tradition of F. R. Leavis, the 'line of excellence' that runs through the works of the major English novelists, connecting these disparate writers with the mystical thread of outstanding achievement? It may be; but reference to Amis junior and Rushdie – while it is true that both these writers appear to be well on the path to some form of canonical status – shows us that the editors also have a broader range of writers in mind. Poetry and the poetic are deemed unsuitable, as Rule 2 makes very clear, though such a rejection might be said to depend on a rather superficial view of poetry as a genre that is always and only elusive and elitist (a view that is also blind to the possibility – one that Thomas Hardy showed in the clearest of ways – that fiction can be as compulsively detailed in its outlook as poetry, and that poetry can be as forcefully narrative as any fiction). So just what sort of writing is it that Thorne and Blincoe are striving not to replicate? Actually, both the reference to Amis and Rushdie and the discussion of poetry serve to clarify – if incompletely – those literary 'principles' that are rejected in *All Hail the New Puritans*. These include the (to them) undesirable manipulation of narrative sequence, seen to be 'a cheap trick' (p. xiii), whereas linear narrative produces 'simplicity and solidarity' (p. xiv), and the irrelevance of literary forms that no longer reflect 'the way we think … the way we write' (p. x). Other issues of contention are genre-imposed limitations (Rule 3); 'devices of voice' (Rule 4); 'elaborate punctuation' (Rule 6) invented contexts and objects (Rule 7); and past or future speculation (Rule 8), all of which I will be discussing more fully at a later stage.

What the two editors appear to reject, then, is – in the absence of a better term – 'literary' writing, by which I mean writing that is unashamedly conscious of itself as a form of artistic expression, fully open to using the rhetorical means available to this end, including formal, stylistic and linguistic unorthodoxy. It probably goes without saying that this term could be used to describe authors whose writing is evidently complex (Modernist authors are obvious examples), but without a doubt, this blanket epithet could equally be applied to novelists who are generally markedly less experimental, or really not experimental at all in the Joycean or Woolfian sense,[1] such as – to name a handful entirely at random and from different periods – Jane Austen, George Eliot, William Thackeray, Arnold Bennett, E. M. Forster, Kingsley Amis, Doris Lessing, Ian McEwan, Maggie O'Farrell, Zadie

Smith or indeed any other of those writers, similar to these or wholly distinct in scope and style, whose work a commonality of readers would probably readily agree to call 'literature'.

In contrast to this, the New Puritans saw their writing as breaking away from any unnecessary ornateness, from what I assume they hold to be the needless *rhetoricity* typified by some or many of the authors, works and styles mentioned above. To them, in the sense that we can gauge this from the Manifesto, the essence of good writing lies precisely in avoiding all forms of expression that are anything other than an unadorned reflection of reality (whatever that is); it is writing that engages directly with a simple, basic mode of framing the narrative, much as Dogme 95 sought to free itself from what it perceived as the intrusiveness of elaborate cinematographic technique.

Having briefly pointed to what I see as the target of Thorne and Blincoe's objection, the next step is to look more closely at the Manifesto itself, at least at a reasonable number of its points, and to decide on the validity and fairness of the ideas forwarded by the editors, again as a means of determining whether this prefatory instrument can be accepted as something that leads to better writing.

The Manifesto starts off, I think, rather promisingly,[2] if perhaps a little gauchely: 'Primarily storytellers, we are dedicated to the narrative form'. Not much to take exception with, though personally I would have avoided the use in this context of that knotty word 'form' at all costs, since 'narrative form' may not necessarily be read as synonymous with simple *'narrative'* and, as a somewhat unnecessary padding aimed at making a basic notion sound a little more complex, it looks unhappily like an avoidance of textual clarity (see Rule 4).

However, if at this stage I am to be wholly candid in my assessment, I would say that things begin to break down – for me at least – with point 2: 'We are prose writers and recognise that prose is the dominant form of expression. For this reason we shun poetry and poetic licence in all its forms'. Of several things that could be said here (I have already touched on poetry), just what is 'poetic licence *in all its forms*'? We might reply that Shakespeare's historical plays are a clear example of this concept, and some may even find that type of writing objectionable for this reason. We might even go a step further and say that this term would cover, for instance, a fictional account of Shake-speare's life in which imaginative reconstruction were given a free rein. Again, some might find this an objectionable form of writing. Perhaps this is what the editors were referring to (though this issue is actually more directly dealt with in their Rule 7). But 'in all its forms' poetic licence – *licentia poetica* – must surely be taken to mean quite simply *any* fictional account of *anything*. All fiction is a parallel version of what we conveniently agree to call reality; it is an artistically en-hanced or at least modified version of something (more or less plau-sible, more or less adjusted to the parameters of our expectations and experience shaped by the external world of 'real' events) that might be, but that actually is not. Blincoe complains that 'there is a marked tendency of authors to set contemporary fiction in a parallel reality: one where car names are slightly modified, the pop stars are slightly different, the slang is artificially modified' (Blincoe and Thorne, 2001: xiv–xv). For my own part, I have to say that I am not acquainted with any such fiction, but even if I were the essential point surely remains the same, which is that however much or little an author may choose to adapt fiction to the contours of that 'real' external world, the reality of the fictitious world is *always* parallel. Nathaniel Hawthorne said of Trollope's writing that it seemed 'just as real as if some giant had hewn a great lump out of the earth, and put it under a glass case, with all its inhabitants going about their daily business, and not suspecting that they were made a show of' (Trollope, 1879: 203). A wonderful idea, but – of course – a mirage of truth, not the real thing. So the shunning in Rule 2 of poetic licence, which I define here as the freedom to cre-ate any form of parallel world through fictional narrative, appears to be devoid of any meaningful value. And this is something that bodes ill, I think, for the other rules still to come.

Rule 3 is largely unexceptionable, though it is effective, for the edi-tors, in its rather blustering iconoclasticism and the (surely pardon-able) self-promotional '... we will always move towards new openings, rupturing existing genre expectations'. *Vive l'avant-garde*! But then, in repetition of the splendidly hollow Rule 2, comes Rule 4's 'We believe in textual simplicity and vow to avoid all devices of voice: rhetoric, authorial asides'. Can they really mean *all* devices? I take it by this that the editors actually meant that they subscribe to the entirely worthy views on writing of George Orwell, curiously unmentioned in this Manifesto ('Never use a metaphor, simile, or other figure of speech which you are used to seeing in print; never use a long word where a short one will do' [Orwell, 1946: 156], and so on), and that they proscribe elaborate figures of speech and 'complex' narrative arrangements of the – to some – intrusive sort, such as the 'Reader, I married him' variety. What else could a device of voice mean? I would suggest that it pertains not only to very specific rhetorical figures (that is, to discrete aspects of style) but also to *all* narrators themselves, identified or not, third person or first, omniscient and omnipresent, partly absent or wholly unreliable. The narrator, a stylistic construct *par excellence*, is nothing more but most certainly nothing less than a 'device of voice'. And, seen in this light, what then is the essential characteristic of all narrators? Surely – beyond telling the tale – it is that of attributing sympathy and antipathy here and there, now to this person, now to that, shaping and re-shaping our understanding, our opinions and our expectations. Manipulating the reader, so to speak, in order to forward the writer's broader objectives, for which the narrator is a mere rhetorical agent. And this essential work – which in turn depends vitally on the inevitable unreliability of all narrators – goes on in all works of fiction (indeed, it is inherent to any kind of writing). Claiming to avoid devices of voice is, to me, something of a smokescreen in that it taints more obviously literary uses of narrative strategy but attempts to liberate itself from similar charges. As if any form of fiction were a transparent stream of truth or a 'great lump' of the real world. In this sense, I would suggest that the editors' rhetorical zealousness at this point is yet another rather vacuous affirmation: impressively articulated but ultimately untenable.

As Thorne and Blincoe go through their rules, the readers are presented with the editors' more detailed thoughts on each item, reinforcing the underlying 'philosophy' of the particular rule itself, but also reinforcing the two writers' shared sense of commitment to the project. In Rule 5, though, we get a glimpse of discrepancy, a slight sense that the unswerving fidelity to the cause that all manifestoes call for may not always be so readily available. It is here that the Manifesto states its belief in 'temporal linearity' and rejects 'flashbacks, dual temporal narratives and foreshadowing'. Blincoe is clearly uncomfortable with this: 'There are many examples of great literature that use dual narratives, flashbacks and other effects that aim at unsettling notions of identity and of time. So the fifth rule could be seen as perverse. And yet...' (Blincoe and Thorne, 2001: xii). He continues, far from convinced, to justify this particular mandate until Thorne brings him back into line with the stinging 'Flashbacks are a cheap trick ... if the characters are strong, we need only know what they are doing now. Leave the psychoanalysis to the literary critics' (Blincoe and Thorne, 2001: xiii), one of whom (James Wood) aptly retorts 'So: out with memory, because memory is undramatic' (Wood, 2000). But, to pick up on Blincoe's own term, this prohibition does indeed seem to be somewhat perverse; certainly, it is needlessly dogmatic. For one thing, it would restrict any narrative more or less to the present tense (since anything other than the most immediate futurity is unknowable), a limitation that is both artistically and psychologically in counterposition to the needs of storytellers to root the here and now in a 'once upon a time' and to let their narratives move forward into the future. Additionally, whatever rules we may choose to limit fiction writers to, the result can only ever be fiction; a present-tense fiction, however 'now' it may appear, is no less a fiction than one that moves about in time. To pretend otherwise is patently false. Are the great nineteenth-century English novels of realism any the less realistic because of their broad temporal sweep? Is the compelling realism of a work such as H. G. Well's *The Sleeper Awakes* made any the less absorbing by locating its action in a distant future? Yet Rule 5, together with Rules 7 and 8 – all of them attempting to ensure that New Puritan texts should exude a palpable realism based on the strictest limitation to the present – are drawn up to support what seems to me a quite unnecessary injunction, one that has no coherent, justifiable connection with narrative vitality.

I have to admit that Rule 9 confuses me: 'We are moralists, so all texts [in the collection] feature a recognisable ethical reality'. Leaving aside the editors' view that the difference between morality and ethics is mere 'quibbling' and the difficulty of understanding quite what is meant by an ethical 'reality', I find myself asking what this rather *provincial* notion is doing prefacing a work of contemporary fiction, not simply as an underlying attitude but as a point of order. Why should a literary manifesto wish to impinge on this terrain? Thorne and Blincoe argue that 'writers' dependency on ethics ultimately affords ... greater freedom' (Blincoe and Thorne, 2001: xvi). But there seems to be some deal of uncertainty in their discussion as to what is actually implied by ethics, in this context. The editors, perhaps not unreasonably, point to the 'many, many writers who have embarrassed themselves by trying to keep pace with the myth of the degenerate artist' (Blincoe and Thorne, 2001: xvi); but is that all? Apparently not, for this notion also appears to involve the never-easy task of 'changing life itself' (Blincoe and Thorne, 2001: xvi), presumably for the better. (Ironically, given their rejection of literary tradition, in this somewhat unexpected insistence on morality – every other point in the manifesto touches on issues of style or form – the editors are in alignment with F. R. Leavis' view on the need for moral purpose in literature, as a basis for the achievements of the great writers who thereby provide 'awareness of the possibilities of life' [Leavis, 1950: 2].) Nevertheless, I find it hard to see the presence of this rule in several of the stories in the collection, including that of one of the editors. And this makes me wonder whether this is simply empty posturing – as if Thorne and Blincoe perhaps felt that the very word 'puritan' required some reference to morality, but were unconvinced of things beyond that – or whether the editors' initial conviction failed to impress itself on their colleagues and collaborators, or even on themselves.

Which leads me now to enquire further into these texts, to determine just how faithfully they reflect this manifesto, and to assess how successful the outcome appears to be.

The stories by the two editors, Blincoe's 'Short Guide to Game Theory' and Thorne's 'Not as Bad as This' are polar opposites. If we are to see a text in this collection as virtuous by dint of its compliance with the Manifesto, then Blincoe's story certainly has its virtues. It is a fairly neat little tale with a plausible enough central episode that, rather like the writings of Roddy Doyle, explores the potential drama, comedy and ludicrousness of a mostly ordinary situation and does so through linguistically very straightforward means (a simple, running inner monologue and a basic dialogue between the two protagonists). The time frame is almost entirely 'to the moment', as Samuel Richardson – that great writer of present-tense happenings – would have it, insistence on this being marked by a high frequency of actions described exclusively in the present simple tense, though this at times appears rather too laboriously list-like as page upon page of first-person simple present indicatives are reeled out (see later). On balance, Blincoe manages to create a story that is a 'faithful representation of the present' (Rule 8), avoids flashbacks and foreshadowings and most definitely keeps the text free of any elaborate or stylistically complex device. That said, some aspects appear forced to me, as if they were contrived merely to conform to this or that point in the Manifesto. For example, I find that the insistence on Daniel's lactose intolerance (pages 40 and 48) is a little unwarranted. It makes no thematic contribution, it plays no real part in the plot; in fact, we get the sense that Daniel's need to eat chocolate while staving off his aggressive nemesis, Duncan, has been brought to the fore simply to give attention to this medical condition. Why insist on it? I suppose that the answer must be that something like lactose intolerance is a clear marker of contemporary reality (we recall that the New Puritans 'recognise that published works are also historical documents': Rule 7). But if so, is this not needlessly and rather inelegantly bending the text to fit the checklist? And does Blincoe's sparse writing help in giving us a deeper understanding of Daniel or Duncan, even accepting that this is a very short tale? I do not find this to be the case; indeed, through such a limited description of personal 'interiority', how could it? What we might call Daniel's *inner monologue* is actually far more an attempt at listing a series of actions, devoid of interpretation, to thereby attain a measure of objectivity ('I haul my suitcase up to the gallery'; 'I visit a bar'; 'I have fish and chips again for breakfast'; 'I apologise'; 'I say, "Hello..."'; 'I am happy to sign', all from p. 38 and entirely representative of the narrative as a whole). This, however, prevents us from any fuller relationship with the character as we are kept at the most superficial level of 'acquaintance'. But perhaps that is part of the point; perhaps this is a form of fiction that – precisely through its imposed simplicities – reflects the ways in which contemporary society only disconnects. Or then again, perhaps the result of these restrictions is the inevitable inability to create anything of deeper literary worth. In all events, though I find the story competent if somewhat mediocre, it has to be said that, as a New Puritan text, 'Short Guide...' is a veritable model.

The same might also be said about Thorne's story 'Not as Bad as This' (perhaps a plea by the author to other writers to excel his efforts?). It, too, broadly conforms to the Manifesto and were we to read it with a checklist in hand, we could probably agree to tick off most of the points as being present and accounted for. Yet in this compliance, it brings the whole New Puritan enterprise into serious question. The text's refusal to shift its temporal perspective beyond the more or less immediate present may appear to some to create a sense of tension or mystery as we struggle to understand the reason for its characters' current actions and attitudes; but another interpretation of this is that it is simply a debilitating dislocation of background events from their description. This is acceptable and valid in the opening scene at Waterloo station since it is entirely normal for fiction to move us from initial confusion to gradual comprehension, indeed – particularly in contemporary fiction – this is practically a conventional function of openings. But when, page after page, we are still effectively no closer to understanding the 'Why?' that underpins the story, it becomes reasonable to ask ourselves just what, if anything, this text gains by *not* filling in the details. And what it gains, sadly, is an amateurish sense of narrative confusion that seems not to know how to sort itself out.

To make things worse, Thorne's understanding of textual simplicity leads him, I believe, to create entirely gratuitous moments that, deriving from nothing, relating to nothing, connecting nothing together, hang needlessly over the tale. These moments may be stimulating to some, but too readily give the impression of being rather more the product of a sixth-form writing project than the well-wrought work of a competent professional. Here, for instance, is Chloë's mother commenting on the portrait of her naked daughter that hangs in her bedroom:

'I'm not sure she [the artist] got Chloë's cunt quite right ... it's more impressionistic than the rest of her body.' (Thorne, 2001: 87)

There is no organic, textually rooted reason for this observation. I suggest that it brings no sense of any deeper understanding of the characters or of their context.[2] It merely adds to the impression of a thin story line padded out by risqué fillers, in the vain hope that the stylistic 'directness' on show will somehow be deemed vital and meaningful and will in this way promote the tale to a higher level of appreciation. Another example; consider this passage from a slightly later point in the narrative:

'Have you and Chloë fucked yet?' [the mother, once again]

I put down my spoon. No point in lying. 'Yeah.'

She clapped her hands together. 'I knew it. Oh, it's so good for her. She gets so uptight. Can I ask you a question? Does Chloë like oral sex?' (Thorne, 2001: 96)

It might be possible to conjecture that such absurdly inappropriate breakfast-table dialogue (proffered over the toast and jam, as it were) makes a deeper, postmodern point that contemporary communication no longer conforms to adequate and coherent social expectations. It might, perhaps, be taken as a marker of the dysfuncionality of Chloë's mother, or of the entire cast of misfits that this tale presents us with. As with aspects of Blincoe's text, we might read this sort of episode in that sort of way. But equally – and, I suspect, with greater insight – we might also conclude that this is actually nothing more than poor writing, however much it conforms to the dictates of the Manifesto. It makes no attempt to integrate the mother's disturbing obsessions more fully into the broader fabric of the narrative; it appears – like the story itself – to exist simply for effect, for show. There is the possibility here to develop the plot beyond this shadow of an idea that we encounter (the disconcertingly passive Chloë, for instance, is an obvious consequence both of her parents' convoluted and unexplained circumstances and her own poor emotional choices; and other elements of the story – not least the brutal egoist who is her boyfriend – might have been expounded to delineate a deeper image of Chloë's damage and disconnection). But the rules set out in the Manifesto actually prevent the necessary stylistic modifications that would be warranted in fleshing out this story, in transforming it into something more profound. We are allowed no recourse to the past; we are given only the most superficial access to the protagonists' consciousness; the narrative perspective offered through Rob is restricted to the purely *voyeuristic* function of description, never rising to explanation or justification. As if in recognition that he can go nowhere consequential with these limitations, Thorne abruptly shuts down the narrative, quite unable to give it any form of relevant closure. 'I don't know why I freaked, I just suddenly saw myself still here in three years' time, still trying to sort out this family…', Rob informs us (Thorne, 2000: 104). Just like his protagonist, Thorne also resolves his involvement in haste, withdrawing from the confusion that is his text as swiftly as he can. This is writing by numbers, attending not to the aesthetic needs of the narrative but instead to the strictures of a more-than-questionable manifesto.

In light of this, can it be said that compliance with the Manifesto is worthwhile, artistically? My view of the works that most closely appear to conform to the guidelines is that far more is lost than gained by following the rules. Texts such as 'Three Love Stories' (Bo Fowler), 'Two Holes' (Simon Lewis), 'Monaco' (Alex Garland) and 'The Puritans' (Toby Litt) struggle to overcome a two-dimensionality that a fuller development of the formal and stylistic devices ruled out by the Manifesto might have helped to resolve. Each of these stories appears to me to have some potential to become more than the extended anecdote that (by and large) they currently represent, yet this potential cannot be fulfilled under these literary restrictions, leaving them mired in the rhetorical wastelands of a Sunday-supplement article. But the clearest example of why compliance with these guidelines is not a good artistic choice must surely be the regrettable 'Better than Well' (Daren King), an attempt to recreate the sense of limited awareness that anti-depressant drugs induce. This text, one that – I presume – sees itself as an absorbing stylistic experiment, is actually about as rhetorically engaging as a cash-machine printout, with a concomitant level of literary interest:

> He got out of bed and crossed the room and lifted the curtain. It was morning: the source of light was the morning sun. He stood by the window and held the curtain open and looked around the room... [*ad nauseam*] (King, 2001: 66)

The many limitations of this approach in creating meaningful and insightful writing are obvious; but the deeper point is that – on the whole – King is well within his New Puritan remit. As Judith Shulevitz observed in the *New York Times*:

> The story consists entirely of the interior monologue of an idiot or, as it turns out, a man on strong antidepressants, who monotonously catalogs every aspect of his empty room. Squint and you might think you were reading a midcentury French experimental novel, in all its repetitive rigor. But no, 'Better Than Well' is actually the perfect New Puritan narrative, set exclusively in the moment, with no past, no future and all due "textual simplicity". (Shulevitz, 2001)

Happily, though, a good number of writers eschew the rules, and in doing so create stories that are far more interesting and effective. This is very much the case for texts such as 'Poet' (Tony White), 'Skunk' (Geoff Dyer), 'A Ghost Story' (Ben Richards), 'Mr Miller' (Candida Clark), 'Facing the Music' (Anna Davis) and 'Lovers' (Rebecca Ray). In all of these otherwise quite distinct stories, there is a poignancy to the narrative that brings with it the insight and deeper suggestiveness of writing if not wholly unshackled by stylistic constraint, then at least never really paying much more than lip service to the Manifesto. In each of these stories – though I find this to be particularly so in the works by Anna Davis and Rebecca Ray – the writers communicate a rich interior narrativity that is never forced, never arbitrary and never gratuitous, forgoing limitations on voice, ignoring prescriptions on content and overriding restrictions on temporal reference.

The rejection of the literary tradition posited in the Manifesto would replace it instead with something freed from that stylistic complexity we associate both with 'great' literature and with 'literary' writing in general, some of the components of which would include experimentation with narrative form; a multiplicity of narrative consciousnesses; a consciously imagistic or symbolic use of language; and the use of memory and conjecture in telling a tale. But, as I have suggested, the outcome of the New Puritan initiative is not a liberation at all; rather, straightjacketing any true stylistic creativity, it is an undermining of the necessary rhetorical freedom that allows a writer to turn a draft idea into something artistically more consolidated. Further, my assessment of the application of these rules to the collection has led me to suggest that the only texts of any marked literary worth – texts that are written, we might say, in continuity of a broader tradition of *literariness* – are precisely those that choose not to slavishly follow these guidelines. Otherwise, the best that we can hope from close compliance – as Blincoe's own story shows – is a sort of mediocrity; the worse – as Thorne and King reveal – is very poor work indeed.

In effect, the editors sought to liberate writing from what Harold Bloom – defining his understanding of the special nature of canonical literature (though I am speaking here not only of that rarified stratosphere but rather of any and all literary writing of a certain quality) – has often called its 'strangeness'.[4] It is undoubtedly wrong to suggest that the greatness of such writing is beyond definition, or that it cannot be delineated; clearly, it can. In fact, it is our task as readers and (especially) as critics to do exactly that. But what we *can* say is that such writing is ultimately irreducible; it evades any final denotation. Just when we think we have fully surveyed its frontiers, we discover another work, equally powerful, equally 'strange', but totally distinct. We can identify the components of its literary goodness or greatness, but listing those components as mere building blocks that can be put together—or, indeed, mandatorily avoided—to create effective texts is a chimera. For it is certainly as impossible to restrict genuinely good writing to ten short points in a manifesto (or to demarcate it in this way, or to set out the formal, rhetorical conditions required for it to flourish) as it is to define or create true happiness through an instruction manual. In such cases, having an idea of what it is we want to achieve will simply not be enough; it requires something much deeper than knowledge alone to bring it about.

And that would be the case even if we were discussing a manifesto for good writing that elicited our unreserved admiration and approval. Where this is not so, that is – as with the current collection – where the rules themselves are of little or no constructive value, then what lasting validity can such a document be said to have?

In concluding the assessment that I set out as my objective in the opening paragraphs of this discussion, I cannot help but endorse the view of the critic Sam Trainor that, if we really *do* want rules, if we really feel that good writing *depends* upon such guidance, then 'more poetic imagination should be the commandment' (Trainor, 2000). This is the only blueprint that we should ever need.

Notes

1 What does or does not constitute literary experimentation is, of course, a controversial notion, and some exception might be taken to the list of authors indicated here. Clearly, highly evident experimentation of the sort that radically alters expectations of narrative transparency can quite readily be identified, but I recognize that this need not imply that experimentation is absent from more 'conventional' modes of writing. For a recent discussion of this in relation to Austen, for example, see Mullan, chapter 20 ('How Experimental a Novelist is Jane Austen?').

2 Except for one minor but I think quite telling detail, which is the statement that 'this collection shows how British fiction is currently among the most exciting in the world' (p. vii). How can the editors possibly know such a thing? The answer, of course, is that they cannot. As a soundbite, as self-promotion, this is excusable. But it is also wholly devoid of any real meaning. This is telling to me as it reflects, rather faithfully, the general pattern through much of the main body of the Manifesto, namely, the nicely turned and well-balanced phrase that – sometimes quite splendidly – denounces and proclaims, but which hides the presence of any deeper significance.

3 I suppose that the obvious comparison to be made at this point is with the notorious use of this word in *Lady Chatterley's Lover*. But Lawrence's use of such language is never gratuitous; it has a direct and vital function in his text and is a visceral expression of the earthiness and simplicity of

Mellor's ideas on love, ideas that root him to a profoundly different world to that of Connie.

4 This notion forms a central part of Bloom's ideas on canonicity, forwarded most notably in *The Western Canon*. For a recent further example of Bloom's views on strangeness, see http://www.dogfilm.net/2012/06/harold-bloom-shakespeare-strangeness-and-meaning/ (consulted September 2012).

Works Cited

Blincoe, N. and M. Thorne (2001[2000]) 'Introduction: The Pledge', in N. Blincoe and M. Thorne (eds) *All Hail the New Puritans* , pp. vii-xvii. London: Fourth Estate.

Bloom, H. (1994) *The Western Canon: The Books and Schools of the Ages.* Chicago, IL: Houghton Mifflin Harcourt.

King, D. (2001[2000]) 'Better than Well', in N. Blincoe and M. Thorne (eds) *All Hail the New Puritans,* pp. 65–9. London: Fourth Estate.

Leavis, F. R. (1950) *The Great Tradition.* New York: George W Stewart.

Mullan, J. (2012) *What Matters in Jane Austen: Twenty Critical Puzzles Solved.* London: Bloomsbury.

Orwell, G. (1946) *Politics and the English Language.* London: Horizon.

Shulevitz, J. (2001) 'The Close Reader; The Puritan Ethic', *The New York Times,* 11 March, http://www.nytimes.com/2001/03/11/books/the-close-reader-the-puritan-ethic.html (consulted September 2012).

Thorne, M. (2001[2000]) 'Not as Bad as This', in N. Blincoe and M. Thorne (eds) *All Hail the New Puritans,* pp. 83–104. London: Fourth Estate.

Trainor, S. (2000) 'More Poetic Imagination Should Be the Commandment', *The Sunday Herald. HighBeam Research,* 1 October, http://www.highbeam.com/doc/1P2-19057874.html (consulted September 2012).

Trollope, A. (1879) 'The Genius of Nathaniel Hawthorne', *North American Review* (CCLXXIV): 203–22.

Wood, J. (2000) 'Celluloid Junkies', *Guardian,* 16 September, http://www.guardian.co.uk/books/2000/sep/16/fiction.reviews1 (consulted September 2012).

CHAPTER 4

GENDER TRACES IN NEW PURITAN
WOMEN'S FICTION

Sonia Villegas-López

The femininity of a text can hardly let itself be reined in or corralled.
Who will bridle the navigation? Who will put the outside behind walls?
Hélène Cixous, 'Coming to Writing'

Introduction

All Hail the New Puritans (2000) includes fifteen stories, four by
women writers and 11 more authored by men. At first sight, gender
does not seem to be a primary concern, or even an issue of importance in their stories, but only a part of the writers' mark of identity.
The stories penned by Scarlett Thomas, Candida Clark, Anna Davis
and Rebecca Ray merge with the tales of their male colleagues, drawing on issues such as mourning, suicide, adolescent musings and flirt-
ing, and updated versions of romance. In matters of style, both male
and female-authored stories follow the New Puritan principles that
vertebrate the collection, but as topics are concerned the treatment
of sex and gender, the representation of women both as narrators and
characters, and their keen eye on related issues such as family dynam-

ics, domesticity, and love and its discourses make us read the stories unmistakably from a gender perspective. The purpose of this chapter is then to search for 'traces' that may help us interpret the stories in such a light. After providing a definition of trace that might be suitable for the aim of working on gender in the stories, they will be approached both at the levels of content and style and of reading. I argue that the reading of traces, often apparently effaced in the texts or merely hinted or alluded to, helps us to reconstruct the figure of the woman author in these writers' stories, as well as to analyse them as examples of 'gendered' New Puritan writing.

The four authors under analysis belong to a young generation of writers who were born in the early 1970s and began publishing in their late twenties and early thirties. Scarlett Thomas has so far published five successful novels – *Bright Young Things* (2001), *Going Out* (2002), *PopCo* (2004), *The End of Mr Y* (2006), and more recently, *Our Tragic Universe* (2011). She is also the author of the Lyly Pascale mysteries and of a number of articles and short stories, including 'Mind Control' in the New Puritan collection. Thomas has been longlisted for the Orange Prize and shortlisted for the South African Boeke Prize. She is currently teaching Creative Writing at the University of Kent, UK. Thomas' interests are varied, including science and philosophy, literary criticism and politics. Her most recent novels show this much, as they draw on the dangers of exacerbated consumerism in a global culture, the anxieties of the academic world, the very act of writing and the figure of the author – she claims, for example, that the intended title for *Our Tragic Universe* had been 'Death of the Author' (Thomas, n.d.) – and definitely sexual politics. Candida Clark has also published profusely from 1998 (*The Last Look*), 2001 (*The Constant Eye*), 2003 (*The Mariner's Star*), 2004 (*Ghost Music*), 2005 (*A House of Light*), and 2006 (*The Chase*). As in her story 'Mr Miller', Clark focuses intensely on narrative voice as she explores the implications of mourning and loss, one of her favourite topics in novels such as *The Mariner's Star* or *Ghost Music*. Like Thomas and the other two women writers in the collection, she contributes with articles to various publications. Five novels by Anna Davis have seen the light, starting in 1999 with *The Dinner*, which was soon followed by

Melting (2001), *Cheet* (2002), *The Shoe Queen* (2007) and *The Jewel Box* in 2009. Moreover, Davis' short stories have appeared since year 2000 in different collections. Some of her works – *The Shoe Queen* or *The Jewel Box*, where she travels back to the 1920s and figures out the complexities of romance – have been described as bordering chick-lit. Drawing closely on popular genres like fairy tale, Davis sets *The Shoe Queen* against the background of modernist aesthetics and plays with diverse topics like women's emancipation, and the revision of romance and eroticism. Last but not least, Rebecca Ray's two novels to date – *A Certain Age* (1998) and *Newfoundland* (2006) – have been received differently by critics. She instantly won recognition with her first work, written at 17, whereas her most ambitious novel, *Newfoundland*, has been often reviewed on the basis of its length. Be as it may, it is a thorough project, almost an epic work in its length, title and approach.

Working on traces

'Trace' is generally the term used to refer to the physical or immaterial remnants of the past. More often than not, traces may be effaced due to the passing of time or to memory's *lacunnae*. This concept has been critically addressed in the works of philosophers such as Jacques Derrida, particularly in *Of Grammatology* (1976), and more recently by critics like Paul Ricoeur, most significantly in *Memory, History, Forgetting* (2005), or phenomenologists like Maurice Merleau-Ponty in *Phenomenology of Perception* (2002). In its relation to memory, though, the critical interest in the notion of trace comes from late antiquity, starting with Plato, Aristotle and reaching later philosophers like Augustine. The problem of memory has also entranced Locke, Hume, Kant and Heidegger, and more recently has been instrumental in the development of new disciplines like psychoanalysis and trauma studies. Since the late twentieth century, postcolonial and feminist critics alike have also paid attention to the dyad memory-history. For them, the critical notion of 'trace' has been of use to reconstruct formerly fractured identities. Benedict Anderson's *Imagined Com-*

munities (1983) reads trace in this very sense, as the presence of an absence which invariably arouses the need to write a narrative of identity: 'Awareness of being embedded in secular, serial time, with all its implications of continuity, yet of "forgetting" the experience of this continuity ... engenders the need for a narrative of "identity"' (Anderson, 1983: 205). In a similar light could be interpreted Maurice Halbwachs' (2007) work on collective memory, and Pierre Nora's notion of the 'archives' of memory. On the other hand, Marianne Hirsch and Valerie Smith (2007) have proposed a gender reading of culture, and try to analyse feminist practices of cultural memory and appropriation.

Also adopting a gender perspective, Elizabeth Grosz approaches the notion of trace in *Space, Time, and Perversion* (1995) from a different stance. In a controversial and polemical essay, Grosz uses the concept as the remnants or vestiges of women's authorial presence in literary texts, and radically questions the *a priori* reading of feminine, feminist or even female traces in them. She challenges the assumptions that there is a particular content or style that might identify a text as feminist, or that the female author leaves some 'traces' that might be later interpreted by a specific female or feminist reader (Grosz, 1995: 14). She follows Benveniste in distinguishing between the 'I' of the author, outside the text, and the 'I' of the fictional speaking subject, the 'I' of the utterance and the 'I' producing the utterance. Grosz also claims, though, that there is always some inscription in the production and composition of a text (Grosz, 1995: 19). The forces operating in the literary text are complex and varied, and work simultaneously to transmit unmistakable messages from the author to their readers:

> The signature not only signs the text by a mark of authorial propriety, but also signs the subject as the product of writing itself, of textuality; it functions as a double mark, a hinge, folding together (or separating) the author/reader or producer and the text or product. The signature cannot authenticate, it cannot prove, it cannot make present the personage of the author; but it is a remnant, a remainder of and a testimony to both a living past and a set of irreducible and ineliminable corporeal traces. It is not that author/reader and text are

entirely other to each other: the otherness of the other is also the condition of self-consolidating subject. The subject is necessarily impli-
cated in the other's otherness, even when this other is a text. (Grosz,
1995: 21)

This argument might lead us to the third reading of trace in this
chapter, as part of the narrative experience itself. We will approach
the subject from the stance of the text as fiction, and as the reflection
but also the creation – and Mario Valdés (1991: 130) would argue,
'augmentation' – of life. Original and simulacrum contribute to the
formation of traces, to which the text is witness.

Traces of the feminine: topics and ends

'Literature is political' is the opening sentence of Judith Fetterley's
classic work *The Resisting Reader* (1977: xi). She accounts for the phenomenon of reading a text 'against the grain', or as she claims, to bring
subjectivity 'to bear on the old "universality"' that texts provide. Fetterley suggests that no text is 'innocent', but that it is always ideologi-
cally and socially charged. It is the 'resisting' reader's role to look for
those meanings and implications – present or absent – in texts, which
irrevocably speak about identity.

Later critics have contended that texts and written fictions are like
bodies. They are material objects and are 'sexually marked' (Lanser,
2004: 126). Further, they are construed in acts of performance and
are socially articulated (Butler, 2004: 2). Texts are self-explanatory
through denotative and connotative clues: what they tell about themselves, and what we can infer about them. Gender might be applied
to and worked on both bodies and texts in two different ways or directions: 'Gender is the mechanism by which notions of masculine
and feminine are produced and naturalized, but gender might very
well be the apparatus by which such terms are deconstructed and de-
naturalized' (Butler, 2004: 42). Gender inscriptions – gender 'traces'
– might be found in texts and bodies physically, socially and symbolically. Like gender, sex and sexuality might be also performed in texts
in normative and descriptive ways (Lanser, 2004: 127).

We must draw on traditional feminist literary criticism to study the connection between women's writing and female or feminine topics, thus establishing a link between texts and gender. Elaine Showalter's essay *A Literature of their Own* (1982) and Sandra Gilbert and Susan Gubar's work on the figure of the woman writer in the nineteenth century, *The Madwoman in the Attic* (1979), were pioneering in developing the methodology of gynocriticism and approaching the motif of the woman author and the expression of the female literary imagination, respectively. Later works, like Maggie Humm's *Border Traffic* (1991) and Patricia Duncker's *Sisters and Strangers* (1992) have also engaged with the actual practice of contemporary women's writing and celebrated their literary and critical achievements since the 1970s, the latter focusing specifically on genre fiction.[1] In their revisions of women's literature they all seem to agree on the recurrence of certain topics like the association of femininity and space, the appropriation and supersession of women's images in the text, and the exploration and revision of romance and sentimental conventions. Despite the obvious contextual differences between the treatment of these topics in nineteenth-century and contemporary women's fiction, the recurrence of these motifs reaches the present day.

Psychoanalysis and the medical profession furthered the connection of women's bodies with matter – based on the inevitable reference to their *matrix* – and by extension with closed spaces, like the home. As Gilbert and Gubar (1979: 93ff.) aptly remarked, the woman writer and the prototypical female characters in nineteenth-century texts were physically and notionally 'immured', or even buried in life. They were meant to explore and later to abandon Plato's cave – the cave of fiction, of imagination – after a process of self-development and vital and intellectual enlightenment. This end, that could be symptomatic of many female narrators-*cum*-characters' transformations in much later fictional texts, could be further applied to these contemporary short stories under inspection. A close connection could be established between the spaces that (female) characters occupy and inhabit, and identity, especially if domestic environments are at stake. As Grosz (1995: 122) concludes, quite often the seclusion – willing or unwilling, I would add – of women within spaces they have not projected or do not own may end in their alienation and in a sense of 'homelessness'. This physical enclosure, Grosz argues reading Irigaray,[2] is very similar to their metaphorical habitation in men's imaginary universes. In this light, the first step in an advantageous renegotiation of women and space is precisely a move on from space – 'as territory which is mappable, explorable' – to place – 'occupation, dwelling, being lived in' (Grosz, 1995: 123).

Family dynamics have also been the focus of attention in many women's narratives, and in the chosen stories in particular. Freud's theory about the organization and reproduction of traditional family types has often been the model to interpret relationships among members of older and younger generations, and more specifically among men and women. In his 1909 essay 'Family Romances' he explains the politics of family succession in Oedipal terms as a means of liberation (Freud, 1991: 221). Though followed by Jacques Lacan among others, French feminists like Luce Irigaray decisively contested Freud's theories. Instead of reproducing Oedipus' narrative, Irigaray chose the episode of Orestes killing his mother Elektra and following the Law-of-the-Father to represent family dynamics in the West: 'The murder of the mother results, then, in the non-punishment of the son, the burial of the madness of women – and the burial of women in madness – and the advent of the image of the virgin goddess, born of the father and obedient to his law in forsaking the mother' (Freud, 1991: 37–8). Irigaray went on claiming that the bond with the mother always leaves a 'trace' – again a remainder of a former presence – the scar left by the umbilical cord (Freud, 1991: 39). The social order, she argued, prevents the (bodily) encounter with the mother. From a source of nurture and comfort, this figure turns into a 'devouring monster', and maternal power is deemed excessive and symbolically castrating. For the philosopher it is essential to find a language, which far from reproducing the paternal model, embraces the corporeal, more akin to maternal culture (Freud, 1991: 43).

The selected stories by these four women writers engage with the topic of a renewal of traditional family types. They are peopled by individuals who find difficult to fit in conventional families, and by others who try to find their place. Sometimes, the reader is exposed to generational conflicts, and other times to the consequences of the lack of family ties. Scarlett Thomas' 'Mind Control' illustrates the latter point by narrating the story of a young woman whose boyfriend Mark dies unexpectedly and she decides to continue living with his parents for the time being. The story focuses specifically on setting and space, a central topic in Thomas' fiction.[3] Action takes place in Mark's parents' house, where the narrator is in charge of some chores for her keeping, like doing the shopping or the housework, but is relieved from others, like doing the laundry, which they have stopped doing. The female voice of the narrator tries to impose common sense on a broken family – including herself – , and on a house in a state of stagnation. Mark's father lives obsessed by the advent of the apocalypse while he takes care of his fish everyday. Mark's mother's illness gets worse after her son's death, and she finds refuge in her room, unable to cope with the new turn of events. Ironically, the house's mad routine stops when one morning Mark's father discovers that his fish have disappeared. This apparently unremarkable fact sets ironically his grief in motion, as the narrator perceptively observes: 'This is the first time I've ever seen Mark's dad cry' (Thomas, 2000: 5). The world that they had known so far is crumbling down, and Mark's father interprets this sign as a supernatural warning.[4]

Candida Clark's 'Mr Miller' portrays the tragic ending of a man without family connections. The anonymous narrator is at the bar where Miller used to go and explains how he arrived one night and reminded her of a previous conversation they had in which she said that someone who speaks about committing suicide will never seriously attempt to do so. Miller tells her how he had been abandoned by Veronica, the woman of his life, and how since then he lacked reasons to go on living. Clark's story also reflects on the remorse the narrator feels when she finds out that Miller has carried out his plan and has hanged himself. Domesticity is replaced in the story by the communal space of the bar, and the reader is led to assume that it is precisely the lack of effective affective ties that takes Miller to a state of depression. This is a topic that Clark has later developed in a novel such as *The Mariner's Star*, where a mariner's wife and mother mourns the deaths of her husband and son at sea, and after considering suicide, takes another turn and chooses life.

Anna Davis presents a family conflict in 'Facing the Music'. Jane is an adolescent who has fallen for Sean, the singer of Citizen Duane, 'the best band in Cardiff' (Davis, 2000: 107). She tries to follow him everywhere even if in so doing she needs to lie to her mother. The whole story portrays the conflict between Jane's incontrollable impulses to follow her desires and the need to conform to family norms and respect her mother's wishes. She appears as the figure of authority in the house, whose suffocating surveillance Jane must evade to fulfil her plan. In Jane's mind, her mother becomes the 'castrating' mother of Freudian imagination. Jane needs to counteract her control by resorting to silence and lies, and by alienating herself from the mother figure. We could apply here Irigaray's words in relation to the problematic encounter with the mother:

> The relationship with the mother is a mad desire, because it is the 'dark continent' *par excellence*. It remains in the shadows of our culture; it is its night and its hell ... The maternal function underpins the social order and the order of desire, but it is always kept in a dimension of need. (Freud, 1991: 35–6)

In the end, she lets herself go and disobeys her mother only to find out that Sean is still living with her girlfriend. Davis' title refers not to the band's music, but to the fact that Jane will have to face her mother's fury back at home (Davis, 2000: 120). Family dynamics will be later explored by Davis in texts like *The Shoe Queen*, illustrating Genevieve Shelby King's traumatic relationship with her mother, on the one hand, and with her husband whom she abandons to follow her lover, on the other, together with the comforts of her luxurious life. As in 'Facing the Music', however, the shoemaker Paolo Zachari will be a huge disappointment for Genevieve, who will have to face a new life from then on. 'Facing the Music' also focuses on the importance of domestic spaces, as Jane needs metaphorically to abandon the house as part of her growing process. As in Ray's narration that will follow, Davis' story focuses on Jane's feeling of guilt for transgressing family norms and neglecting her duties.

Finally, 'Lovers' by Rebecca Ray centres on tradition and on the unconditional love that parents feel for their offspring. It deals further with the feelings of remorse and guilt that accost the protagonist when she tells them that she will move out of the family house to share a flat with her boyfriend. Ray's story reproduces the protagonist's conflictive emotions:

> The next two weeks before she moved were strange. Her father started fixing little things of hers that had been broken for a while. Her mother cooked a lot of food for her and she remembered this long article she'd read about a family where the mother was dying of cancer and they knew she only had a while left. This article said that it had brought the family together and that they'd spent all the time they had with each other, it said that they'd touched each other more. She thought that this was true, in a little way, in her family right now. But she also thought that even though they felt closer, they really felt further apart. (Ray, 2000: 193)

Two different strands of meaning collide here: the gratitude towards her parents and the drive to begin a new life, both of them symbolized by the wooden box that the protagonist is given as a goodbye present and that she will keep in her new house. 'Lovers' is, even more clearly than the former stories, about creating a sense of home which is in no way alien to the protagonist, and that is inevitably built on her experience.[5]

Love is an integral part in the four stories, and although it is obviously not a topic restricted to women's fictions, it is interesting to analyse the treatment – and at times the act of revision – that Thomas, Clark, Davis and Ray carry out, respectively. 'Mind Control' shows the effacement of love and the muffling of desire when the loved one dies; 'Mr Miller' also draws on the notion of absence by approaching suicide; 'Facing the Music' represents an adolescent's infatuation; and, 'Lovers' constructs a whole discourse on the topic.

Mark's girlfriend and his parents react similarly to his sudden death in Thomas' story. As Roland Barthes would argue, Mark stands for the other who departs. If it is true that the loved one always performs this role, Mark's death precipitates absence: 'The other is in a condition of perpetual departure, of journeying; the other is, by vocation, migrant, fugitive; I – I who love, by converse vocation, am sedentary, motionless, at hand, in expectation, nailed to the spot, *in suspense* –' (Barthes, 1990: 13). That is truly what the characters in 'Mind Control' seem to experiment with, unable even to speak Mark's absence, or to proceed further with their lives. A woman in love who waits for the absent one has usually voiced the discourse of absence and loss in the form of female complaint.[6] Therefore, the expression of lament for the lover's temporal or permanent absence is primarily feminized (Barthes, 1990: 14). Mark's girlfriend, however, does not give free rein to any of the physical signs associated to loss, like sighs or tears. On the contrary, she manages to exert 'mind control' and never lets sadness show.

Candida Clark chooses a topic that will be recurrent in her production – the loved one's death. In *The Mariner's Star*, for example, another nameless narrator is about to commit suicide after her life has been wrecked by her husband and son's deaths, and in *Ghost Music* a similar topic – how to react to the imminent death of one's lover – is also the source of interest. 'Mr Miller' portrays a case of suicide for love, or better for unrequited love. In Barthes' (1990: 218) terms, '[i]n the amorous realm, the desire for suicide is frequent: a trifle provokes it'. Miller considers this act carefully, even listing the reasons for and against it, and weighing death more dearly: 'But if you think it more in terms of a person trying to live their life *freed from desire*, then I think you're getting closer to the thing I mean: death as an ideal state' (Clark, 2000: 55). The story actually functions like Miller's legacy for the narrator, who had earlier trivialized the idea of death and from then on knows better.

In 'Facing the Music', Davis also singles out a topic that will reappear later in her production: the conflict between following one's desires or submitting to authority and rules. That is clearly the case with Jane in Davis' New Puritan story. 'Stealth is essential', reads Jane's sentence in one of her interior monologues (Davis, 2000: 114), as she wears her stilettos to meet Sean, words that we could also expect from Genevieve's mind in *The Shoe Queen* when cheating her husband to meet her lover. Julia Kristeva speaks about the experience of love in similar terms:

> Both a fear and a need of no longer being limited, held back, but going beyond. Dread of transgressing not only proprieties or taboos, but also, and above all, fear of crossing and desire to cross the boundaries of the self ... The meeting, then, mixing pleasure and promise or hopes, remains in a sort of future perfect. (Kristeva, 1987: 6)

The whole story is constructed around this unfulfilled meeting with the loved other, frustrated and never granted at the end.

Finally, 'Lovers' plays with the commonplaces about love. It reproduces the ironic declaration 'I-love-you', a manifestation of parental and romantic love, respectively. According to Barthes:

> The word (the word-as-sentence) has a meaning only at the moment I utter it; there is no other information in it but its immediate saying: no reservoir, no armory of meaning. Everything is in the speaking of it: it is a 'formula,' but this formula corresponds to no ritual; the situations in which I say *I-love-you* cannot be classified: *I-love-you* is irrepressible and unforeseeable. (Barthes, 1990: 148–9)

In the story, characters use the word-as-sentence as formula, to start a different turn:

> And then he told her that he loved her. He looked into her face and he really told her, like he was trying to say something else. Like he was trying to say that because he loved her, that should make this other thing better. Like she should think about him loving her and that would make her feel good again. (Ray, 2000: 193–4)

Ray goes deeper into the meaning and functions of language, moving from words to emotions.

In the pages that follow words and form will become the focus of attention, as we will read these four examples of New Puritan fiction in the light of the strategies and practice of feminist narratology.

New Puritanism and feminist narratology

The New Puritan manifesto was meant as a renewal of narrative form for all the writers who subscribed it in Blincoe and Thorne's anthology. They signed out their nonconformism with rhetorical excess and the predictability of genre fiction,[7] and were in favour instead of textual simplicity that implied a new look at narrative conventions like beginnings and endings, voice and time, and the ethical function of narrative texts, among other aspects. Interestingly, many of these issues have also been of great concern for feminist narratologists since the 1970s until the present day, as it will be shown.

Feminist narratologists have applied the axis of gender to the study of women's fiction. Sally Robinson published in 1991 *Engendering the Subject: Gender and Self-Representation in Contemporary Fiction*, a pioneering essay on the way that gender subjectivities can be produced in literary texts. Stemming from influential concepts like Judith Butler's performativity, Robinson contends that 'feminist discursive practices have a stake in bringing the subject to light' (Robinson, 1991: 190), and that women's texts must necessarily propose a number of strategies to do so, mimicry and masquerade among them (Robinson, 1991: 193). These female-authored texts interact with other canonical or official texts, leading to gender interpretations from socio-cultural and narratological perspectives:

> Homogenous representations of Woman and women's heterogeneous self-representations exist in a complex and often contradictory relationship. I have charted this relationship here by arguing that contemporary women's texts strategically engage with official narratives of sexual difference, of subjectivity and of history; that this engagement proceeds by a movement 'inside' and 'outside' gender as ideological representation; and that it is in the interstices between these two types of cultural and narrative positioning that female subjectivity is engendered in discourse. (Robinson, 1991: 190–1)

She suggests further that there always remains a 'trace' of Woman-as-Other in the texts (Robinson, 1991: 89).

In her essay 'Guilty Cravings: What Feminist Narratology Can Do for Cultural Studies' (1997), Robyn Warhol deals with the strategies that narratology has at hand to study gender in women's texts. Warhol suggests the need for an analysis that combines close readings and the study of historical context to any given text. She mentions two main projects or practices: focusing on women's fictions which seriously challenge official narratives and 'reading in detail', using Naomi Schor's expression, 'applying the analytic categories narratology made available to scrutinize texts very closely and arrive at gender-conscious interpretations of narratives' (Warhol, 1997: 343), or even more recently to concentrate on gender not as a preconceived category but as a textual effect.

Similarly, Kathy Mezei engages with the practice of close reading in *Ambiguous Discourse: Feminist Narratology and British Women Writers* (1996) and seeks to demonstrate 'how feminist narratology locates and deconstructs sites of ambiguity, indeterminacy, and transgression in aspects of narrative and in the sexuality and gender of author, narrator, character, and reader' (Mezei, 1996: 2), that might be so interesting for our purposes. Her vision of the aims and scope of feminist narratology is all-encompassing, as it would pay attention to narrative voice, historical context, topics and ends, and also to the act of reading and reception. In tune with this comprehensive analysis of the narrative text, Susan Lanser offers the clues that make us support a gender reading of narrative and take us back to the notion of 'trace' explained above: '[S]ex could constitute an ideal model for a narratology that recognizes absences and presences, texts and contexts, sameness and difference and their movements over time and place. A historical poetics would be especially enriched were we to take on sexual questions as narratological elements' (Lanser, 2004: 135).

In *Fictions of Authority* Lanser focuses on the topic of narrative voice as 'a trope of identity and power' in the narrative text, following the impulse of second-wave feminists like Luce Irigaray (Lanser, 1992: 3). Lanser argues that the act of writing is imbued with power and engages with aesthetic and social conventions: 'I maintain that both narrative structures and women's writing are determined not by essential properties or isolated aesthetic imperatives but by complex and changing conventions that are themselves produced in and by the relations of power that implicate writer, reader, and text' (1992: 5–6). This argument implies that a feminist appropriation of voice in narrative must entail a double process of accommodation and subversion of textual and rhetorical practices. Lanser claims that these strategies are particularly helpful in the case of narrators who engage in 'extra-representational acts' (Lanser, 1992: 16). That is not the case, however, with the female narrative voices who take the floor in Thomas, Clark, Davis and Ray's stories. Following New Puritan imperatives, their narrative voices explicitly reject rhetorical excess. In general terms, they 'efface authoriality' – to use Lanser's expression (1992: 104) but not subjectivity. The female narrator in 'Mind Control' uses strategies to distance herself from what really matters to the story: the unspoken grief of the characters, herself included, after Mark's death. Thomas manages to create 'presence' out of absence – the absence of mourning for the lover's loss, for the son's loss. In this story, the mysterious disappearance of the fish stands for Mark's unutterable absence, one day and without warning. The narrator also concentrates on other events that might attract her attention, like the experiment about watering the plants with different types of mineral water, and then assesses the results. As the characters' vital space is gradually restricted to the house and the garden – 'Mark's dad has become housebound. Mark's mother's bedridden' (Thomas, 2000: 1) – they concentrate on the here and now, their few anxieties reproduced in the present tense: the past cannot return and the future does not exist.

'Mind Control' and 'Mr Miller' both engage with an innovative presentation of beginnings and endings. Peter Brooks' famous essay 'Freud's Masterplot' argues convincingly about the way in which narratives are invariably determined 'by the sense of an ending' (Brooks, 2004: 264). From the early tradition of English fiction this has been the *leit-motif* of narrative: to arrive at a sense of closure, to fulfil the pleasure of reading (and writing) by reaching the end. The end *par excellence* is death, as Brooks argues quoting Walter Benjamin: 'For Benjamin, this death is the very "authority" of narrative: we seek in fictions the knowledge of death, the classic instances of the genre is so often literal – quickens meaning: it is the "flame," says Benjamin, at which we warm our "shivering" lives' (2004: 264). Thomas and Clark's stories begin with death, thus following one of the principles of their manifesto – 'New openings, rupturing existing genre expectations' – in their search for narrative freedom. 'Mind Control' and 'Mr Miller' narrate the unexpected, and in so doing they also alter the traditional time linearity.

In some of the stories the discourse of romance and sentimentality undergoes a revision. In *Writing Beyond the Ending* (1985), Rachel DuPlessis marks the importance of appropriating and subverting the romance plot for women writers in an effort to go beyond narrative expectations:

> Romance plots of various kinds, the iconography of love, the posture of yearning, pleasing, choosing, slipping, falling, and failing are, evidently, some of the deep, shared structures of our culture. These scripts of heterosexual romance, romantic thraldom, and a *telos* in marriage are also social forms expressed at once in individual desires and in a collective code of action including law: in sequences of action psychically imprinted and in behaviours socially upheld. (DuPlessis, 1985: 2)

Rebecca Ray carries out the revision of these features in 'Lovers'. In her story Ray goes 'beyond the ending' not by altering the customary 'they lived happily ever after', but by querying the very conventions of the popular genre. She complies with DuPlessis' theory about the uses of romance for feminist writing and narratology: 'The romance plot in narrative thus may be seen as a necessary extension of the processes of gendering, and the critique of romance that we find in twentieth-century female authors, as part of the oppositional protest lodged against both literary culture and a psychosexual norm' (DuPlessis, 1985: 38).

New Puritan norms dictate that all the stories in the collection are about 'change and escape' (Blincoe and Thorne, 2000: xii), another masterplot that engenders social and ethical implications. These short tales – and women's stories in particular – speak forth about how those changes question the validity of institutions, like the family or heterosexual love, we could add. The four stories articulate, for example, a sense of loss, reproduced as mourning in 'Mind Control' and 'Mr Miller', and as the need for a reassessment of ethical responsibility in 'Facing the Music'. Freud's acute definition of mourning is still a point of reference: 'Mourning is regularly the reaction to the loss of a loved person, or to the loss of some abstraction which has taken the place of one, such as one's country, liberty, an ideal, and so on' (Freud, 2001: 243). Like melancholia, mourning is only appeased with time. Both manifest as pathologies with specific symptoms. Similarly to mourning, melancholia undergoes a process of dejection which conveys 'self-reproaches and self-revilings, and culminates in a delusional expectation of punishment' (2001: 244). The female narrator in 'Mind Control' shows a complete inability to utter Mark's death, and skirts his loss by following other events closely, like Mark's parents' own mourning. Clark's 'Mr Miller' is told by a seemingly female voice that tries to 'redeem' herself and relieve her guilt by the very telling of the story.[8]

'Facing the Music' enacts another ethical reality, as it shows the need to mend the conflictive relationship between mother and daughter, severed by Jane's passion for Sean. This has been critically diagnosed by Irigaray in *An Ethics of Sexual Difference*, where she speaks about 'the love of self among women': 'Traditionally, it is left in the undifferentiation of the mother-daughter relationship. And this relationship has to be given up, Freud tells us, if the woman is to enter into the desire for the man-father' (Irigaray, 1984: 101). Irigaray wonders whether this often-effaced link can work only by substitution or, on the contrary, if there exists the possibility of surmounting this rivalry between women. The answer is that women must reassess themselves symbolically to find valuable models to imitate, significantly by means of a different language (1984: 104).

Conclusion

Our purpose in this chapter has been to support a study of traces – gender, textual, etc. – to discuss the stories written by Scarlett Thomas, Candida Clark, Anna Davis and Rebecca Ray, subscribing the New Puritan aesthetics. We have proposed to track the presence of author, topics and style where many of these signs had been apparently effaced from the texts. The analysis has consisted, then, in tracing marks, and thus giving substance to elements and details that could be interpreted from the perspective of gender without necessarily being a priority for the authors themselves. In the way, our work as 'resisting' readers has come to full view. In so doing, we have been inspired by Elizabeth Grosz's essay on the topic, whose conclusions we subscribe: 'there are ways in which the sexuality and corporeality of the subject leave their traces or marks on the texts produced, just as we in turn must recognize that the processes of textual production also leave their trace or residue on the body of the writer (and readers)' (Grosz, 1995: 21). If we could argue that the demise of postmodernism has come – though this might be the topic of another essay – the sex of the (she) author – their materiality – strikes back. In this context, Hélène Cixous' thoughts in 'Coming to Writing' sound remarkably modern:

> How what affects me comes into language, comes out fully worded, I don't know. I 'feel' it, but it is a mystery itself, which language is unlikely to let through.
> All that I can say is that this 'coming' to language is a fusion, a flowing into fusion; if there is 'intervention' on my part, it's in a sort of 'position,' of activity – passive, as if I were inciting myself: 'Let yourself go, let the writing flow, let yourself steep; bathe, relax, become the river, let everything go, open up, unwind, open the floodgates, let yourself roll ... ' A practice of the greatest passivity. At once a vocation and a technique. This mode of passivity is our way – really an active way – of getting to know things by letting ourselves be known by them. You don't seek to master. To demonstrate, explain, grasp. And then to lock away in a strongbox. To pocket a part of the riches of the world. But rather to transmit: to make things loved by making them known. (Cixous, 1991: 57)

Cixous' text is partly an enigma, surely a beautiful metaphor – but not an overwrought one – of women's material access to writing, and it could well be the gist to interpret the four selected stories. 'Mind Control' ends with the mystery of the fish in the pond. The whole story could be read as a means of 'getting out' of an uncomfortable situation and of looking for answers when there are none or they are not at hand. 'Mr Miller' dissects the puzzle of life and death, and the thin line between them, without providing full answers. The narrator confronts the terrible episode of Mr Miller's suicide, for which she finds neither explanation nor comfort; and, as in the former story, though, the events have been minutely described and arranged in the present time. 'Facing the Music' explores personal relations and plays with the implicit and the unsaid as it dramatizes a girl's momentum. It shares the taste for allusion with the story that closes the collection, 'Lovers', which portrays a young woman's independence and the way she wavers between sincerity of feeling and complying with a senti-mental discourse that might lessen for her parents the effects of her departure.

The adherence to life and the validity of personal experience in the replication of reality are two features that these writers contemplate, as Rebecca Ray declares in an interview:

> I believe in recording life. I've reached the point where I know that fiction matters to me most for its ability to record – and juxtapose – what I've really experienced. This is important to me for several reasons.
>
> I have an extremely poor long-term memory. I can very rarely recall anything much beyond a few months previous; images, maybe a few moments. This has made it very significant for me to commit life to paper – to know that it's stored somewhere.
>
> I also believe in the transformative process of documenting life. There are many intractable sadnesses in this world; to be able to recognize and record them has value. It gives love.
>
> Finally, for me, the truth is more important than invention. Arguably, fiction is never truth. I can't answer that. I can only say that I gain a greater satisfaction from documenting the real in a way that does it justice than I have ever done from imaginative creation. (cited in Villegas-López, 2012)

Far from aesthetic flourishes the four stories are inscribed in the here and now, and approach the gutters of reality, sometimes provokingly and always evading imposture, aided to this end by the format of the short story.

Notes

1 Maggie Humm wrote a comprehensive chapter on the achievements of feminist literary criticism in Stevi Jackson and Jackie Jones' edited work *Contemporary Feminist Theories* (1998) that includes these and many other sources chronologically arranged.

2 In her chapter, Grosz quotes profusely from *Elemental Passions* (1992) by Luce Irigaray. In this work, the French philosopher explains the relationship between women and space in terms of the physical and notional demarcations associated to women's bodies and daily experiences, and also in relation to property (or the lack of it).

3 Both the PhD student Ariel Manto in *The End of Mr Y* and Meg, the professional writer in *Our Tragic Universe*, experience a sense of homelessness and are in need of a place they can claim their own. Ariel's sense of space is related to dislocation and alienation: she loses the privacy of her office and shares her place with other academics, shares a flat with another student, and experimenting with troposphere she even loses substance and abandons the materiality of her body for the sake of extra-corporeal episodes and time travelling. After a failed relationship, Meg leaves her boyfriend and rents a cottage by the sea where she will find a place to write, the Woolfian 'room of one's own'.

4 Thomas evokes the same image in her novel *Our Tragic Universe*, where Frank recounts the anecdote of another mysterious disappearance of goldfish, for which he provides a rational explanation, however (Thomas, 2010: 419).

5 Ray expands this idea in her late novel *Newfoundland*, a story of transformation and about creating a sense of home and community.

6 So it happens in Ovid's *Heroides*, a collection of letters of love and dejection, and later in *The Wife's Lament*, an Old-English poem contained in the *Exeter Book*, or in the *Portuguese Letters* (1669) by Guilleraques. See John Kerrigan's study on the topic (1991).

7 In an interview with Rebecca Ray, she comments the following in relation to the use of genre fiction in her writing: 'Genre fiction is a successful

concept invented by sales teams. I just write whatever comes naturally to the story. I think each story has an aesthetic that's inherent to it. Consequently the stories I've written, short or long, have differing styles.' (cited in Villegas-López, 2012).

8   Candida Clark shows a similar concern in *The Mariner's Star*, in which the protagonist surmounts her depression by releasing her grief and facing her fears.

Works Cited

Anderson, B. (1983) *Imagined Communities: Reflections on the Origins and Spread of Nationalism*. London: Verso.

Blincoe, N. and Thorne, M. (2000) 'Introduction: The Pledge', in N. Blincoe and M. Thorne (eds) *All Hail the New Puritans*, pp. vii–xvii. London: Fourth Estate.

Barthes, R. (1990[1977]) *A Lover's Discourse: Fragments*. Harmondsworth: Penguin.

Brooks, P. (2004) 'Freud's Masterplot', in M. Bal (ed.) *Narrative Theory: Critical Concepts in Literary and Cultural Studies*. Vol. III. Political Narratology, pp. 261–75. London: Routledge.

Butler, J. (2004) *Undoing Gender*. London: Routledge.

Cixous, H. (1991) 'Coming to Writing', in D. Jenson (ed.) *Coming to Writing and Other Essays*, pp. 1–58. Cambridge, Mass: Harvard UP.

Clark, C. (2000) 'Mr Miller', in N. Blincoe and M. Thorne (eds) *All Hail the New Puritans*, pp. 51–64. London: Fourth Estate.

Clark, C. (2002) *The Mariner's Star*. London: Review.

Clark, C. (2005) *Ghost Music*. London: Review.

Davis, A. (2000) 'Facing the Music', in N. Blincoe and M. Thorne (eds) *All Hail the New Puritans*, pp. 105–20. London: Fourth Estate.

Davis, A. (2007) *The Shoe Queen*. London: Black Swan.

Derrida, J. (1976) *Of Grammatology*. Baltimore, MD: The Johns Hopkins University Press.

Duncker, P. (1992) *Sisters and Strangers: Introduction to Contemporary Feminist Criticism*. Oxford: Blackwell.

DuPlessis, R. (1985) *Writing Beyond the Ending*. Bloomington. Indiana University Press.

Fetterley, J. (1977) *The Resisting Reader: A Feminist Approach to American Fiction*. Bloomington: Indiana University Press.

Freud, S. (2001[1917]) 'Mourning and Melancholia', in *The Standard Edition of the Complete Psychological Works of Sigmund Freud. Vol. XIV (1914–*

1916): On the History of the Psychoanalytic Movement, Papers on Metapsy-chology and Other Works, pp. 237–58. London: Vintage.

Freud, S. (1991[1919]) 'Family Romances', in S. Freud, *On Sexuality: Three Essays on the Theory of Sexuality and Other Works*, pp. 221–5. London: Penguin.

Gilbert, S. and Gubar, S. (1979) *The Madwoman in the Attic: The Woman Writer and the Nineteenth-Century Literary Imagination*. New Haven, CT: Yale University Press.

Grosz, E. (1995) *Space, Time, and Perversion: Essays on the Politics of Bodies*. New York: Routledge.

Halbwachs, M. (2007) 'From *The Collective Memory*', in M. Rossington and A. Whitehead (eds) *Theories of Memory: A Reader*, pp. 139–43. Baltimore, MD: The Johns Hopkins University Press.

Hirsch, M. and V. Smith (2007) 'From *Feminism and Cultural Memory: An Introduction*', in M. Rossington and A. Whitehead (eds) *Theories of Memory: A Reader*, pp. 223–9. Baltimore, MD: The Johns Hopkins University Press.

Humm, M. (1991) *Border Traffic: Strategies of Contemporary Women Writers*. Manchester: Manchester University Press.

Humm, M. (1998) 'Feminist Literary Theory', in S. Jackson and J. Jones (eds) *Contemporary Feminist Theories*, pp. 194–212. Edinburgh: Edinburgh University Press.

Irigaray, L. (1984) *An Ethics of Sexual Difference*. Ithaca, NY: Cornell University Press.

Irigaray, L. (1991) 'The Bodily Encounter with the Mother', in M. Whitford (ed.) *The Irigaray Reader*, pp. 34–46. Oxford: Blackwell.

Irigaray, L. (1992) *Elemental Passions*. New York: Routledge.

Kerrigan, J. (ed.) (1991) *Motives of Woe: Shakespeare and 'Female Complaint'. A Critical Anthology*. Oxford: Clarendon Press.

Kristeva, J. (1987) *Tales of Love*. New York: Columbia University Press.

Lanser, S. S. (1992) *Fictions of Authority: Women Writers and Narrative Voice*. Ithaca, NY: Cornell.

Lanser, S. S. (2004) 'Sexing Narratology: Toward A Gendered Poetics of Narrative Voice', in M. Bal (ed.) *Narrative Theory: Critical Concepts in Literary and Cultural Studies*, Vol. III: Political Narratology, pp. 123–39. London: Routledge.

Merleau-Ponty, M. (2002[1945]) *Phenomenology of Perception*. London: Routledge & Kegan Paul.

Mezei, K. (1996) 'Introduction: Contextualizing Feminist Narratology', in K. Mezei (ed.) *Ambiguous Discourse: Feminist Narratology and British Women Writers*, pp. 1–20. Chapel Hill: The University of North Carolina.

Nora, P. (2007) 'From *Between Memory and History: Les Lieux de Mémoire*', in M. Rossington and A. Whitehead (eds) *Theories of Memory: A Reader*, pp. 144–9. Baltimore, MD: The Johns Hopkins University Press.

Ray, R. (2000) 'Lovers', in N. Blincoe and M. Thorne (eds) *All Hail the New Puritans*, pp. 191–200. London: Fourth Estate.

Ray, R. (2005) *Newfoundland*. London: Penguin.

Ricoeur, P. (2005) *Memory, History, Forgetting*. Chicago, IL: The University of Chicago Press.

Robinson, S. (1991) *Engendering the Subject: Gender and Self-Representation in Contemporary Women's Fiction*. New York: State University of New York Press.

Showalter, E. (1982) *A Literature of Their Own: British Women Novelists from Brontë to Lessing*. London: Virago.

Thomas, S. (n.d.) 'About Scarlett Thomas', http://www.scarlettthomas.co.uk (consulted July 2012).

Thomas, S. (2000) 'Mind Control', in N. Blincoe and M. Thorne (eds) *All Hail the New Puritans*, pp. 1–8. London: Fourth Estate.

Thomas, S. (2006) *The End of Mr Y*. Edinburgh: Canongate.

Thomas, S. (2010) *Our Tragic Universe*. Edinburgh: Canongate.

Valdés, M. J. (ed.) (1991) *A Ricoeur Reader: Reflection and Imagination*. New York: Harvester Wheatsheaf.

Villegas-López, S. (2012) Interview with Rebecca Ray, e-mail message, 22 June.

Warhol, R. R. (1997) 'Guilty Cravings: What Feminist Narratology Can Do for Cultural Studies', in D. Herman (ed.) *Narratologies: New Perspectives on Narrative Analysis*, pp. 340–55. Columbus: Ohio State University Press.

CHAPTER 5

New Puritans/New Labour

José Francisco Fernández

If New Labour had been a literary movement, there are reasons to believe they would have created something along the lines of *All Hail the New Puritans*. In other words, the New Puritans seem to share some of the features of New Labour, at least in terms of presentation and 'news management', but within the context of a literary movement. It is my intention in this chapter to examine to what degree the volume of short stories edited by Nicholas Blincoe and Matt Thorne encapsulates the spirit of an era in Britain, the end of the 1990s, and particularly the euphoria surrounding Tony Blair's first term in office.

There are indeed striking similarities between both phenomena, the rise of New Labour to government and the emergence of this particular group of young writers to a position of literary pre-eminence, taking into account of course the different milieus to which the protagonists of both events belonged. But still, the verve, the sharpness and perhaps a certain lack of substance of these projects lend themselves to a common consideration of both events, which is the final aim of this section.

But first, some thought must be given to the politics of the generation of young British writers who had just begun their careers before the end of the millennium and were on the brink of becoming professional writers by the year 2000. There is common agreement as to the disillusion of British society at large with politics over recent decades. Experts have pointed to the influence of television and other media in becoming the sounding board for discussion of matters that were previously the object of debate in Parliament, with the result that 'politics have faded from the public consciousness' (Sampson, 2005: 3). A certain weariness brought on by the alternation in power of two big parties which gradually resemble each other, the complacency of a political class in a position of privilege that appears removed from the economic hardships of the population and a pervading atmosphere of low intensity corruption (spin doctoring, sleaze, smear, cash for honours, etc.) have led to a general loss of faith in the traditional system of political parties, together with the ensuing side-effects of an increase in the numbers of non-voters, especially among those under 24, and a shift from belief in party politics to a concern with consumer power (Childs, 2005: 8).

After a convulsed decade of protest during Margaret Thatcher's terms in office, John Major, British Prime Minister during most of the 1990s, personified a period of tranquillity in which citizens were told that things were back to normal: 'He [Major] is the epitome of sweet reason. He reassures us that nothing truly alarming need ever happen' (Young, 1993: 113). This lacklustre image that traditional politics held for young voters was bound to be reflected in the literature written at the time by members of this age group. Instead of turning their fiction into an enquiry of the evils of their time, some new authors turned their writing into a political attitude, expressing a desperate rebelliousness that in itself implied a reaction against a worn-out and obsolete system, as in this fragment from *Ecstasy*, by Irvine Welsh:

> It was the party: he felt that you had to party, you had to party harder than ever. It was the only way. It was your duty to show that you were still alive. Political sloganeering and posturing meant nothing; you had to celebrate the joy of life in the face of all those grey forces and dead spirits who controlled everything, who fucked with your head and livelihood anyway, if you weren't one of them. You had to let

them know that in spite of their best efforts to make you like them, to make you dead, you were still alive. (Welsh, 2004: 26–27)

In this period of 'slumbering acquiescence' (Young, 1993: 116) that was Britain in the 1990s, the feeling of detachment from politics can be perfectly represented by Richard, the protagonist of Alex Garland's *The Beach* (1996). In his life as a traveller through South-East Asia he gets by with what could be called the Westerners' qualms kit, a standard set of scruples that helps him handle troublesome situations: 'I don't like dealing with money transactions in poor countries. I get confused between feeling that I shouldn't haggle with poverty and hating getting ripped off' (Garland, 2007: 52). Apart from this minimum baggage in terms of political consciousness, consisting of a basic awareness of class distinctions, enough to make him question his own position as regards injustice, he lacks any coalesced ideas on how society should work, having only vague concepts that belong to a past tradition. When he finally arrives at the remote beach where an alternative lifestyle commune live secluded from the rest of the world, he is somewhat disappointed at finding that their main ambition is to live as carefree as possible, free of the burden of morals: 'It's silly really. I think I was expecting an … an ideology or something. A purpose' (Garland, 2007: 96). Although set in a distant part of the world, the novel does reflect the lack of commitment that was rife in Britain at the time, an ethical wasteland in which 'the media – along with sport, fashion and celebrity – has moved from the margins to the very centre of our cultural life, filling the vacuum left by the outflow of intellectual interest from politics and progressive ideas' (Cowley, 1999: 12).

Richard, the protagonist of Garland's novel, is the epitome of the world of *kidults*, twenty-something-year-olds who are unwilling to abandon adolescence and who understand life as a videogame: constantly moving on, dodging obstacles (responsibilities) in pursuit of an unspecified aim without the possibility of pausing and assessing each situation. The arrival of Tony Blair's New Labour to power in 1997 did nothing but reinforce the ideology-free landscape of a generation of young people in Britain. Despite the Prime Minister's revolutionary stand against the establishment and his moves towards constitutional reform, what he represented was in fact 'not so much a politician of traditional left or right, but a moderniser' (Blair, 2010: xvi) which in real terms meant someone above the dialectical fray of confrontation, a public figure who offered a ready-made discourse fit for all tastes, as the leader of the opposition at the time remarked: 'Tony Blair was elected because he claimed to believe in almost everything. Before long people may decide that it is the same as believing in nothing, with delivery to match' (Hague cited in Sampson, 2005: 81). The 'Brave New World' of Blair, as Will Self named it, however, was achieved at a heavy cost, the loss of diversity, the homogenization of society and a certain indifference towards discordant discourses: 'With everyone middle-class, childless and a restful shade of beige, we're living not so much in a melting-pot as in a Cup-a-Soup. Or so we wish to believe' (Self, 2006: 259).

The group of authors that have been associated with the label of New Puritans grew to maturity with the final decline of the Tories after 18 years' uninterrupted exercise of power and the rising star of Tony Blair. The emergence of the soft left in Britain at the end of the 1990s was part of their emotional background and in their presentation they adopted some of the attitudes that were already the trademark of New Labour. This does not mean that they were committed supporters of Tony Blair's policies. Toby Litt, for one, considers that the New Labour governments represented a missed opportunity to transform the country into a less market-orientated society:

> I don't think we do, except if it's to be a provider of financial services with lower standards of regulation, for the world to use as a kind of economic junction box, where we skim up a little bit of money because it passes through, and a tourist site and some kind of begrudged art venue, some kind of out of town barn where you put up some Damien Hirst and some Tracey Emin. (cited in Navarro Romero, 2011: 280)

It must be stated too that in the stories of the collection references to British politics are missing, as if the authors and their characters lived in a vacuum in which someone was already taking care of that cumbersome aspect of social governance and therefore they did not need to address such concerns. For Nicholas Blincoe, it was all part of the cultural atmosphere of the times:

> It's interesting how un-political we were considering the horrendous legacy of Tony Blair's dysfunctional, illiberal and incompetent government. But that all came later. The collection reflects the times, which was always the aim ('faithful representations of the present'). In 1999, the three big things that had overshadowed our childhood and teens (as, loosely, Gen X or post-baby boomers) had been the misery of boom-and-bust economies, terrorism and nuclear annihilation. A stable and growing world economy, the advent of peace in Ireland and the end of the Cold War had created a curious political vacuum: it really was a time without ideology. (Blincoe, 2011)

The New Puritans were not any different from the originators of other cultural manifestations of the same age group working at that time in Britain. As Roger Luckhurst has clearly stated, complicity with the centre of power was the dominant note in art produced after the 1980s: 'The Young British Artists dominated the British cultural scene in the 1990s with an avant-gardism that was evacuated of any political sense' (Luckhurst, 2005: 81).

However, if not in their subject matter, the New Puritans did work in parallel to the political scheme of New Labour in terms of their aims and ambitions, in what they were trying to achieve. The 'Third Way' was notoriously the approach to the perceived end of history that New Labour's ideologists had elaborated, imagining a middle ground between the harsh liberal forces of the market advocated by the Right and the monolithic reliance on the state associated with the traditional Left. The pundits of New Labour felt that 'an alternative politics, involving new thinking and innovative policies, must be developed which can comprehend and confront major contemporary transformations in our social and economic life' (Lukes, 1998: 3).

The 'Third Way' was, in short, a compromise between the different approaches that had been offered in the past for managing the economy in order to find imaginative and effective solutions. Likewise, the New Puritans contemplated an old division in the world of literature between low and debased forms of writing (pulp fiction, SF, fantasy, thrillers) and the literary novel, fraught with already-seen experiments and worn-out personal marks of style. They too imagined the possibility of new forms being born of past traditions that would offer fresh perspectives to a fast-moving technological era. They would modulate different genres to create, for instance, thrillers with lyrical intensity, erotic writing infused with high literary pretensions or local-colour narrations that fizzed with media-inspired energy. Taking this into account, despite all its shortcomings, *All Hail the New Puritans* must be credited with imagining a Third Way in literature, as was admitted by critics: 'There is something refreshing in the New Puritan desire to find middle ground between simple genre fiction on the one hand and playful postmodernist stylization or pure artiness on the other hand' (Rosenquist, 2007: 8).

If the 'Third Way' in politics was considered to be not a perfectly drafted programme for the future but 'a vehicle for debate about the purpose of social democracy in a global economy' (Seldon, 2005: 175), the whole idea of setting up the volume of *All Hail the New Puritans*, preceded by a polemical manifesto, was not meant to set the standards for the practice of literature in the twenty-first century but to open a debate about changes in contemporary fiction (Thorne, 2011). Young writers perceived that the advance of literature had reached a period of stagnation and a fresh approach would stimulate creativity. Like the Prime Minister, the New Puritans had no inkling of what the outcome of the debate would be, but having the right attitude was an essential element of both projects.

The New Puritans were charged with the same electricity that sparked from Blair's propagandists during his first term in office, when New Labour's honeymoon with the voters seemed in full swing. The mood surrounding Blair's first years in No. 10 was that of euphoria, being the result of a vast majority (179 seats) achieved in May 1997, but also due to the energy displayed by the government just after taking charge of the destiny of the nation, and everything seemed possible: 'At the same time,' wrote columnist John Lloyd in September 1997,

Blair's millennial rhetoric, the dynamism of his person and the enthusiasm of his Government have combined to give the impression that
the Union will be renovated, the health service restored, the pensions
safe-guarded, education made efficient, the excluded included and
Britain the envy of the West. (Lloyd, 1997: 4)

When reading 'The Pledge', the introduction written by Nicholas
Blincoe and Matt Thorne to their collection of short stories, it is difficult to abstract oneself from the period when it was written and not
to see in the text the influence of New Labour English, a jargon which
owns much to advertising and management. What they lacked in
specific proposals they made up for with the promotional style com-
monly used when launching a new product. On the first page, when
the editors present the anthology, Blincoe and Thorne exult in the excellence and brilliance of their book with an enthusiast's conviction:

The aim of this anthology was to bring together a group of like-
minded writers and set them a challenge ... see if something exciting
emerges ... what makes recent fiction so original and challenging ...
how British fiction is currently among the most exciting in the world
... the beginning of a new wave. (Blincoe and Thorne, 2001: vii)

The repetition of the same message brings to mind the government's
communication strategy, which a Whitehall head of information characterized as the three 'Rs': rhetoric, repetition and rebuttal (Franklin,
2004: 90). The style of 'The Pledge' contains tremendously positive
language that continues in the dialogue that ensues, and it is similar
to the official discourse by the representatives of the government of
the day; it exuded self-belief and it put up a brave face for the new
times ahead.

Blair himself had been the originator of this kind of messianic language, drawn from an inner belief of being chosen for a higher aim,
which he still used when remembering his victory 13 years later:

On our side, we had the mood ... We had the self-belief that the start
of a new adventure often bestows on the ignorant. We had the confidence that in reaching this stage we had swept all before us, con-
quered with ease, strode out with abandon. Hadn't we fought a great

campaign? ... Hadn't our strategies, like something derived from destiny, scattered the proud in the imagination of their hearts? (Blair, 2010: 4)

It is difficult not to find echoes of Blair's emotional rhetoric of triumph in Blincoe and Thorne's call to arms: 'But the stories in this collection are so obviously both new and fantastic, I think it presents a real challenge to the critic to explain just why they work so well' (Blincoe and Thorne, 2001: xvii).

Before the campaign for the general elections of 1997 and afterwards, with the intention of maintaining the momentum achieved by the victory, Blair usually addressed the best qualities he saw in the character of his fellow citizens, like courage and innovation (Blair, 2004: 166), using this as the foundation for the Britain of the new millennium. Similarly, Blincoe and Thorne theorized on the need to redress the direction of British literature as they saw it by counting on the best qualities of their chosen writers: simplicity, contemporaneity, integrity. Both projects based their survival on something unattainable, the hopes for a different future to which they would make a decisive contribution. The future that the New Puritans might imagine in the world of literature would correspond to what New Labour imagined as the perfect scenario for British politics, 'a permanent consensus under its permanent management' (Finlayson, 2003: 11).

A consequence of this forward looking ethos in the world vision of both projects is their rejection of the past. Blincoe and Thorne famously declared that 'Story-telling does not need the validation of tradition. New Puritanism is about looking to the future' (Blincoe and Thorne, 2001: viii). Theirs was the opportunity to 'blow the dinosaurs out of the water' (Blincoe and Thorne, 2001: vii), meaning that the time of the practitioners of the literary novel of the previous 20 years had finished; they would not have anything to do with their epic style. Again, it is very likely that the influence of New Labour, as the dominant political project of the day, was paramount in this respect. If there was anything Blair wanted to dissociate himself from, it was not the Tories, whose economic policies he had quickly adopted, but old Labour: its lack of internal democracy, its liaison with the unions, its tradition of tax, spending and borrowing, its unsuitable members of the loony left ... all that smacked of rancid, unstylish, stagnant old times: 'much of the New Labour project rested on Blair's broad personal appeal and importantly his lack of Labour Party baggage' (Bennister, 2009: 174). As befitted movements born at the end of the millennium, for New Labour and New Puritans everything related to the past was out, the way forward lay in their promises for the future. What Alan Finlayson describes as an essential feature of New Labour can be easily applied to the New Puritans if we think in terms of the literary world: 'The future is where the problems are and whoever can advance the solution to things that are going to happen can claim to be the natural party of government' (Finlayson, 2003: 51).

There are additional elements that reinforce the idea that the New Puritans drew from the same source as New Labour to paint their picture of reality. If we look for further similarities, in both cases the friendship established between blokes was instrumental in their coming into being, with Blair firmly ensconced with Alasdair Campbell and Peter Mandelson in a closed circle that very few could enter. Before Blair became leader, he and Gordon Brown had appeared as a twosome. The birth of the New Puritans can be ascribed too to the synergy between Blincoe and Thorne, and their invitation to a number of friends of theirs to join the project.

The moral content that the editors advocated for the New Puritans in point 9 of their manifesto can also be detected in a New Labour leader who talked about responsibilities, about the distinction between right and wrong, about duties of citizenship and whose firm beliefs never wavered as time went on.

Tony Blair felt dazzled by the media and was adamant about never relaxing on matters concerning presentation. He also felt attracted by pop culture, which brought him closer to the world of celebrities and fashion. The editors of *All Hail the New Puritans*, for their part, were willing to make the most of the publicity surrounding the project and of course favoured the explicit mention in the stories of contemporary films, songs, and other cultural products of the day. Both New Labour and the New Puritans received the allure of cosmopolitan environments. New Labour projected to the world the image of being the promoters of an innovative country in the fields of music, art and design through the concept of Cool Britannia. In the stories of *All Hail the New Puritans*, the fictions of Alex Garland and Geoff Dyer, set in Monaco and Paris respectively, do account for continental European glamour among the objects of desire for the contributors to the anthology. But these concomitant features do not really tackle the core of the matter: being New Labour a political party with a project, however vague, for the society of its time, how does the New Puritan movement assimilate its model of society in their narrations? To what extent do the stories in *All Hail the New Puritans* reflect New Labour society? In order to provide an answer to this, I will focus on four stories in the anthology ('Mind Control' by Scarlett Thomas, 'A Ghost Story (Director's Cut)' by Ben Richards, 'Not as Bad as This' by Matt Thorne and 'The Puritans' by Toby Litt) in which social relations can be studied in detail. In all four of these stories a group of individuals spend a considerable amount of time together, and issues such as domination, control, power and negotiations between people can be conveniently analyzed.

Let us consider first the outline of Blair's ideal society. As is well known, in order to win the favour of the majority of voters, Blair pushed his party towards the centre, adopting for its credo values and principles that had until recently been associated with the Right, such as a firm stance against delinquency – 'Tough on crime, tough on the causes of crime' had been one of Blair's catchphrases during his time as leader of the opposition. Building a solid ideological principle around the concept of family was also one of his concerns, and family for Blair was strongly based on his belief in the concept of responsibility. The Prime Minister frequently insisted on the need to reinforce the duties of citizenship, to instil in the people the conviction that the rights they enjoyed were strongly connected to a number of obligations to the community and to other members of the family unit, especially children: 'rights and opportunities without responsibility are engines of selfishness and greed' (Blair, 2004: 191). Similarly to the 'Third Way' vision he promoted for politics, consisting of the economic tenets of the Right adopted by a progressive social democracy, his view of the family combined elements of tradition (decency, respect, order) with more modern attitudes (end of discrimination as regards different types of families, recognition of the role of technology, openness to the outside world). His view of a thriving society, expressed in the rhetorical language of politics, was 'to bring to the self-interested consumer age the value of solidarity. Not to cease to want the best for oneself but to wish it for all' (Blair, 2004: 259).

But it is notorious that, despite emerging from a powerful source of energy at the centre, the Blairite project for Britain did not find the means to reach the layers of society it had meant to and its delivery got diluted along the way. Tony Blair's policy in domestic affairs was blocked by the Chancellor, Gordon Brown, who did not easily accept any meddling in the huge areas of governance he controlled (from social welfare to income tax rates, from higher education fees to Third World debt). An administration not sympathetic to the Prime Minister's impulses towards modernization, despite his personal charm, his appeal and his relentless energy, did not help much in the transmission of Blair's values for the nation. True, in Blair's first term many constitutional changes were implemented, with devolution taking place in Scotland and Wales, the establishment of a Northern Ireland Assembly, the election of a London major and the partial reform of the House of Lords, but these policy reviews were 'instructed that ideological thinking was out, and that "what counts is what works"' (Ludlam, 2004: 2), that is, they lacked the conviction of a carefully designed plan. As Terence Casey writes, 'in rather typically British fashion, these changes were haphazard, without an underlying vision of the proper balance of power and responsibilities between institutions' (Casey, 2009: 10).

Tony Blair's form of governance, avoiding discussions with the whole cabinet and leaning on consultations with a selected group of advisors might have contributed to the ebbing away of his initial message to the nation. His style of leadership, more focused on direct intervention rather than on a lengthy process which depends on the concourse of many agents, led Blair gradually to pay more attention to the world stage than to home affairs: 'domestic politics is negotiation, bureaucracy, incrementalism, whereas foreign affairs more readily lends itself to giving a strong lead and direct decision making' (Dyson, 2009: 38). Whatever the reasons, the truth is that in the stories of *All Hail the New Puritans* in which families (or at least some people living together under the same roof) are portrayed, there is a significant lack of response to New Labour's values of responsibility and solidarity. It is as if, when actual writing took place, the stories clearly diverged from the rosy panoramic view of the introduction.

In the four stories where people gather in family-like units and in which the action centres on their living together dysfunction is the norm, as if the structure of the family had been subject to a radical shake-up and the different elements had been joined together at awkward angles, producing asymmetrical figures. In Scarlett Thomas' story, 'Mind Control', the narrator is living with the parents of her dead boyfriend, taking somehow the role of the deceased child. She is in charge of the housekeeping and takes care of her surrogate parents, carrying on with a normal life, except for the fact that the mother is permanently in bed and the father is insane: 'While Mark's father surfs the internet looking for other people's experiences of missing fish, I continue to clean, take ice-cream to Mark's mother and play on the Dreamcast. I'm addicted to Shenmue, and the plants are suffering because of it' (Thomas, 2001: 6). There is no chaos, nor disorder, but no explanations are provided and there is no cohesion either.

Jim, the protagonist of Ben Richards' narrative, 'A Ghost Story (Director's Cut)' has suffered a mental breakdown after the fiasco of his film getting no distribution and no attention from critics. His girlfriend too has left him, so, searching for a place to restore his peace of mind, he travels north to stay with Martha, an old friend, who lives with her husband. While the married couple are at work during the day, he strikes a friendship with Karen, the cleaning-lady. She is an uninhibited girl who takes to the sick man and they watch films together and keep each other company. When tragedy strikes this fragile relationship and Karen dies, the filmmaker discovers with disgust that the visual culture that he voraciously consumes equally plays its part in the banality of the girl's death, turning it into a unit of information to be broadcast in the evening news: 'when I thought about that burning car I knew that I was seeing more than the sad and untimely death of a girl of whom I had grown very fond. I was seeing the blazing wreck repeated and reflected on the eyeballs of popcorn-crunching spectators' (Richards, 2001: 33).

Matt Thorne's 'Not as Bad as This' is probably the most accomplished example of a corrupted version of a family in the whole collection of stories. Under an apparent normality, in which the people in the house carry out their duties as if nothing had gone wrong, basic rules of decorum are broken, cruelty and punishment are enacted for no apparent reason and, again, the head of the family and supposed figure of authority has a deranged mind and behaves erratically. The narrator of the story, Rob, goes back temporarily to his ex-girlfriend's house to help her father recover his sanity by creating an illusion of former happier times. Following a previous arrangement, Chloë allows and encourages Rob to mistreat her while the other members of the family continuously interfere in each other's privacy. The initial plan of creating a bogus happy family seems doomed and Rob finally leaves the house: 'I don't know why I freaked, I just suddenly saw myself still here in three years' time, still trying to sort out this family' (Thorne, 2001: 104).

Finally, in 'The Puritans' by Toby Litt, Jack and Jill are a couple who live together in a house by the sea, but they are far removed from being a conventional family. They are the visible part of a team who illegally copy sadistic and pornographic videos. The other member of the team is John, an ex-convict whom they do not trust, and living together is not devoid of tensions: 'Most of the time, Jack kept quiet. He knew that his attempts to peacemake only inflamed the others. John accused him of being in Jill's pocket. Jill tried to force him to agree with her. Generally, he did agree with Jill. But, because of that, he worried that John was right, and that he *was* in Jill's pocket' (Litt, 2001: 171). Jack and Jill meet another couple who are apparently unaware of their clandestine activities and they get entangled in the newcomers' manipulative strategies, keeping information from each other and letting distrust grow in their relationship. At the end, the brutal force of the sordid business they are involved in breaks through their routine and their lives are shattered.

What can be gathered from the examination of the four narratives is that there is a problem with power. Either it is avoided or dismissed, as in the stories by Scarlett Thomas and Ben Richards, or it is exerted arbitrarily or forcibly, as in the stories by Matt Thorne and Toby Litt. Power in the family stories of *All Hail the New Puritans* is difficult to locate, it is ungraspable, with unidentified agents. It is highly significant that fathers, when they appear, are ridiculously unbalanced figures, in whom the authors of the stories have not invested any dignity: 'He [Chloë's father] was squatting in a muddy ditch, naked apart from a pair of baggy white underpants and thick-lensed glasses. The moment he saw us he broke into a run' (Thorne, 2001: 91–2). As a consequence of this empty space which no one is willing to occupy, there is no negotiation for living together, and responsibilities for one's acts are avoided for the most part. Relationships, consequently, are a game of chance, following random patterns. In Toby Litt's story there certainly are strict rules that concern the shift-system by means of which the copying machines keep working 24 hours a day, but apart from that the protagonists are at the mercy of forces outside their control. The only authentic, protective and warm relationship based on mutual trust is the one formed by the filmmaker and Karen in Ben Richards' story, but it is brutally cut by the girl's accident when it was beginning to take shape.

Another common feature of the four stories is that in all cases myths functioning as metanarratives, which provide governing structures for the texts, are degraded and diminished. In Scarlett Thomas' piece, there is a subtext taken from religious fundamentalism, represented by a preacher from the US that Mark's father picks up on the radio. The preacher advocates strict adherence to the Scriptures, but in the story the symbols taken from the Bible are ridiculously brought down in scale: 'The fish pond is Mark's father's pride and joy. The fish are all right-wing Christians, by the way. Or, at least, they must be after listening to the stuff Mark's dad plays to them on his short-wave radio' (Thomas, 2001: 2). One day all the fish in the pond disappear, including Matthew and John, Mark's father's favourites, in a reverse and reduced version of the miracle of the loaves and fishes.

In Ben Richards' story the subtext is provided by Pendle Hill, a mountain that lies behind the town of Clitheroe, where the action takes place. In the early seventeenth-century it was the site of a famous case of witchcraft where a number of women 'were accused of cow-killing, milk-souring and general curse-laying before being taken to Lancaster jail and hanged' (Richards, 2001: 22). If the hill looked imposing and foreboding to Jim on his first night in town, the day Karen dies it looks inoffensive and benign: the black magic has been transposed to the images on TV which recreate the car accident, implying that it is in the media where evil resides nowadays.

In Matt Thorne's disturbing story, 'Not as Bad as This', the myth of the English Rose is defiled. Chloë, a model of cool English beauty and responsibility, accepts to undergo various kinds of degrading experiences at the hands of her ex-boyfriend, who stretches the limits of the young woman's resistance, as if by unveiling her basest instincts he was making her as contemptible as the people in the house.

Finally, Toby Litt chooses as a general frame for his narrative the myth of the Cold War, a favourite topos of the author. The basement in the cottage by the sea where the protagonists have set up a clandestine workshop is in fact an atomic fall-out shelter, built in the late 1970s, when the threat of nuclear annihilation was felt as real by millions of people in the West. They even wear a kind of uniform (navy blue coat, Breton jumper, blue jeans, army surplus boots) that might in different circumstances give them the air of a commando or resistance group. However, the course of the action reveals that in their line of business there is no place for great schemes involving the world super powers, and that reality is violently prosaic.

There are no references to current British politics in the stories of the collection, and no connection can be made between the lives of the characters and the policies of any government. What can be concluded when examining the fictional families of *All Hail the New Puritans* is that the uplifting rhetoric of the most salient political figure of the times, which was somehow present in the editors' introduction to the volume, was counteracted by the blunt narratives of young writers. Contrary to what journalist David Boyle states when assessing the New Puritan project, I believe that it is in the stories themselves, and not in the manifesto, where one can find 'the determined rejection of spin or manipulation and the demand for something real' (Boyle, 2004: 142). Their fiction, in which big concepts are downsized and reduced to a manageable format, could be taken as the necessary counterpart to the discourse of power, as a way of coming to an understanding of the reality of Britain during this period of history.

Acknowledgements

This chapter is part of the I+D research project FFI-2012-35872, funded by the Spanish Ministerio de Economía y Competitividad and the ERDF (FEDER).

Works Cited

Bennister, M. (2009) 'Tony Blair as Prime Minister', in T. Casey (ed.) *The Blair Legacy: Politics, Policy, Governance, and Foreign Affairs*, pp. 165–77. Basingstoke: Palgrave.

Blair, T. (2004) *Tony Blair in his Own Words*, ed. P. Richards. London: Politico's.

Blair, T. (2010) *A Journey*. London: Hutchinson.

Blincoe, N. (2011) Answers to questionnaire on the New Puritans, e-mail message, 7 July.

Blincoe, N. and M. Thorne (2001[2000]) 'Introduction: The Pledge', in N. Blincoe and M. Thorne (eds) *All Hail the New Puritans*, pp. vii–xvii. London: Fourth Estate.

Boyle, D. (2004[2003]) *Authenticity: Brands, Fakes, Spin and the Lust for Real Life*. London: Harper Perennial.

Casey, T. (2009) 'Introduction: How to Assess the Blair Legacy?', in T. Casey (ed.) *The Blair Legacy: Politics, Policy, Governance, and Foreign Affairs*, pp. 1–19. Basingstoke: Palgrave.

Childs, P. (2005) *Contemporary Novelists: British Fiction since 1970*. Basingstoke: Palgrave.

Cowley, J. (1999) 'Searching for England', *Waterstone's Magazine* (Summer/ Autumn): 3–14.

Dyson, S. B. (2009) *The Blair Identity. Leadership and Foreign Policy*. Manchester and New York: Manchester University Press.

Finlayson, A. (2003) *Making Sense of New Labour*. London: Lawrence and Wishart.

Franklin, B. (2004) 'A Damascene Conversion? New Labour and Media Relations', in S. Ludlam and M. J. Smith (eds) *Governing as New Labour*, pp. 88–105. Basingstoke: Palgrave.

Garland, A. (2007[1996]) *The Beach*. London: Penguin.

Litt, T. (2001[2000]) 'The Puritans', in N. Blincoe and M. Thorne (eds) *All Hail the New Puritans*, pp. 165–90. London: Fourth Estate.

Lloyd, J. (1997) 'The Self-Inventors', *TLS* (26 September): 3–4.

Luckhurst, R. (2005) 'British Science Fiction in the 1990s', in N. Bentley (ed.) *British Fiction of the 1990s*, pp. 78–91. London and New York: Routledge.

Navarro Romero, B. (2011) 'Coming to Terms with 21st Century British Politics: An Interview with Toby Litt', *Journal of English Studies* 9: 277–86.

Ludlam, S. (2004) 'Introduction: Second Term New Labour', in S. Ludlam and M. J. Smith (eds) *Governing as New Labour*, pp. 1–15. Houndmills, Basingstoke: Palgrave.

Lukes, S. (1998) 'Left Down the Middle', *TLS* (25 September): 3–4.

Richards, B. (2001[2000]) 'A Ghost Story (Director's Cut)', in N. Blincoe and M. Thorne (eds) *All Hail the New Puritans*, pp. 19–33. London: Fourth Estate

Rosenquist, R. (2007) 'All Hail the New Puritans', in A. Maunder (ed.) *The Facts on File Companion to the British Short Story*, pp. 7–8. New York: Facts on File.

Sampson, A. (2005[2004]) *Who Runs this Place?* London: John Murray.

Seldon, A. (2005[2004]) *Blair*. London: The Free Press.

Self, W. (2006) 'The Media Estate: Big Brother', in *Junk Mail*, pp. 255–61. New York: Black Cat.

Thomas, S. (2001[2000]) 'Mind Control', in N. Blincoe and M. Thorne (eds) *All Hail the New Puritans*, pp. 1–8. London: Fourth Estate.

Thorne, M. (2001[2000]) 'Not as Bad as This', in N. Blincoe and M. Thorne (eds) *All Hail the New Puritans*, pp. 83–104. London: Fourth Estate.

Thorne, M. (2011) Answers to questionnaire on the New Puritans, e-mail message, 6 July.

Welsh, I. (2004[1996]) *Ecstasy*. London: Vintage.

Young, H. (1993) 'Reinventing the British Disease', in M. Bradbury and A. Motion (eds) *New Writing Two*, pp. 109–17. London: Minerva and British Council.

Chapter 6

Brits Abroad
The Travelling Perspectives of Geoff Dyer and Alex Garland

Bianca Leggett

The role of place in the stories of *All Hail the New Puritans* (2000) is key to the shared sympathies and ideas that bind the collection together. Place names are prominent, acting to anchor the stories in a recognizable and contemporary reality. Nicholas Blincoe admonishes writers for attempting to 'erase all the specifics of a culture ... to create a sense of timelessness', an act which shows 'contempt not just for the everyday, but for everyone now alive' (Blincoe and Thorne, 2000: xv). The specifics of place, likewise, show that New Puritans accord importance to the role that place plays in the texture of everyday life. The kind of lives most often on show in this collection are provincial ones: New Puritans often shun the metropolitan centre, preferring to stage their dramas at Britain's forgotten margins. In setting their stories in places like Preston, Warwick and Newport, the authors register a complaint against British fiction not unlike the Angry Young Men before them, bringing demotic and regional voices into the hallowed halls of culture. Likewise, the New Puritans seem to combine the Angry Young Men's anarchic energy and alienation with their rejection of the academy and the avant garde. James Wood recognises this tendency in *All Hail the Puritans* in none too flattering terms: whereas Wyndham Lewis applauded the attempt to 'Kill John Bull with art', he writes, this collection is 'more likely to kill art with John Bull' (Wood, 2000). Wood draws a connection between the New Puritan collection, whose prefacing Pledge calls for an end to 'poetic licence' and 'the retreat to the campus' (Blincoe and Thorne, 2000: ix) and a British aesthetic whose roots are in the realist tradition, proving suspicious of any tendencies in art which might be perceived as elitist or fanciful.

Since the locations of most of the New Puritan stories is closely in harmony with the collection's ethos, thematic emphasis and style, we may ask, how does this resonance change when one of its stories is set in a glamorous Continental location? Alex Garland's story 'Monaco', is set at the Grand Prix racing track in the country of its title, while Geoff Dyer's 'Skunk', a kind of psychogeographic fable set in Paris, are alone in representing the New Puritans abroad. Travel abroad retains, for the most part, a connotation of privilege, associated with holidaying and dilettantism. The traveller is a cosmopolitan figure, assumed to have both a degree of disposable income and a lack of responsibilities. In this sense, the protagonists of these stories are already at odds with most of the characters we meet elsewhere in the collection. Yet, while these stories represent a straying from the geographic terrain of the rest of *All Hail the New Puritans*, we should not assume too readily that their thematic ground is likewise a deviation. By examining the depiction of the British abroad in these two stories, this chapter argues that a portrait of contemporary experience emerges which suggests that life in Paris and Monaco is not so different from that in Preston or Newport after all.

The cosmopolitan location of Geoff Dyer's 'Skunk' is representative of Dyer's reputation as a cosmopolitan author, both as a well-travelled man and an author whose literary influences are spread far and wide. His novel, *Paris Trance* (1998), contains references to Albert Camus and Ernest Hemingway; *Jeff in Venice/Death in Varanasi* (2009) credits Nietzsche, Gramsci and (naturally) Thomas Mann, while elsewhere Dyer has written about his admiration for Rainer

Maria Rilke and Günter Grass. It is perhaps surprising, then, to note that Zadie Smith has compared him to one of Britain's most famously xenophobic authors, calling Dyer a 'post-modern Kingsley Amis' going on to suggest that Dyer's 'acute and bad tempered' writing is 'in the great British tradition' (Smith, 2009). The comic tradition of which Smith speaks is one that, like Kingsley Amis' work, often draws on the social embarrassment of an English protagonist, and is charac-terized by an authorial voice which uses understatement and bathetic humour to create its effects. While Dyer's authorial voice may draw on a British comic tradition, however, perhaps the key influence to acknowledge in understanding the type of cosmopolitanism which Dyer represents is a writer who both shared Dyer's taste for travel and who was the subject of Dyer's first work of travel fiction, D. H. Law-rence. *Out of Sheer Rage* (1997) tells the story of a man who is trying to write a book about D. H. Lawrence, and moves from place to place in imitation of his subject in the hope of finding inspiration. He feels tempted to return to England, but decides against it saying 'moving back to England meant moving back into what, in my notes, I referred to by the Lawrentian phrase "the soft centre of my being". Being abroad – anywhere – meant being at the edge of myself, of what I was capable of' (Dyer, 1997: 13). Elsewhere, Dyer quotes a proliferation of writers, including Lawrence, whose letters included variations of the question 'Where does one want to live?' (Dyer, 1997: 13). While 'Skunk' exhibits Dyer's writing at its most prosaic and anecdotal, its positioning of the writer as artist in exile and interest in the creative experience of lostness stems from the cosmopolitan spirit of Modern-ism and the elite form of nomadism it engendered in a generation of writers.

If Dyer was suggested to be 'a post-modern Kingsley Amis' then Alex Garland was given a similarly flattering, but somewhat mislead-ing, comparison when dubbed 'the new Graham Greene' (Gluck-man, 1999). Garland is quick to shrug off the label, calling such high praise 'a bit ridiculous' (cited in Gluckman, 1999). Garland is right to acknowledge that his work lacks the political and theological scope which Greene's novels achieved, insisting that 'literature about back-packers is pretty limited' (cited in Gluckman, 1999), yet Garland's novels contain an ethical enquiry about the figure of the traveller which justifies a degree of comparison. The Thailand Garland depicts in *The Beach* (1996) and aspects of The Philippines in *The Tesseract* (1998) have something of Greeneland about them, taking us into seedy foreign underworlds in which flailing antiheroes find themselves quickly drawn into morally murky situations in which they feel out of their depths. When asked what drew him to such 'seedy' subjects, Greene said: 'I think it's the same draw that a child has towards making a mud pie. Perhaps it's a certain remaining infantility in one's character. The seedy is nearer the beginning isn't it – or nearer the end, I suppose' (cited in Donaghy, 1992: 49). Greene suggests simultaneously that the 'seedy' contains some kind of essence (or seed) of the human condition and that its draw for the author is one of complicity of the thrills of base things. This idea links Greene, not only to Garland and his work's preoccupation with violence, but to another author to whom Garland claims to owe the greatest debt, J. G. Ballard. While most of Ballard's work is domestic in setting, he cites his time spent growing up in Shanghai and internment in a Japanese concentration camp as an influence on his work: 'I don't think you can go through the experience of war without one's perceptions of the world being forever changed. The reassuring stage set that everyday reality in the suburban West presents to us is torn down; you see the ragged scaffolding, and then you see the truth beyond that, and it can be a frightening experience' (cited in Clute, 2009). *Empire of the Sun* (1984) was reportedly one of Garland's greatest influences in writing *The Beach* and indeed there is some resemblance between the boy protagonist of that story and the boyish protagonist of Garland's novel, both of whom share a delight in the paraphernalia of war, a fierce desire for survival and a disturbingly amoral playfulness. 'Monaco', however, bears a stronger relationship to one of Ballard's most controversial novels, *Crash* (1973). Like *Crash*, 'Monaco' juxtaposes motor-racing violence and sexuality, which prompts troubling questions about the relationship between both sex and technology, and desire and death.

'Monaco' also has something of the Ballardian stylistic character in Garland's spare and lapidary prose style, in the neutrality of the authorial voice and in his forensic eye for detail and expert pacing which builds tension as he draws out the build-up towards the story's explosive conclusion. Garland's style, like Dyer's, corresponds well to the dictates of the Manifesto that heads the anthology. Alex Clark wrote, in the *London Review of Books,* that 'Monaco' 'makes a virtue out of the understatement and pared-down prose that the Pledge demands' (Clark, 2000). The simplicity of expression in both stories is also suggestive of hostility to academicism, or a refusal to 'retreat to the campus' as the Pledge has it, which is also a part of the spirit of *All Hail the New Puritans.*

Alex Garland's reputation at this point in time was more that of a writer of blockbusters than a scholarly writer, indeed the popularity of *The Beach* was somewhat to the detriment of the 'anti-traveller' message it was intended to carry (Gluckman, 1999). Either oblivious or indifferent to the novel's satirical intent, *The Beach* became a smash hit with backpackers and was approved by the Thai tourist board as a piece of positive publicity. While Garland's popular success has sometimes given him a reputation as a writer of pulp fiction, which belies the complexity of his work, he is in some sense a genre writer. Like his novels *The Beach* and *The Tesseract,* 'Monaco' is a story whose element of ethical enquiry is framed as a visceral, rather than intellectual, thriller.

The anti-intellectualism of Geoff Dyer's narrator in 'Skunk', however, is more questionable. His tone verges on the boastful when he considers the fascination that his anti-intellectualism might hold for a Parisian woman:

> I think she *was* curious because I did not fit any of the moulds from which Parisian men were cast. This was the first afternoon she had spent with a forty-year old intellectual who had nothing intelligent to say about – and little interest in – anything except night-clubs and smoking dope. (Dyer, 2000: 72)

If we are to identify the narrator with Dyer himself, and certain overlapping biographical details between author and narrator encourage such a reading, this is somewhat disingenuous. Dyer, a writer who began his career with a book of academic criticism and who was recently named by the *Observer* as one of 'Britain's Top 300 Intellectuals' (Naughton, 2011), can hardly himself claim to be a man whose interests are confined to drugs and clubbing.

If Dyer and Garland's anti-intellectualism is more apparent than actual, this could be argued to be in line with a British tradition. The perception of British culture as anti-intellectual, particularly when contrasted to that of the French, is a phenomenon that Stefan Collini historicizes in his study *Absent Minds: Intellectuals in Britain* (2006), dating the trend back to Burke whose 'celebration of the lack in Britain of those "political men of letters" who allegedly help foment the French Revolution prefigures a good deal of twentieth century writing on the subject' (Collini, 2007: 80). Interestingly, the character of anti-intellectualism in Britain according to this genealogy is conservative, whereas for Nicholas Blincoe and Matt Thorne, the move towards a fiction which deals in the 'everyday' is equated with the attempt to create a new order. By dubbing the writers of the anthology 'Puritans', Thorne and Blincoe suggest, like the Angry Young Men before them, that the old order is corrupt. Their choice of analogies reveals a preoccupation with ageing and decay: New Puritans will 'blow the dinosaurs out of the water', dispense with 'disco dads' and banish 'carefully poised sentences' which are 'nothing but make-up on a corpse' (Blincoe and Thorne, 2000: vii, viii, xvi).

The anti-intellectualism which Garland and Dyer share with the spirit of the New Puritans is not only a British phenomenon, then, but part of a cultural moment of rebellion. While it is debatable whether Geoff Dyer, aged 42 at the time that *All Hail the New Puritans* went to press and a published author for over 10 years, could claim to be part of a new wave of young writers, the spirit of a certain youthful defiance runs through his work as it does through Garland's. Dyer and Garland's supposed anti-intellectualism is perhaps better understood, not as a rejection of high culture, but an emphasis on the importance of the experiential, particularly the sensational and the dangerous. The fact that, in Dyer and Garland's work, the real is better experienced abroad, implies a numbing quality in British life. Dyer's idea of travel as a means of 'being at the edge of myself' finds a correlative in the desire Richard expresses in *The Beach* to become 'worldly and interesting' through travel (Garland, 2000: 163). Richard hopes to acquire 'a store of memories', which should ideally include witnessing 'extreme poverty', '[b]eing in a riot' and most important of all 'having a brush with my own death' (Garland, 2000: 163).

Drugs occupy a prominent position both in *The Beach* and in much of Dyer's work because, like travel, they are associated with embracing danger in pursuit of hedonistic highs and deeper self-knowledge. Lindsey Michael Banco uses the word 'Tripping' to suggest the confluence of travel and drugs, often experienced together, but also motivated by similar desires. In 'Monaco', however, the central focus is on neither travel nor drugs, but a different kind of thrill-seeking and dangerous pursuit, Grand Prix racing. Ayrton Senna, the champion racing driver, whose premature death at the San Marino Grand Prix in 1994 this story inevitably recalls, spoke of racing driving as a kind of brinkmanship of self-discovery: 'The harder I push, the more I find within myself. I am always looking for the next step, a different world to go into, areas where I have not been before. It's lonely driving a Grand Prix car, but very absorbing. I have experienced new sensations and I want more. That is my excitement, my motivation' (cited in Collings and Edworthy, 2002: 238). It is striking too that, like 'tripping', Senna uses a spatial metaphor: to reach ever higher speeds is to enter 'a different world'. Travel, drugs and motor racing alike are portrayed as both hedonistic and yet heroic in becoming a means to confront existential truths.

There is, however, another way to read travel. Reading Garland's *The Beach* or Dyer's *Jeff in Venice/Death in Varanasi* we learn that travel can be motivated, not so much by the attraction to the unknown as detachment from home; not so much by self-discovery as a descent into solipsism. The Generation X protagonists of these novels both leave England as a means of escape. 'Escape through travel works', Richard argues. 'Almost from the moment I boarded my flight, life in England became meaningless' (Garland, 2000: 115). But in rendering life at home meaningless, do these travellers enter into a life which is more meaningful? In the case of Richard, the conclusions are doubtful. When the social structure of 'the beach', a utopian island community, violently implodes, Richard escapes with his life concluding, 'I carry a lot of scars. I like the way that sounds. I carry a *lot* of scars' (Garland, 2000: 438). This glib and self-satisfied sound-bite suggests that Richard's experiences have not tempered his enthusiasm for glossy violence nor produced a more sophisticated aspiration than to model himself on celluloid machismo. In *Jeff in Venice/Death in Varanasi*, Dyer's alter-ego 'Jeff' does not so much find himself as lose his mind. During a trip to India he becomes increasingly isolated and, in a parody of spiritual enlightenment, ends the story by apparently embracing insanity.

We will keep these anticlimactic conclusions in mind as we consider what comment both 'Monaco' and 'Skunk' make on the connection between being abroad and self-discovery or improvement. In the case of the Englishman abroad in these stories, the narrators are abroad for professional reasons rather than soul-searching, yet these professions link them to the idea of the traveller and outside observer. The narrator of Garland's 'Monaco' is a photographer in the high-octane world of Grand Prix racing who captures the conjunction of two sensational events: the first, a striptease by a young 'Eurotrash' woman standing at the sides of the track and the second, the disastrous crash of a Ferrari on the final stretch of track of Monaco's racecourse (Garland, 2000: 9). Dyer's tale is of a travel writer who, at a dinner party with friends in Paris, invites an attractive woman to join him the next day to 'enter the dreamspace' of Paris by smoking skunk, an excursion which ends badly when the drug prompts a paranoid episode in his companion who subsequently takes flight and leaves the narrator afraid for her safety (Dyer, 2000: 74).

The positions of the photographer and the travel writer demand inside information and confer authority on the traveller's perspective, differentiating them from that lowliest of creatures, the tourist. Garland's character in 'Monaco' defines himself against the 'Eurotrash', a moneyed group who watch the racing from behind high protective fencing. In contrast, the photographer narrator stands on a 'narrow strip' which is:

> No-man's land as far as the public is concerned ... there to service the race marshals and medics and fire crews and journalists ... To stand

here, you must first sign a piece of paper that says you take full responsibility for any harm that befalls you in this exposed position.
(Garland, 2000: 10)

The photographer is both spatially and symbolically closer to the dangerous world of the racing driver's rather than the posing spectators
on the margins. Dyer's character 'insider' status is instead linked to
his *savoir faire* in Paris, indicated by his longstanding friendship with
a French couple and evident familiarity with the geography of the
city. He decides to observe Paris from his own 'narrow strip', that is
the privileged 'dream space' (Dyer, 2000: 74) of the city which he attempts to access through smoking the strong marijuana which gives
the story its name, 'Skunk'.

In Banco's analysis, drugs are a key part of how the 'anti-tourist
tourist' distinguishes his or herself from the pack, signalling both
'countercultural solidarity and access to an osmotic blend of familiarity and alterity' (Banco, 2009: 132). Dyer seems to use skunk in this
way, wishing to gain a new perspective on the city, but enacting rituals
of marijuana smoking which give the activity a quality of nostalgia.
The element of 'countercultural solidarity' which he hopes to share
with Marie is, however, horribly misjudged. Instead, the drugs leave
Marie feeling paranoid about the narrator's intentions towards her,
notably that he is planning on 'putting me in a novel' (Dyer, 2000:
76). Marie's fears are justified: shortly after her exit, the narrator tells
us: 'When I returned to my table I made a few notes, of things she had
said, in case, one day, I wanted to use what had happened in a novel
or story' (Dyer, 2000: 80). The incident can be read as a kind of joke
or metafictional allusion to Dyer's tendency to blur the line between
travel writing and travel fiction, as he does in the other stories in *Yoga
for People Who Can't be Bothered* (1998), from which 'Skunk' is taken,
and *Jeff in Venice/Death in Varanasi* (2009). Sometimes published as
fiction in one country and travel writing in another, Dyer is keen to
perpetuate the confusion, saying that he likes, 'to write stuff that's
maybe only an inch from what really happened ... The test is hopefully
that you can't tell when I go from faithfully transcribing what happened to completely inventing something' (cited in Hansen, 2003).

Like Nicholas Blincoe, Dyer is interested in generic classifications only in so far as they can be 'subverted, reinvented and modernised' (Blincoe and Thorne, 2000: xi).

In terms of travel writing, however, there is an ethical question at stake when the difference between travel fact and travel fiction is flattened. Writers of guidebooks, the kind of travel writer represented by Dyer's narrator, usually have a contractual responsibility to their publishers to produce an account which is accurate and research-based. The writer of travel fiction is at the other end of the spectrum, having full license to treat the host country as raw material, ready to be bent to suit the conventions of his or her story. As Marie's drug induced disorientation sets in, she seems to accuse her companion of appropriating the city in a way which recalls the liberties of the novelist: 'I want to be in my city. Where is my city? Why can't we be in my city?' (Dyer, 2000: 75). The advantage has shifted from Marie, a self-possessed Parisian with 'a Parisian fondness for debate and strident argument' (Dyer, 2000: 70–1), to the writer and outsider, a figure of blankness and suspicion. As Mary Pratt argued in *Imperial Eyes*, the travel writer's portrayal of the foreign allows him or her to master that which they describe, conveying to their readers a sense of 'ownership, entitlement and familiarity' (Pratt, 2008: 3). In contrast, Marie feels like an alien in her own city since the narrator has transfigured it, either by intoxicating her with a disorientating drug or by appropriating her as a character in a fictional Paris which she cannot recognize.

Marie's sense that the narrator wishes to possess her is also, perhaps, an effect of the half-articulated undertow of sexual tension between the characters. While the narrator claims he has 'no sexual feelings towards her ... partly because I had a girlfriend in England', he adds in mischievous parenthesis '(though I did not mention this, of course)' (Dyer, 2000: 72). The association of travel with sex generally finds its explanation in the liberating possibilities that come with leaving behind one's usual social context and milieu, so that the consequences of one's actions are unlikely to outlast the holiday itself. Dyer (2010: 298) suggests as much in a short essay in which he considers the sexually liberating effect of hotels: 'By becoming a temporary resident of this non-place you become a non-person,' he argues, 'you are granted an ethical equivalent of diplomatic immunity. You become morally weightless ... You have no history'. He goes on to suggest that, for the same reason, 'men are less liable to be impotent' in hotels (Dyer, 2010: 298). 'Skunk' carries the suggestion that the 'dream space' of Paris has some of the 'morally weightless' and aphrodisiacal conditions of the hotel.

The narrator's desire to form a bond with Marie through smoking skunk is a failure, yet he believes that the paranoid episode allows him to gain a truer sense of her character: 'she was not the adventurous free spirit she had seemed [but]... someone who often spent evenings hanging out on the phone, chatting to friends, many of whom had boyfriends and did not live nearby' (Dyer, 2000: 77). According to the narrator, she is not a 'free spirit' but a needy single woman, and one whose vulnerable state requires his 'custodianship' (Dyer, 2000: 79). When Marie escapes into a taxi, the narrator's sense of failure becomes associated with feelings of failed masculinity: 'My penis, as happens when I am nervous or stoned ... had shrunk dramatically', he notes (Dyer, 2000: 80). Only when he narrates the story to his attractive friend Mimi, emphasizing 'the funny side' and drawing 'attention to how correctly I had behaved' (Dyer, 2000: 81) does he regain confidence. As author, Marie is once again in Dyer's 'custodianship' and the rambling and frightening episode is shaped to assume the logic of an anecdote of comic mishap. We can read the story as Mimi hears it, as a comically anticlimactic tale of drugs and a city walk, or we can read it as a metafictional parable. In this second version the travel writer becomes a kind of villain, both a detached and a powerful figure who manipulates and gains possession of his subject in order to fashion a narrative which flatters his own position.

Garland's story too can be read as a kind of metafictional enquiry into the ethical responsibilities of authorship, investigated through the photographer narrator. The narrator is allowed no more biographical detail than his profession, rather as he attempts to keep his subjects from realizing 'that I had eyes behind the lens' for fear of disrupting their exhibitionist display (Garland, 2000: 13). Like Christopher Isherwood's 'camera' narrator (another Englishman who finds thrills overseas), 'shutter open, quite passive, recording, not thinking' (Isherwood, 1989: 9), the narrator suggests that he is a neutral observer into this world rather than an agent within it. At a dull part of the track as the cars make their practice laps, he begins to take pictures of an attractive 'Eurotrash' girl, whose boyfriend does not object because 'that's what she was there for, and that's why he was sitting at Rascasse' (Garland, 2000: 11). In so doing, the narrator directs attention away from his own objectification of the girl by deflecting blame on to her 'Eurotrash' boyfriend. On spying the lens, the girl performs a succession of poses from the demure to the provocative: 'She was as comfortable with a camera as that' (Garland, 2000: 11), the photographer comments. The photographer's passivity is emphasized by the girl's professionalism, even enthusiasm, as she becomes more daring and begins to masturbate: 'She tilted her head provocatively and continued to gaze straight at my camera' (Garland, 2000: 12).

According to Laura Mulvey in her analysis of the male gaze in cinema, '[P]leasure in looking is split between active/male and passive/female'. She goes on to explain: 'The determining male gaze projects its fantasy onto the female figure, which is styled accordingly' (Mulvey, 1999: 383). If we read the scene through Mulvey's analysis, the photographer becomes the active participant in the scene in that it is his lens, and the masculine fantasies that it represents and propagates, which provoke the girl's display, which she has passively tailored according to male fantasy. As studies like Ariel Levy's *Female Chauvinist Pigs: Women and the Rise of Raunch Culture* (2005) have noted, however, in a seeming backlash against the second wave feminism which Mulvey represents, it is an increasingly accepted notion that women choose to embody male fantasy figures, not because they have internalized their objectification, but as an authentic expression of their own empowerment and sexuality. Levy argues against such a notion, suggesting that the women are hoping to 'get ahead' by 'conforming to someone else's – someone more powerful's – distorted notion of what you represent' (Levy, 2005: 106). We are blocked from deciding whether the girl's display of desire represents her own arousal or a projection of male sexuality because of her lack of interiority, and our inability to move beyond the 'male gaze'. A feminist critique alerts us, however, to the subtle ways in which the photographer may have greater responsibility for the scene which he photographs than his narrative encourages us to recognize.

In order to get the perfect shot, the photographer explains, he needs the conjunction of both girl and car, recalling the iconic advertising image that conflates the appeal of a shiny new car with that of an attractive woman by picturing the two together. And if the association of cars with girls makes racing sexy, the association of girls with racing suggests that they too are fraught with danger. As they await the speeding car, the girl attempts to delay orgasm and the photographer, in parallel, restrains himself from using his last few shots, prompting the photographer's meditation on the term *petit mort*: 'When the French come, they think they're dying' (Garland, 2000: 15). The close association of the car's approach with the girl's climax creates an expectation that the car too will experience a dark *petit mort* of some kind, which it duly does when it 'loses its back end in a cloud of burning rubber' (Garland, 2000: 18).

The story ends with a tableau, the photo itself, allowing the narrator to end the story abruptly in the moment of 'liberation' in which the different forces held in check during the story – sex, money, violence and the sheer kinetic energy of the car – seem to collide. Ending in stopped animation, the story leaves room for the reader to react to the conclusion without recoil or distress but instead to find a kind of beauty and thrill in the show of destruction. By ending with the pyrotechnics of the crash rather than the gore of its consequences, we are licensed to view events from an artistic point of view rather than a sentimental or ethical one.

Even so, Garland seems to encourage us to find something heroic in the driver through the insertion of an apparent non-sequitur, the story of Williams, the first winner of the Grand Prix who, in wartime, became an undercover agent. Williams' subsequent capture and execution by the Nazis suggest a connection between the nerve of the racing track with a kind of moral courage. This anecdote, inserted just before the crash which ends the story, has the effect of associating the blank figure of the racing driver, known only as the Ferrari, with Williams, and as such his death acquires a quality of martyrdom.

But what, exactly, is the Ferrari a martyr to? We might read it as a kind of *memento mori*, the means by which death punctures the celebration of youth, beauty and money represented by La Rascasse. The simultaneity of the photographer's shot, the girl's climax and the Ferrari's crash creates, however, more than this: a sense of causation, even culpability. The 'Eurotrash' couple's taste for thrill-seeking and transgressive behaviour finds a nihilistic expression in the ultimate car crash, which seems like a kind of morbid wish fulfilment. Henri Lefebvre describes the role of the car in contemporary life as a paradoxical one, both insulating us from stimulation and social contact ('simultaneity without exchange, each element remaining ... tucked away in its shell') yet also seeming to offer relief in the form of violent contact, that is 'taking risks' through dangerous driving (Lefebvre, 2002: 101). Lefebvre argued that dangerous driving was provoked by the stultifying effect of urban capitalist life, offering a 'paltry ration of excitement and hazard... a substitute for eroticism, for adventure....' (Lefebvre, 2002: 101). The result is, Lefebvre argues, a kind of 'psychosis' that drives motorists to both feel detached and to desire violence and collision. The appeal of racing driving might be understood as the same phenomenon by proxy, the business of spectating requiring the racing enthusiast to be passive and still, yet encouraging identification with the dynamism of the drivers who take potentially lethal risks. While racing driving seems to offer 'excitement', 'hazard' and even 'eroticism', Garland's depiction of the 'Eurotrash' world at La Rascasse is one of ostentation and ennui rather than action. It offers a view of a 'slow corner' behind a 'high fence' which is better suited for people-watchers than true racing fanatics (Garland, 2000: 9). The fusing of the girl's climax with the crashing of the car suggests that violence provides an erotic release from the stagnation of La Rascasse.

Finally, however, the role of the photographer, for whom the final tableau is the culmination of his desire for the perfect photograph, raises more nagging questions. While the photographer's narration emphasizes his role as a coolly detached and amoral observer, the story's conclusion provokes us to reconsider whether he is in fact an agent in this scene and, accordingly, whether he bears some moral responsibility. Laura Mulvey's (1999: 383) analysis argued that in film

the male gaze renders the subject passive, since it is the male eyes behind the lens which direct the way we view the subject who is 'styled
accordingly'. In this scene, both the behaviour of the girl and the
speeding car are similarly 'styled' towards the photographer's gaze,
which demands sex appeal, speed and danger.

The question of what kind of moral responsibility the photographer bears his subject echoes the more obviously metafictional question raised in Dyer's 'Skunk', in which the narrator's treatment of
Marie as material for comical anecdote produces a similar unease. In
both stories, the link between the artist and the misfortunes suffered
by his subject is more symbolic than actual and as such the metafictional parable is lightly sketched. Not only this, but it is compromised
by a sense of complicity between narrators and authors. Garland's
prose positively revels in the girl's lurid display of sexuality just as the
lyricism of the final passage seems to celebrate the crash; the comedy
of Dyer's writing finds much to enjoy in the bizarre paranoia of Marie
and the dilemma faced by the story's narrator. Furthermore, the stories refuse closure by ending in a moment of suspended animation:
Garland's with the frozen tableau of the photograph and Dyer's with
the phone ringing, not yet answered, so we cannot be sure if it is news
of Marie's safety or something less reassuring. The effect is thoroughly
in the spirit of the New Puritans collection which, according to its
editors, wishes to recognize an 'ethical reality' (point 9 of the New
Puritan Manifesto) without using story-telling as a means to moralize.

The narrators of these stories are removed from their subjects
twice, not only as artists but also as foreigners. I have argued that for
Dyer and Garland, like Lawrence and Ballard before them, the attraction abroad represents both the desire for experience and the rejection of a life of torpid detachment in Britain. They follow in a tradition in which the traveller has often been compared to the artist, both
products of a self-imposed exile, cultivating detachment as a means
of sharpening their perceptions of a society from which they stand
apart. Like Geoff Dyer's argument that one becomes a 'non-person'
in a hotel, however, these narrators seem detached from their human-
ity: while travel abroad has brought them sensation, they seem further than ever from community or empathy. While Dyer and Garland

have written about travel time and again, they are in a sense both anti-travellers who strike at the heart of the myth of travel as a means of acquiring self-knowledge, spiritual wisdom or cosmopolitan sophistication. In these stories, Dyer and Garland's Englishmen abroad find a kind of adventure and profit from it artistically, but their troubling detachment, linked to their outsider status, undermines the value of their experience. As such, these stories represent, less a cosmopolitan escape from Britishness, but rather a continuity with the concerns of the New Puritans on native soil. It seems that problems of anomie, like our globe-trotting narrators, are not confined by British borders.

Works Cited

Banco, L. M. (2007) 'Trafficking Trips: Drugs and the Anti-Tourist Novels of Hunter S. Thompson and Alex Garland', *Studies in Travel Writing* 11: 127–53.

Banco, L.M. (2009) *Travel and Drugs in Twentieth Century Literature*. London: Routledge.

Blincoe, N. and Thorne, M. (2000) 'Introduction: The Pledge', in N. Blincoe and M. Thorne (eds) *All Hail the New Puritans*, pp. vii–xvii. London: Fourth Estate.

Clark, A. (2000) 'No Dancing, No Music', *London Review of Books*, (2 November), http://www.lrb.co.uk/v22/n21/alex-clark/no-dancing-no-music (consulted May 2011).

Clute, J. (2009) 'J. G. Ballard: Writer whose Dystopian Visions Helped Shape our View of the Modern World', *Independent* (21 April), http://www.independent.co.uk/news/obituaries/jg-ballard-writer-whose-dystopian-visions-helped-shape-our-view-of-the-modern-world-1671634.html (consulted May 2011).

Collini, S. (2007) *Absent Minds: Intellectuals in Britain*. Oxford: Oxford University Press.

Collings, T. and Edworthy, S. (eds) (2002) *The Formula One Years: A Season-by-Season Account of the World's Premier Motor Racing Championship from 1950 to the Present Day*. Glasgow: Carlton Books.

Donaghy, H.J. (ed.) (1992) *Conversations with Graham Greene*. Jackson: University Press of Mississippi.

Dyer, G. (1997) *Out of Sheer Rage*. London: Little, Brown.

Dyer, G. (2000) 'Skunk', in N. Blincoe and M. Thorne (eds) *All Hail the New Puritans*, pp. 70–82. London: Fourth Estate.

Dyer, G. (2010) 'Sex and Hotels', in *Working the Room*, pp. 297–302. Edinburgh: Canongate.

Dyer, G. (2011) 'Sleeping Under Four Stars', (14 May), http://www.nerve.com/content/sleeping-under-four-stars (consulted May 2011).

Garland, A. (2000[1996]) *The Beach*. London: Penguin.

Garland, A. (2000) 'Monaco', in N. Blincoe and M. Thorne (eds) *All Hail the New Puritans*, pp. 9–18. London: Fourth Estate.

Gluckman, R. (1999) 'More Postcards from The Beach', 19 February, http://www.gluckman.com/BeachGarland.html (consulted October 2010).

Hansen, S. (2003) 'A Drug User's Guide to not Writing', (24 February), http://dir.salon.com/story/books/int/2003/02/24/dyer/email.html (consulted May 2011).

Isherwood, C. (1989[1939]) *Goodbye to Berlin*. New York: Random House.

Lefebvre, H. (2002[1971]) *Everyday Life in the Modern World*. London and New York: Continuum.

Levy, A. (2006) *Female Chauvinist Pigs: Women and the Rise of Raunch Culture*. London: Pocket Books.

Mulvey, L. (1999) 'Visual Pleasure and Narrative Cinema', in J. Evans and S. Hall (eds) *Visual Culture: The Reader*, pp. 381–9. London: Sage.

Naughton, J. (2011) 'Britain's Top 300 Intellectuals', *Guardian* (8 May), http://www.guardian.co.uk/culture/2011/may/08/top-300-british-intellectuals (consulted June 2011).

Pratt, M. L. (2008) *Imperial Eyes: Travel Writing and Transculturation*. London: Routledge.

Smith, Z. (2009) Quoted on cover notes of Geoff Dyer, *Geoff in Venice/Death in Varanasi*. Edinburgh: Canongate.

Vale, V. and Juno, A. (1998) *J. G. Ballard*. Hong Kong: V/Search Publications.

Wood, J. (2000) 'Celluloid Junkies', *Guardian*, (16 September), http://www.guardian.co.uk/books/2000/sep/16/fiction.reviews1 (consulted April 2011).

Chapter 7

New Puritanism between Page and Screen
Alex Garland

Sara Martín

1. Garland's (atypical) career: Moving away from the novel

Point two of editors' Nicolas Blincoe and Matt Thorne's smug, impractical ten-point manifesto for the collection *All Hail the New Puritans* reads: 'We are prose writers and recognise that prose is the dominant form of expression. For this reason we shun poetry and poetic licence in all its forms' (Blincoe and Thorne, 2000: ix). Their expanded comments are worth quoting at length. Since poetry is 'less of an influence than film, technology, music or television...' Thorne argues, 'fiction should be focusing on the dominance of visual culture' (Blincoe and Thorne, 2000: ix) in order to supersede it:

> *Nicholas*: Film undeniably enjoys a kind of cultural primacy – at least it did in the twentieth century. Without doubt, this represents a positive challenge, reminding writers that fiction must constantly reinvent itself, as other technologies deliver new ways to tell stories.
>   Yet no matter how much I love films, I believe that prose fiction remains the inspiration for all other kinds of story-telling...

Matt: Fiction is the most immediate form of expression. Anyone who has tried to get a film through to production has probably faced all kinds of compromises that (most of the time) can be avoided in fiction. (Blincoe and Thorne, 2000: ix)

Blincoe and Thorne's manifesto took its inspiration from the Danish 'Dogme 95' manifesto, a call to eschewing the artificiality of cinema in order to make purportedly more 'authentic' films. Cinema casts a long shadow on the anthology as the somewhat mystified editors struggle to suppress the truth: whether poetry or prose, the printed word matters less and less in our adamant audiovisual culture.

Reviewers were quick to grasp this inherent tension. Stressing that the manifesto is just 'Back to Basics (yet Again),' his *Independent* review title, Boyd Tonkin notes that 'The NP editors pay predictable homage to the "cultural primacy" of film narrative (that deeply Victorian invention)' (Tonkin, 2000). As Tonkin points out, a surprising number of characters in the collected short stories 'serve or monitor the audio-visual imperium'. He detects in this a certain conflict between the editor's technophilia and the authors' technophobia, which is traced back to Wordsworth for 'In fact, ambivalence towards hi-tech media lies behind most of back-to-basics crusades since the Romantic era' (Tonkin, 2000). James Wood, on his side, mocks Blincoe and Thorne's state of denial. Calling his *Guardian* review 'Celluloid Junkies,' Wood opens fire by declaring that the manifesto:

> flourishes the possibility of a new kind of fiction, but in fact it represents a kind of hidden shame about literature, *and an embarrassment that fiction is not more like film*. It is really a manifesto for the New Philistinism. (Wood, 2000, emphasis added)

For Wood, and I concur, it is quite transparent that the manifesto 'is really a commercial or pragmatic argument posing as an aesthetic and puritanical argument.' Whereas Dogme 95 was furiously anti-Hollywood, the New Puritans 'really want to embrace Hollywood' (Wood, 2000).

Of the 15 New Puritans, Alex Garland is the one whose career has been most deeply conditioned by this tension between page and screen to the point that it is now impossible to say whether he is a novelist, a screenwriter or both. Worldwide success reached Garland (born: London, 1970) in 2000 thanks to the Hollywood adaptation by Scottish director Danny Boyle of his best-selling novel *The Beach* (1996). By that time, Garland had already published a second novel, *The Tesseract* (1998), later filmed by Oxide Pang Chun (2003). Before publishing his third and, so far, last book, the novella *The Coma* (2004) illustrated by his father Nicholas Garland, Garland had written the hugely successful zombie film *28 Days Later* (2002), also directed by Boyle. He wrote next, in 2005, the screenplay for a film based on the popular computer game series *Halo*, now finally out of development hell. Garland has more recently invested time and talent on the scripts for *Sunshine* (again Boyle, 2007), *Never Let me Go* (Mark Romanek, 2010, from the novel by Kazuo Ishiguro) and *Dredd* (Pete Travis, 2011, from the *2000AD* comic by John Wagner and Carlos Ezquerra).[1]

Add to this heady mix his work as co-writer of the computer game *Enslaved: Odyssey to the West* by Ninja Theory. A gamer himself, Garland explains that games are now at the stimulating stage cinema was in the 1920s and 30s but developing their 'unbelievable potential' at 'a more accelerated pace' (in *Edge* Staff, 2010). This is why he wished to be 'at the coalface ... trying to figure out that potential'. As Garland further contends:

> If games are going to achieve at least one area of their true potential, they need to do a lot of work. They need to involve and respect writers and place them in a particular position within their structure. That, I would also make clear, doesn't necessarily mean me. I'm not ever going to write *Hamlet* or make *Goodfellas*, but my limitations don't stop me from being able to recognise what's true. At some point, there will be someone who's able to do that, and when you combine the immersion and projection of the game experience with that level of characterisation, you're going to have an art form that's obliterating in its impact and importance. (cited in *Edge* Staff, 2010).

In the 21st century Shakespeare, screen and computer game writers are all deemed to be doing the same job: *writing* stories. And why not?

This is what post-modernity does to the writer: the more media appear to write for, the more possibilities materialise for the next *literary* revolution to happen outside the printed page, even in games.

The problem to be solved regards the relative reputation as *literary* means of expression of each medium. The stage and the page combine now with radio and all kinds of screens (cinema, TV, computer ... tablet, smartphone) to increase the number of public platforms for writers. Indeed, the list of novelists turned occasional or habitual screenwriters is immense, whereas in the fields of drama, in which income is even less guaranteed, writers just never limit themselves to the stage. Garland belongs, thus, to a 'tradition' old enough to includes names as diverse as Aldous Huxley, F. Scott Fitzgerald, William Faulkner, Nathaniel West, Raymond Chandler, William Goldman, Richard Price, Michael Tolkin, John Irving, Dennis Lehane, Elmore Leonard, Ian McEwan, Hanif Kureishi, Kazuo Ishiguro, Roddy Doyle, Michael Chabon, Nick Hornby ... What is now changing is the perception that literary writers only write for the screen media for money, a change due not only to well-known cases such as Harold Pinter (Nobel prize winner as a dramatist and first-rate screenwriter), but also to the changing reputation of the screenplay as a *literary* text. Screenplays, which, unlike stage plays, were seldom ever published are now available independently from films. Garland himself has published (with Faber and Faber) those for *28 Days Later, Sunshine,* and *Never Let me Go,* as many as novels he has now in print.

The reputation of cinema screenplays as literary texts has unquestionably benefitted from the work for the screen of revered literary authors, who have carried over to cinema the authorial respect which screenwriters are still denied. TV (and games) are now the new frontier to conquer in view of Hollywood's current disregard of solid writing. The new wave of quality TV has even led to the recent announcement by Salman Rushdie that he is to write an SF TV series, *The Next People,* for the US cable network Showtime. This was, apparently, suggested by his US agents in view of the difficulties met in raising financing for Deepa Mehta's film adaptation of *Midnight Children* (2012), co-scripted by Rushdie himself (Thorpe, 2011). Still fully convinced about the superiority of novels, Rushdie sees nonetheless the advantages for the writer of TV in comparison to cinema. Unlike what happens in movies, where, as Rushdie grumbles, 'the writer is just the servant' (cited in Thorpe, 2011), the writer's name matters in TV as much as in literature. As Rushdie stresses, 'The Sopranos was David Chase, West Wing was Aaron Sorkin' (cited in Thorpe, 2011).

Garland himself has so far written for TV just the episode 'Sunrise' (2009) for the animated series Batman: Black and White, and is quite busy with more cinema projects in pre-production (The Sweeney, Logan's Run). His return to the novel seems, in these circumstances, less than certain. In this he is, arguably, atypical among his generation. Garland's combined writing career is, however, also atypical as it is by no means wholly successful. To begin with, Boyle's version of The Beach was a box-office success thanks to the presence of Leonardo Di Caprio post-Titanic (1997); yet, unlike the novel, the film was not particularly well-received because, as Roger Bowen rightly protests, it 'sanitizes the story for the very culture and age group Garland's novel is at pains to critique' (Bowen, 2007: 55). The film version of The Tesseract simply flopped, which sank further the novel's modest reputation. This is a perverse effect of adaptations, particularly if we consider that Pang Chun's film uses too few plot elements from Garland's novel to really call it an adaptation. The Coma was heavily criticized by reviewers. Garland's original screenplay for 28 Days Later has no doubt given him the high reputation as a (screen)writer he enjoys now, perhaps even above that gained for The Beach, even though this film is not quite a (horror) masterpiece. This reputation has, strangely enough, survived the fiasco that was the pseudo-Solaris sf film Sunshine (2007). Garland himself attributes its box-office 'catastrophe' to the fact that he, director Danny Boyle and producer Andrew Mac Donald overstepped the lower budget zone in which they are 'more comfortable' (in Ehrlich, 2010). Proof of this is that Garland has finally carried out a much cheaper, more personal project: the adaptation of his friend Kazuo Ishiguro's Never Let me Go (2005, Booker Prize short-listed).

David Poland's excellent interview with Ishiguro and Garland explains in just 30 minutes, possibly better than any lengthy volume, how film adaptations are made and how the generational gap between the British writers born in the 1950s and in the 1970s operates. These two friends met when Ishiguro (b. 1955) learned that a piece of dialogue in *The Beach* had been modelled on a scene in his novel *An Artist of the Floating World* (1986). This is significant as Garland, inspired by his father's career, wanted originally to be a comic book artist. 'In fact, the first version of *The Beach*,' Garland admits, 'was a 62 page comic strip (62 pages because Tintin books were always 62 pages)' (cited in Widmyer, 2007). Only his lack of talent for this medium pushed him onto the novel (cited in Leith, 2004). Ishiguro became his main literary referent, whereas Garland became for the older writer a generational referent, as part of the younger generation for whom sf, computer games, TV and comics are indeed part of their writing experience. Both, significantly, enjoy reading graphic novels, which might be the genre on which the literary and the visual best converge. Ishiguro, who clearly admires Garland's screenwriting skills, confesses nonetheless that as a spectator 'I don't like this idea that film is a collaborative effort' (Poland, 2010), preferring to think there's an 'author' communicating with the audience. Ironically, as directors have been absurdly identified as the only 'author' in films, screenwriters are not granted the (literary) credit they deserve. Asked by Poland whether he is concerned that his reputation is suffering for this, Garland candidly answers that what would frustrate him is not having the capability to carry out a project, by which he clearly means a film. Ishiguro comes to his rescue arguing it is all a matter of convention and there's no reason why screenwriters should not be respected, as playwrights are. This sounds, to say the least, unrealistic as screenwriters are under great pressure from directors anxious not to lose their authorial status and from producers anxious to control films.

Today computer games are already, worldwide, much bigger business than movies, whereas, as noted, TV is attracting bigger audiences for quality writing than cinema itself. Bombarded with so many exciting games, TV series and films, even committed readers feel less inclined to read novels. In the field of drama practically all outstanding British playwrights born in the 1960s and 1970s claim to have found their inspiration in cinema (the film *Trainspotting* is often mentioned) not in reading. I very much suspect not only that their novelist peers might make a similar claim but also that they are read by a dwindling readership that might eventually dwindle down to the tiny size of the readership for poetry. Asked about the supposed writer's block ascribed to him in recent years, Garland frankly acknowledges that 'If you are asking were there times when I thought, "Fuck this, I've had enough of writing, I don't like the book world. I don't like most books, even. I don't like sitting on my own in a room for hours on end," then yes, there were loads of times like that' (cited in Adams, 2004). There are still peculiar cases, like that of Nadeem Aslam (b. 1966), who spent 11 years working in anachronistic technological isolation on his dense, beautiful novel *Maps for Lost Lovers* (2004). Yet Garland represents, in my view, a more common trend among the younger (British) writers: use your writing talent whenever it brings the highest projection (not necessarily money) and the greatest creative freedom in the shortest possible time. Note, in any case, that for Garland to become a highly regarded screenwriter he had to start first as a novelist and gain the kind of literary reputation that someone focused only on screenwriting can never achieve due to sheer prejudice. His New Puritanism has led him in the end to prove not that written fiction is equal to any other high-impact audiovisual media but that it is fast becoming just a means for the literary writer to become a rising star in them.

2. Garland's (literary) writing: Not just prose

Garland is often asked whether he prefers writing films or novels. He tends to be evasive – 'I'm not sure I like either better' (cited in Widmyer, 2007) – insisting that both are about 'words serving the function of telling a story, creating characters, integrating themes;' for him, film making tends to be 'more stressful than novel writing, but also more fun' (cited in Widmyer, 2007). Garland candidly grants that writing novels is not always a lonely pursuit and that if *The Beach* had been a screenplay his editor should have received a writing credit for her efforts (Poland, 2010). He stresses that, in any case, 'when I sit down to write a script I'm not planning to write a script, I'm planning to make a film' (cited in Ehrlich, 2010), whereas, logically, when writing a novel the text is the end product.

Similar motifs find an echo across the thin line dividing Garland's scripts and novels: *28 Days Later* and *The Beach*, for instance, connect through their allusions to 'globalization and consumerism' (Annesley, 2004: 568); all his works show 'an obsessive kind of detachment from life, an anxiety about connection' (Adams, 2004), and, according to Garland himself, are coloured by his 'atheist perspective' (cited in Ehrlich, 2010). They are also coloured by an array of influences that, as habitual in writers of his generation, mix non-hierarchically literature with other media. Among his literary influences Garland cites his friend Ishiguro next to Ballard, Salinger, Fenton, Greene, le Carré and Gulag-survivor Valam Shalamov (cited in Widmyer, 2007). His favourite films are the ones most members of his generation would name, from *Alien* to *The Third Man*, mixing sf and horror with the thriller. Garland emphasizes, nonetheless, that he gets 'the confidence to do what I want' from comic book artists – such as Daniel Clowes, Robert Crumb, Chris Ware, Gilbert Hernandez, Peter Bagge, George Herriman and Hergé – rather 'than from any novelists or film-makers' (cited in Widmyer, 2007).

Garland's attraction *and* resistance to being a *literary* novelist first and foremost presents a formidable challenge to any literary critic trying to judge his unusual, irregular career. *The Beach*, rightly called a '"generation-defining" bestseller' (Tayler, 2004), is also 'a terrifically good bad book, impossible to put down even at its silliest' (Tayler, 2004), of the kind that makes young writers' career expectations particularly fragile. Garland opted very intelligently for distancing himself from the novel that gave him the money and the 'launch pad for a working life' but also that '[s]et a precedent I had no interest in following. Created expectations that I was not cut-out to match. Disappointed virtually all of my readers subsequently' (cited in Widmyer, 2007). His wish to remain free from market pressure explains the experimental *literary* fiction of *The Tesseract* and *The Coma*, novels too at odds with *The Beach* and with Garland's film-oriented career to have found the audience they deserve.

As a (print-oriented) writer, Garland is both the perfect New Puritan, since he eschews adorned, poetical prose, and a perfect anti-Puritan, since his work is, nonetheless, intensely poetical in a visual sense. Blincoe and Thorne's manifesto rejects the literary pre-eminence of poetry in favour of prose, as 'great fiction recreates the immediacy and the rhythm of life itself instead of small, frozen movements' (Blincoe and Thorne, 2000: x). This highly questionable statement is flatly contradicted by Garland's own fiction. An example is, precisely, his short story for Blincoe and Thorne's collection, 'Monaco'.[2] Garland depicts an intense, Ballardian moment captured by the stunned photographer protagonist: the image of a Formula 1 Ferrari crashing against the fence of luxury restaurant La Rascasse, dazzled by the view of a narcissistic, teasing Eurotrash beauty masturbating there for the benefit of the camera. The minimalist storyline is just punctuated by comments on the difficulties posed by Monaco's Grand Prix urban circuit along the years. The prose is bare of adjectives and adverbs, polished down to subject and verb with relentless precision and the result is a forceful image that can only be called poetic, in its own dark, cruel erotic sense (with a dash of humour). Despite the florid poetical prose practised by the already mentioned Aslam and other disciples of (post-colonial) writers like Rushdie, or Arundhati Roy, the main trend in contemporary British literary writing seeks, rather, this minimalist, functional prose aimed at eliciting a pristine *visualisation* too often called cinematic when it is actually poetical or simply literary (hence the difficulties to adapt Garland's novels to film). Contemporary British drama, by the way, moves exactly in the same direction, a point often missed but that might explain why Garland's *The Coma* worked well on stage in the production of Marcus Condron's theatre company We Could be Kings for the 2006 Edinburgh fringe festival (Gardner, 2006).

Garland's novels are saturated with this type of unobtrusive prose and intense visualization, elements that help the author construct rather self-contained literary artefacts. This is so even in the case of *The Beach*, which has, however, attracted academic attention, quite reductively, above all in the context of the post-colonial critique of tourism. Lindsey Banco claims that by 'ridiculing tourism, Garland's novel accuses the countercultural 'traveller' of shoring up the same privileged identity with which the hegemonic, vulgar tourist commodifies cultural otherness' (Banco, 2007: 141). Drugs are also found to play a significant role as they 'draw attention to the instability of the authentic/inauthentic and real/imaginary binaries upon which much tourist discourse is based' (Banco, 2007: 145). Law et al. (2007: 146), on the other hand, criticize the exclusion of non-Westerners from the Thai paradise colonized by Western travellers, and in particular the film version for its collusion with 'the western imperial imagination – shaping the desires, cultural expectations and experiences of various sojourners in Southeast Asia'. That the twenty-something English narrator, Richard, can nonchalantly impose from page one 'his Nam and Nintendo-cluttered imagination' (Parry, 1998) onto Thai territory, is a clear sign that Garland is exposing this uncritical, arrogant Western imagination rather than colluding with it. *The Beach*, however, is neither primarily a post-colonial novel, nor a cautionary tale 'about the effects of too many war movies' (Parry, 1998) but a novel about a fairly new literary problem: how to write a literary novel using a narrator in whose cultural background literature plays a decidedly minor role.

Richard, a backpacker of the pre-Internet era in search of the elusive traveller's paradise promised by the Lonely Planet guides, finds it in a remote Thai beach thanks to a map bequeathed to him by a suicidal stranger, calling himself Daffy Duck. Adventure calls, accidental companions are recruited and the mythical island found. Yet, Richard discovers that this is shared in tense balance by hostile Thai drug dealers and a pseudo-hippy community, which he joins, just barely surviving under the leadership of the authoritarian Sally. Predictably, mayhem erupts with Richard's underhand collaboration and paradise is lost, though no significant moral lesson is learned. Bowen (2007: 42) claims that 'Conrad's literary legacy informs *The Beach*' but misses how little relevance *Heart of Darkness* has for Richard (and how, retrospectively, this novel is reformulated by TV series *Lost* and reality show *Survivor*). Highlighting the literary gap between himself and his narrator, Garland (1997: 419) cracks a joke at Richard's expense when he has him fail to recognize Daffy Duck's allusion to 'The horror! The horror!' in their last hallucinated meeting. Mister Duck sighs, dismayed. Garland and Richard may share the 'international language of brands' (Annesley, 2004: 566) and the same 'Eighties vintage' popular culture – 'Atari and Nintendo video games, Airfix models, Tintin and Asterix, David Attenborough's *Life on Earth*, Warner Brothers cartoons, *The Waltons* and *The A-Team*, the film *Zombie Flesh-Eaters*' (Parry, 1998) – shaping the (Western) worldview in *The Beach*. Yet, whereas Garland is a reader of literature, Richard is not (except of Lewis Carroll, apparently, as at one point he feels 'Curiouser and curioser' [Garland, 1997:125]). Banco argues that 'As Thompson does in *Fear and Loathing*, Garland signals his critical stance by calling attention to the constructedness of the text and by undermining his protagonist's authority' (Banco, 2007: 142). This is done precisely by highlighting this crucial difference as regards literary heritage. Richard, after all, feels no artistic impulse to write but the need to make sense of his experiences in Thailand, once back home one year after the events. This ends in failure, as, once written, 'these things' become murkier rather than 'clear' for him (Garland, 1997: 67).

The problem is not only that Richard lacks a literary imagination but that 'as a postmodern subject and chronic cannabis user, [he] not only experiences the [Vietnam] war through film (and as film) but also processes his everyday experience in the same way' (Stephenson, 2005: 375). In narrative terms, 'Richard's mental cinema does not fade away when he reaches *The Beach*; on the contrary, it intensifies' (Stephenson, 2005: 375). Logically, his transparent prose, practically devoid of any attempt at introspection, and his easy-to-follow narrative sequence – split into short episodes rather than proper chapters – result in an effortless film-style visualisation, for Richard's mental-visual codes are Hollywood-based. This is why Parry stresses that this is not a book about South-East Asia, the Vietnam War, travelling or drugs but a book about a narrator fascinated, 'no doubt [like] a large proportion of its many readers' by 'savage, tropical war' (Parry, 1998) that Richard, born in 1974, is too young to have lived except on the screen. This begs the question, of course, of whether Garland's critique addresses specifically young (British) males nostalgic for a military experience of which post-Second World War Europe has deprived them (and which they might not be up to). Leaving this contentious issue aside, what matters in Richard's narrative is that it is representative of his prosaic personality and not of the author's.

Can a prosaic personality generate visual poetry? Not much, beyond brief glimpses in the description of the dreamy beach, the surprising phosphorescent algae that line its rocks or the coveted, unreachable, pretty François. Richard, himself an unreliable narrator, finds, in any case, all means of capturing experience unreliable, wishing for a singular alternative that, ironically, downplays the importance of the visual in the novel:

> I don't keep a travel diary. I did keep a travel diary once, and it was a big mistake. All I remember of that trip is what I bothered to write down. Everything else slipped away, as though my mind felt jilted by my reliance on pen and paper. For exactly the same reason, I don't travel with a camera … If only there were a camera that captured smell. Smells are far more vivid than images. (Garland, 1997: 201)

What may lead a reader again and again to *The Beach*, in my own experience, is Richard's candid, implicit acknowledgement – shared, I believe, by Garland and by most of us, alienated from high culture by post-modernity – that life is banal even at its most extreme and can only be captured by banal narrative codes. When Richard meets Sally and the community, he is, as with too many things in his young (traveller's) life, disappointed. 'It's silly really,' he tells her in justification. 'I think I was expecting an … an ideology or something. A purpose' (Garland, 1997: 96). This aimlessness increases his 'own budding alienation' (Garland, 1997: 243) and vital boredom, or listlessness (Garland, 1997: 254), to the point of driving him, in essence, mad (and murderous) for a while. In the early stages of the novel Richard wonders whether he is alone in never having 'grown out of playing pretend,' simply stating that 'so far there are no signs that I ever will' (Garland, 1997: 33). This is useful to understand how and why he starts projecting his Vietnam movie fantasies onto his disappointing island life, lacking a more substantial literary or high-culture narrative code. A recurring obsession in Garland's work, Richard's telling of his schizophrenic dreams or nightmares, daydreams or hallucinations about Mister Duck (Garland's partial delegate in the text) are crucial to understand the problem. When this Conradian ghost leaves Richard puzzling over what horror he can possibly mean, we realize that neither the depth of Conradian experience nor the density of his poetic prose, designed 'to make you *see*', are viable in the age of trivial backpacking and addictive computer games. They would be ludicrous. Two things stand thus revealed. On the one hand, *The Beach* exudes a certain melancholy since immature, unbookish Richard can by no means be a new Marlow, despite sharing with him the problem of how to make experience accessible to himself and to others. On the other hand, Garland's novel also elicits a nagging suspicion that our audiovisual culture, beginning with Coppola's *Apocalypse Now!* (1979), has exposed Conrad's *Heart of Darkness* as a pretentious, hollow rendering of an experience as preposterous as Richard's. The emperor has no clothes; the upstart can only wear (literary) rags.

Since first novels written in a first-person narrative voice tend to be autobiographical, Garland was too often mistaken by critics and readers for Richard, a predicament that has even undermined his self-confidence as a writer. The relative indifference with which his fine second novel was met is an example of the dangerous typecasting of young writers by unsympathetic, impatient critics and readers, and a key factor in Garland's growing comfort with cinema. As he himself explains:

> I got my fingers burned with *The Tesseract*, because a lot of people said: you've over-reached yourself massively. It almost felt like they were saying: you don't have the intellect to keep up with the things you're trying to talk about; leave it to other people. The problem is, I don't want to stop doing that, because that's what interests me. (cited in Leith, 2004)

In *The Tesseract*, Garland returns to the same place where *The Beach* begins, a seedy hotel where a disoriented young Englishman, the merchant seaman Sean, encounters his fate. Moving from Bangkok to Manila, Garland provides *The Tesseract* with a much more 'vivid sense of place' (Zaitchik, n.d.), though this does not mean this *is* a book about South-East Asia. Undoubtedly, as Parry maintains, '[t]he most absorbing parts of this book are about the ordinary life of the

Philippines and its people, who come off the page with greater depth than the young Westerners in *The Beach*' (Parry, 1998). However, *The Tesseract* is, above all, a subtle narrative experiment in which Garland forces three very different stories to converge, using a fine visual style this time conveyed by his own poetical prose with its 'restrained descriptive capability' (Zaitchik, n.d.). The text is 'neat, near flawless' (Zaitchik, n.d.) and a source, once again, of very potent, haunting images.

The Tesseract 'begins in a recognisable cinematic mode, that of the gangster thriller' (Parry, 1998), yet despite its three interlocking stories, this is not a mere literary descendant of Quentin Tarantino's *Pulp Fiction*. The stories concern first, Sean's panicked attack against the not-too-bright Filipino gangsters he is to re-negotiate a protection deal with; second, the social ascent of a woman doctor, Rosa, from her lowly local hometown to her middle-class Manila suburb, an ascent forced by her mother after ruining Rosa's budding love story with the wrong boy; third, the doctoral research carried on by upper-class psychologist Alfredo on the dreams of two perky street kids, Vicente and Totoy, as a way to overcome his grief over his dead wife. The three stories eventually converge in Rosa's kitchen where Sean's chase by the bumbling surviving gangsters, witnessed by the two fascinated kids, ends tragically.

In *The Tesseract* Garland works, above all, on the interconnection of the three narrative strands. Diverse moments in Sean's final hours are repeated in the other two narratives, giving the book a variety of perspectives but also a singular coherence. If taken in isolation, the harshest images in the novel – Sean's unexpected shooting of the gangsters, his falling into an open sewer, the clumsy killing of a cat, a baby attacked with acid – seem simply lurid but these are all compensated in the text by another array of enticing images suggested by Rosa's sweet teenage beauty, Vincente's attraction for an alien (for him) MacDonald's restaurant and his word-perfect dreams, Alfredo's view of Manila from his exclusive high-rise apartment. This is not meant to be, after all, a two-dimensional 'exotic, speedy thriller' as the back cover blurb promises but, precisely, a literary tesseract, that is to say, a representation of a complex reality we might not immediately grasp by apparently simplified means that, in the end, do provide an impression of that complexity: 'a four-dimensional cube – a hyper-cube – unravelled' (Garland, 2007: 308). In Alfredo's words, meant for Vincente and Totoy:

> A hypercube is a thing you are not equipped to understand.
> You can only understand the tesseract.
> For you and for me, Cente, this is the way it is. We can see the thing unravelled, but not the thing itself. (Garland, 2007: 308)

Later, when Vicente witnesses Sean's brutal execution, he recalls Alfredo's words and concludes that 'Maybe there is nothing here I am meant to understand' (Garland, 2007: 335). As readers, how-ever, since we have access to all the characters' perspectives on the events, we have the privilege of seeing not only the whole hypercube unravelled and understand what has happened but also to grasp that implicit, unrepresentable fourth dimension: how all this impacts on lives so far unconnected, creating an accidental microcosm. Garland works here not so much on a wish to accurately represent Manila but on pure literature, which is what emanates from words used to build a self-contained textuality. This may or may not connect firmly with the real world but provides a fulfilling *reading experience*. This is what *The Beach* partly fails to do, as the reader struggles with his or her sense of the inanity of the story.

Just as he returns to *The Beach* for the beginning of *The Tesseract*, Garland returns to *28 Days Later* for the beginning of his Kafkaesque novella *The Coma*, since in both cases his protagonist awakens from unconsciousness to cope as best as he can with trauma. Garland's mo-tivation to write *The Coma* is reflected in the closing segment of the text, which points back to Alfredo's research in *The Tesseract*. In the words of his protagonist, Carl, as he rises out of his coma:

> Everybody dreams, but nobody has ever managed to tell me what their dream was like. Not so that I really understood what they saw or felt. Every dream that anyone ever had is theirs alone and they never managed to remember it either. Not truly or accurately. Not as it *was*. Our memories and our vocabularies aren't up to the job. (Garland, 2005: unpaginated, emphasis in original)

Technically, Garland cheats as what he narrates is not exactly a dream, or even a coma, but the complex hallucination that the workaholic, lonely Carl suffers between being brutally attacked by a gang of teens on a train for defending a young woman and, presumably, dying as he wakes up. This strongly recalls the plot of Adrian Lynne's *Jacob's Ladder* (1990), written by Bruce Joel Rubin, in which the victim is a Vietnam War veteran, a film of which, surely, Garland must be aware. *The Coma* is increasingly more satisfying in re-reading, as Garland's efforts to make the text as tightly dream-like as possible become apparent. Most reviewers were, however, less than satisfied with Garland's bold attempt to face this challenge. For Scott Lamb, 'Nothing here is fully resolved, and little is fully explained; we are, after all, dealing with a dream world' (Lamb, 2004). Both M. John Harrison and Anthony Quinn insist on attributing *The Coma*'s austere prose to writer's block instead of to its inner oneiric dynamics. For Quinn, 'it might not be fanciful to discern a personal meaning in its tale of a coma victim desperately trying to force his way back into waking life' (Quinn, 2004). For Harrison, the tone is 'spare to the point of anality' (Harrison, 2004). Finding the book 'perfectly readable' thanks to its 'lucid prose,' Muchiko Kakutani criticizes it, nonetheless, as 'ultimately static and unsatisfying as a story and disappointingly slight as a metaphysical meditation about the mysteries of identity and the interface of reality and dreams' (Kakutani, 2004). Intriguingly, Lyn Gardner claims that the stage adaptation, heavily illustrated with video,

> has the edge over the novel itself. It succeeds in making the internal physically manifest, and very unsettling it is too. Watching it, you feel as if you are in a terrible dream from which you can't wake up. It turns you inside out. (Gardner, 2006)

I fully agree with Harrison's impression that the 'meaningless specificity' of Carl's first-person narrative generates 'a terse simplicity rather frightening in the world of padded-up books' (Harrison, 2004). The book calls attention to its very existence as such, and it seems to have been written 'to question the novel as a medium in much the same way as [it] questions the act of consciousness' (Harrison, 2004). This might be plain over-reading, but Garland's tale and Garland senior's rather hermetic woodcuts definitely succeed in disquieting the reader, as entering someone else's dreams would do. Again, as happens in short stories, this novella forces the readers not to miss a single word, which, coming from a novelist who started with a 400-page, small print novel is certainly a comment on the need for any novel to justify its length. Whether in despair or in control, Garland is seemingly writing himself out of the novel, trying to invent as he gives it up something else which is truly New Puritan in its minimalism but quite beyond it in its surreal visual poetics.

Notes

1 See Alex Garland's IMDB page at http://www.imdb.com/name/nm0307497/

2 See the analysis by Bianca Leggett in this volume.

Works Cited

Adams, T. (2004) 'Coma Chameleon' (review of *The Coma*), *The Observer*, 27 June, http://www.guardian.co.uk/books/2004/jun/27/fiction.features2 (consulted June 2011).

Annesley, J. (2004) 'Pure Shores: Travel, Consumption, and Alex Garland's *The Beach*', *MFS: Modern Fiction Studies* 50(3): 551–69.

Aslam, N. (2004) *Maps for Lost Lovers*. London: Faber and Faber.

Banco, L. M. (2007) 'Trafficking Trips: Drugs and the Anti-Tourist Novels of Hunter S. Thompson and Alex Garland', *Studies in Travel Writing* 11(2): 127–53.

Blincoe, N. and M. Thorne (2000) 'Introduction: The Pledge', in Blincoe, N. and M. Thorne (eds) *All Hail the New Puritans*, pp. vii–xvii. London: Fourth Estate.

Bowen, R. (2007) 'Journey's End: Conrad as Revenant in Alex Garland's *The Beach*', *Conradiana: A Journal of Joseph Conrad Studies* 39(1): 39–57.

Boyle, D. (dir.) (2000) *The Beach*. Scr J. Hodge. Figment films.

Boyle, D. (dir.) (2002) *28 Days Later*. Scr A. Garland. DNA Films, UK Film Council.

Boyle, D. (dir.) (2007) *Sunshine*. Scr A. Garland. DNA Films, Ingenious Film Partners, MPC.

Chung, O. P. (dir.) (2003) *The Tesseract*. Scr O. P. Chung, P. Neater. Artist Film, Pang Bros.

Edge Staff (2010) 'Interview: Alex Garland – Part One', *Edge*, 4 October, http://www.next-gen.biz/features/interview-alex-garland-part-one (consulted June 2011).

Ehrlich, D. (2010) 'Alex Garland on Religion, Sex and Adapting *Never Let me Go*', *Moviefone*, September 18, http://blog.moviefone.com/2010/09/18/alex-garland-interview-never-let-me-go/?utm_source=twitterfeed&utm_medium=twitter (consulted June 2011).

Gardner, L. (2006) '*The Coma*' (play review), *Guardian*, 22 August, http://www.guardian.co.uk/culture/2006/aug/22/edinburgh2006.edinburghfestival1?INTCMP=SRCH (consulted June 2011).

Garland, A. (1997[1996]) *The Beach*. Harmondsworth: Penguin.

Garland, A. (2007[1998]) *The Tesseract*. Harmondsworth: Penguin.

Garland, A. (2000) 'Monaco', in Blincoe, N. and M. Thorne (eds) *All Hail the New Puritans*, pp. 9–18. London: Fourth Estate.

Garland, A. (2002) *28 Days Later*. London: Faber and Faber.

Garland, A. (2005[2004]) *The Coma*. London: Faber and Faber.

Garland, A. (2007) *Sunshine*. London: Faber and Faber.

Garland, A. (2011) *Never Let Me Go*. London: Faber and Faber.

Harrison, M.J. (2004) '*The Coma* by Alex Garland: From Dream-Scene to Dream-Scene', *Times Literary Supplement* (18 July): 19, available at *Powell's Review-a-Day*, http://www.powells.com/review/2004_07_18.html

Hodges, J. (2000) *The Beach*. London: Faber and Faber.

Kakutani, M. (2004) 'Trying to Define Yourself While Unsure of Reality' (review of *The Coma*), *New York Times*, June 29, http://www.nytimes.com/2004/06/29/books/books-of-the-times-trying-to-define-yourself-while-unsure-of-reality.html?scp=8&sq=alex%20garland&st=cse (consulted June 2011).

Kirby, I. and Fulton, A. (dirs) (2008–9) *Batman: Black and White*, 'Sunrise' (TV episode), A. Garland (screenwriter). Sequence Post, Warner Premiere.

Kristensen, N. (dir.) (2010) *Enslaved: Odyssey to the West*, T. Antoniades and A. Garland (screenwriters), from the Chinese novel *Journey to the West*. Ninja Theory for Namco Bandai Games.

Lamb, S. (2004) '*The Coma* by Alex Garland', *Salon.com*, July 7, http://www.salon.com/books/review/2004/07/07/coma/ (consulted June 2011).

Law, L., T. Bunnell, and C. Ong (2007) '*The Beach*, the Gaze and Film Tourism', *Tourist Studies* 7(2): 141–64.

Leith, S. (2004) 'It Cuts Both Ways' (interview), *Telegraph*, June 14, http://www.telegraph.co.uk/culture/books/3618820/It-cuts-both-ways.html (consulted June 2011).

Lynne, A. (dir.) (1990) *Jacob's Ladder*, B.J. Rubin (screenwriter). Carolco Pictures.

Parry, R.L. (1998) 'Bratpackers' (review of *The Beach* and *The Tesseract*), *London Review of Books* (15 October): 35–6, http://www.lrb.co.uk/v20/n20/richard-lloydparry/bratpackers/print (consulted June 2011).

Poland, D. (2010) '*Never Let Me Go*, Screenwriter Alex Garland & Novelist Kazuo Ishiguro', *MCN videos*, 18 September, available at *Viddler*, http://www.viddler.com/explore/mcnvideos/videos/219/

Quinn, A. (2004) 'Stream of Unconsciousness' (review of *The Coma*), *New York Times*, 4 July, http://www.nytimes.com/2004/07/04/books/stream-of-unconsciousness.html?scp=7&sq=alex%20garland&st=cse (consulted June 2011).

Romanek, M. (dir.) (2011) *Never Let Me Go*, A. Garland (screenwriter), from the novel by K. Ishiguro. DNA Films, Film4, Fox Searchlight Pictures.

Stephenson, W. (2005) 'Island of the Assassins: Cannabis, Spectacle, and Terror in Alex Garland's *The Beach*', *Critique: Studies in Contemporary Fiction* 46(4): 369–81.

Tayler, C. (2004) 'He Woke up and It Was All a Dream' (review of *The Coma*), *Telegraph*, 11 July, http://www.telegraph.co.uk/culture/books/3620479/He-woke-up-and-it-was-all-a-dream.html (consulted June 2011).

Thorpe, V. (2011) 'Salman Rushdie Says TV Dramas Comparable to Novels', *Observer*, 12 June, http://www.guardian.co.uk/books/2011/jun/12/salman-rushdie-write-tv-drama (consulted June 2011).

Tonkin, B. (2000) 'Back to Basics (yet Again)' (review of *All Hail the New Puritans*), *Independent*, 2 October, http://www.independent.co.uk/arts-entertainment/books/news/back-to-basics-yet-again-638112.html (consulted June 2011).

Travis, P. (2011) *Dredd*. Scr A. Garland, from the comic book characters by C. Ezquerra and J. Wagner for the *2000AD* comic *Judge Dredd*. DNA Films, IM Global, Paradise F.X. Corp., Reliance Big Pictures.

Widmyer, D. (2007) 'Novelist To Screenwriter And Back To Novelist' (interview), *The Cult: The Official Chuck Palahniuk Website*, July 30, http://chuckpalahniuk.net/interviews/authors/alex-garland (consulted June 2011).

Wood, J. (2000) 'Celluloid Junkies' (review of *All Hail the New Puritans*), *Guardian*, 16 September, http://www.guardian.co.uk/books/2000/sep/16/fiction.reviews1/ (consulted June 2011).

Zaitchik, A. (n.d.) '*The Tesseract*, by Alex Garland', *Think Magazine*, http://www.think-magazine.com/books/54-fiction/410-the-tesseract-by-alex-garland.htm (consulted June 2011).

CHAPTER 8

CODE-BREAKING, STORY-TELLING AND KNITTING
CHALLENGING THE BOUNDARIES OF FICTION IN
SCARLETT THOMAS' NOVELS

Miriam Borham-Puyal

One of the most obvious concerns of contemporary fiction appears to be the questioning of pop culture and its impact on society and literature alike. The influence of a shallow culture of consumerism not only on the writing of people's selves, but also on the performance of novelists, which must publish in the 'aesthetical market' that develops a two-fold approach to the novel, the aesthetic and the commercial (Childs, 2005: 17), is present in the work of several of the milestones of contemporary fiction written in English. Authors such as Martin Amis or Zadie Smith, in *Money: A Suicide Note* (1984) or *The Autograph Man* (2002) respectively, have questioned a consumerist- and/or celebrity-driven culture, while novelists and critics alike have readily distinguished between the literary and the *popular* novel, the aesthetically or the commercially successful novel, and have often searched for a combination of both.

Scarlett Thomas, as a participant in a challenging literary and cultural manifesto, and even more so as a teacher of creative writing, has obviously invested much time and energy in considering what constitutes the essence of prose fiction and what makes it ground-breaking or the epitome of convention. Having read and taught Aristotle, Chekhov, Tolstoy and Nietzsche, and having been influenced by experimental and metaliterary contemporary authors such as Julian Barnes, she remains particularly conscious of the boundaries established for story-telling, and the ways in which authors can and should subvert them in order to experiment with form and matter. Abandoning her early ascription to genre fiction, her work has progressively become a series of *what ifs*, of scenarios that resemble the thought experiments she so much enjoys, and which playfully challenge the readers' literary expectations. Every novel in her production becomes then a space for riddles and loose-ends that will blow up the limits of fiction and the ways in which it aims to make sense of reality, exploring postmodern issues such as the impossibility for (dis)closure, the 'arbitrariness and subjectivity and transience of signs' (Scott, 1990: 59) or the emphasis on 'discourse as the shaper of human self-definition' (1990: 65), all matters foretold in Barnes' work, for instance.

Thomas' first novels are a trilogy of detective fictions which revolve around a young English scholar, Lily Pascal. Having focused her academic career on the study of crime fiction, in the first book of the series, *Dead Clever* (1998), she is almost accidentally involved in a crime investigation and is forced to act as a detective to solve the brutal murder of an English undergraduate. In this early work –written before the New Puritan manifesto–, Thomas already presents the correlation between life and fiction as a riddle that needs to be solved employing a series of logical patterns or conventions; in Lily's words: 'the riddle belonged firmly in my area of expertise. I spent all my time unpicking books and poems and if anybody could get to the meaning in a series of seemingly unconnected words then it would be someone like me. I'd never thought an interest in literature would have any practical application but suddenly it did' (Thomas, 2003: 110). The natural impulse of *making sense* in literature and life is again emphasised by Lily when she states:

> One of the things that none of my ex-boyfriends could understand about me was the way I liked working out puzzles and riddles, *solving*

> things. One of the main reasons I'd specialised in crime fiction during my MA was my constant need for the conundrum, the whodunnit, the way I always had to work out who the villain was before the end of the book.
>
> There was something about this situation in particular that both intrigued and infuriated me. *Whodunnit?* Was becoming a real question and I wished I knew the answer. It had to make sense and I couldn't resist the challenge of working it out. (Thomas, 2003: 109–10)

Of course, in such formulaic fiction as classic detective stories usually are, the life of characters ends making sense after a series of, ironically, expected plot twists. There is a mystery, a series of questions, which must neatly be answered as the curtain draws for the reader's satisfaction. One need only recall Agatha Christie's popular novels, for instance, in which the final chapter brought the elaborated disclosure of all the mysteries, the intricate answers to all the questions previously posed, leaving readers jaw-dropped as they consider their inability to perceive what in the end seems so obvious while enabling them to close the book with the satisfaction of absolute knowledge. In an interview, Thomas herself complained of the neat pattern that generic fiction set for writers, and asserted that much of her later experimentation came from starting her career writing formulaic fiction, where, in her own words: 'my editor even went so far as to remind me of the "rules" I should be following. I was writing this inauthentic claptrap that was superficially about pain but was really the furthest thing from real pain and confusion' (cited in Mondor, 2007). In her first novel, the need to fit into a narrative pattern results in a far-fetched explanation of the murder(s), which somehow seems to mock that very same necessity.

In a first-person account of her literary career, Thomas adds: 'writing these novels [the Lily Pascale trilogy] … taught me a lot about plotting, but also showed me that formula fiction is a pretty shallow thing to write and that "being published" is not the same as being a real writer' (Thomas, n.d.). This conflict between what it means to be a published and a *real* author, as well as the portrayal of the difficulties of writing a novel that could break the boundaries of formula, recurrently appear throughout her work in the shape of her alter-egos, female writers who spend their time writing for journals or publishing houses that demand popular genre fiction while they struggle to write a novel about 'real pain and confusion'. In her lectures and interviews, Thomas analyses the formulaic story under the light of Aristophanes' famous *The Frogs*, in which Aeschylus attacks Euripides' tragedies stating that they could all revolve around the loss of a bottle of oil and its later recovery; that is, in Thomas' words, formulaic stories, such as her early detective fiction, start 'with a conflict that is later resolved', but 'less formulaic stories, or stories that use a formula to more interesting effect, while they have similar levels of narrative drive, are about something more interesting than losing a bottle of oil' (in Mondor, 2007). It is the latter that Thomas aimed to develop in her subsequent novel, *Bright Young Things* (2001).

This novel, which meant Thomas' recognition as one of the most promising young authors of her generation, commences with the introduction of six different characters who present their perspective of life and who answer a job advertisement which requires 'bright young things' for a 'big project'. After the job interview, they wake up on a deserted island and must work their way through what has happened and why they have been taken there. In this sense, it resembles her previous detective fiction because the narrative drive lies in solving the initial mystery. However, the readers' expectations are challenged when the accustomed conventions of this form of fiction are unobserved. Thomas explains it thus:

> The idea of *Bright Young Things* was always to try to challenge that view of the island-adventure narrative that says you have to have clashing stereotypes (the nun, the hooker, the family man, the psychotic loner, the natural leader, the disturbed young girl etc. etc.), and that the adventure will basically consist of the group arguing, then electing a leader, then planning an escape while the psychotic loner loses it and then tries to kill them all and so on. I pretty much did the opposite of all that in the book. (cited in Purbright, 2005)

More interested in the characters' inner life than in the action, the point of view shifts from one to another, offering the reader the possibility to explore the different approaches or perspectives to the experience they all share, and therefore to develop a greater empathy by this exercise of imagination in which to 'see oneself as an other' becomes a landmark of the contemporary reflection in literature on the new understandings of identity (Childs, 2005: 276–7).

Again, this provides a space to comment on narrative fiction. Narrative patterns, whether in printed form or in the shape of films or soap operas, act as the mould into which *real-life* people try to fit their vision of the world in order to neatly make sense of it. For example, Jamie, a brilliant mathematician who desires to become a heroic figure in the midst of this adventure, already frames the happenings in a book:

> [Jamie] is trying to be scared about the situation, but all he keeps doing is running through scenarios in his head. He sees himself telling people back home what happened, and how he engineered the dramatic escape. He imagines himself on talk shows, selling the book of his experiences, never having to worry about numbers again, except for the staggering sales figures.
>
> He has briefly considered that being kidnapped might not be fun, and that this could (as the book jacket will suggest) end in tragedy, but even that outcome seems better than his actual life. He remembers how adventurous he felt going up to Edinburgh on the sleeper, fantasizing about a Bond Girl mysteriously popping into his compartment and asking for his help. This situation is real, but it's more like Jamie's fantasy world than reality ever has been before. Being held hostage on a remote island is just so much more exciting than what he expected: boring interview, train home, Carla demanding what the hell he thought he was doing, rejection letter. (Thomas, 2001: 63)

Comedy or tragedy, a narrative with a happy or a sad ending, Jamie relates to it by means of what he has learnt to expect from the mass culture he is immersed in: the shy geek becoming a hero and winning the beautiful girl. Nevertheless, it is Jamie himself who denies the final possibility of a conventional conclusion: in a final twist of the plot, he prevents a potential rescue by destroying the note they were to send to sea. The plot and the characters are then left in suspense, literally and figuratively in the middle of nowhere.

The difference with conventional narrative patterns is also emphasized by means of Annie, a precursor of Thomas' later hallmark heroines such as Alice or Ariel. In relation to the mystery surrounding their appearance on the island and their abductor's intentions, Annie asserts:

> the only real thing about the man is the gaps he left, the gaps which people have to fill in with their imaginations, with guesswork and with bits from old horror films and urban myths. In reality, nothing about him or the threat he posed can ever exist outside everyone's imaginations, and that's the way Anne likes it. (Thomas, 2001: 209)

Films or myths, both narratives that humans create to shape and explain reality, thus frame the expectations of the characters about the world and their circumstances. In addition, Annie finds no meaning in a reality that allows the possibility of suffering, so she studies 'suicide, bizarre conspiracy theories, existentialism, nothingness, postmodernism' because, as she reflects, 'when you're born into a world where everything is false, and in which you are never going to make a difference, what other alternative is there than to just skate around on the surface, making pretty patterns?' (Thomas, 2001: 209). For Annie, then, fiction not only makes more sense than life, but is also aesthetically and morally more appealing than the harsh reality:

> [she believes] most videogames have nicer environments than the real world, better moral structures, and certainly a value on life, even if it is just one hundred coins. If you want morals, you'd better look to fiction, because they're not there in the real world. Life's cheap, but as long as death is cheaper, death will always win. (Thomas, 2001: 209)

Fiction, moreover, allows her to disconnect from reality, to create a parallel universe in which happy endings are possible:

> All the fun [Annie] had ... didn't involve anything real. She loved novels with happy endings, and Hollywood films and, of course, soap operas. In these fictions she knew she would find true love and friendship and gossip and excitement, and she could absolutely guarantee that she would get a happy ending. For Anne it was that simple. If life

wasn't going to be like a Hollywood film, there was only one option: fuck life and rent the film instead.

Annie always makes sure that she never watches war films, never reads a book with a sad ending, never tunes in to charity events … and hardy ever watches the news. When her aunt got cancer, she just tuned her out. She enjoys illness only if it is abstracted; if it happens to a stranger or a minor character on TV. Good characters always re-cover from illnesses anyway, and even if the worst does happen, char-acters on TV can be given beautiful deaths which they can more or less choreograph themselves. They can say the right last words, leave the right will, and make everyone they leave behind happy. And if someone dies in a soap, you usually get a new character to replace them. (Thomas, 2001: 292–3)

Annie is also a product of mass pop culture: following in the steps of the New Puritan's manifesto, Thomas details through her characters' voices contemporary brands, commercials, or even soap operas, and how they delimit people's lives in a fictional pattern of who and how should certain people be or act. As will happen in later novels, Thom-as introduces the idea of a video game that imitates reality, ironically called *Life*. Designed by Annie, it allows *living* through the player's avatar with the advantage of always being in control of the action, much in the same way as the popular *Sims* game does. The charac-ter, then, becomes author in control of another layer of the narrative, which may or may not be inscribed into the norms of conventional life narratives.

With its exploration of the influence of contemporary pop culture on people, *Bright Young Things* became the first of another trilogy: the 'Postmodernism is Rubbish' trilogy, in Thomas' own words, which aimed 'to explore what it means to be trapped in a culture where your identity is defined by pop culture' (Thomas, n.d.). In her next novel, *Going Out* (2002), Thomas will more deeply cultivate the idea of en-trapment within a culture, while she continues to develop the notion of the tendency in fiction to provide the reader with a falsely *realistic* and neat plotting in which the conflict is set and resolved. Luke, the main character, has a rare allergy to the sun which has prevented him from ever venturing outside his home; Julie, on the other hand, lives in constant fear of death and would rather live a neat but entrapped life. Luke's perception of the world is mediated by the books he reads and the shows he watches; Julie's is by the messages of an increasingly paranoid society obsessed with everlasting youth and health. Although the focalization shifts from Luke to Julie and vice versa, it is her voice which is heard throughout most of the novel. A lover of mathematics, puzzles, and paradoxes, she reflects on the possibility of actually living when you are trapped in a limited narrative frame. Early in the novel, a mouse in a cage triggers the following questions: 'What would you prefer? A comfortable, safe, warm, cosy life in a cage; or an uncertain life of freedom? Julie would choose the cage, she suddenly realises, as long as her cage was safe; and fitted with a computer and modem, say, and satellite TV – and lots and lots of puzzles' (Thomas, 2002: 37–8). These questions, addressed to an implied reader, highlight the way contemporary culture favours the safety of the known and expected patterns; Julie at first embraces them: she failed her exams and renounced a promising career to remain at home and do something safe, such as becoming a waitress. However, as she and her friends start a road trip in order to meet a mysterious healer who may cure Luke, she realizes that she has not been living but entrapping herself in a narrative of fearful stories.

More evident of Thomas' discourse on reality and fiction is Luke's situation; comparing it to Schrödinger's cat paradox, Julie thinks about Luke as another being that has been sealed in a box and wonders:

> Before he left his room, was he alive, dead or fifty per cent alive? Or was he some sort of paradox, a trick, or something imaginary like a number you make up because it answers your impossible question? If something's not there, you invent it. If you don't have an answer, you make one up. Is Luke imaginary? Is his life – full of narrative and perfect fiction – just imaginary? (Thomas, 2002: 345)

In the same manner as Annie, Luke only sees the world through the bright eyes of soap operas and reality shows, of films and commercials, those very same forms of fiction which Thomas perceives as reworkings of 'ancient myths' that the story-teller has learnt to repeat *ad nauseam* (in Mondor, 2007), and which are not *real* life, but artificial and implausibly *perfect* narratives which the audience transforms into a frame of reference in order to shape their own culturally-influenced lives.[1]

The fiction which aims to be artificially satisfying by providing a detailed explanation of all the questions posed at the beginning is mocked in the healer's *cure* for Julie's and Luke's disorders: Julie receives mundane advice about everyday healthy habits and a short tale which consists of more questions, while Luke is told that the answer is inside him. Other characters wander through the narrative and their story is also left in suspense: one character remains in the forest to become a witch, others decide to travel abroad and just walk away without looking back or reappearing again. The explanation comes with a final quotation extracted from Baum's *The Wonderful Wizard of Oz*: if Dorothy had known her magic shoes could carry her home, she would not have started a wonderful journey that gave a brain, a heart and bravery to the scarecrow, the woodman and the lion, respectively (Thomas, 2002: 357). Once again, fiction is not a place to find the answers to all questions, but a means by which to explore all the interrogations; after all, the journey to Ithaca may prove more enlightening than the actual arrival.

This fascination for the human need to find answers, together with the dangers of pop culture and the responsibility of the writer in the face of them are more deeply explored in her following novel, *PopCo* (2004), which culminates the trilogy and which inaugurates Thomas' most challenging and characteristic style of plotting. The novel's heroine is Alice Butler, a young creative of a toy company and granddaughter of two renowned cryptologists, described as a 'subversively smart girl in our commercial-soaked world who grows from recluse orphan to burgeoning vigilante, buttressed by mystery, codes, math and the sense her grandparents gave her that she could save the world' (cited in Mondor, 2007). After mysteriously receiving a series of encrypted messages, she joins a secret and subversive anti-commercial society, NoCo, and aims to expose the evils of consumerism writing a novel about a toy company, which also includes the story of a young girl aiming to decipher a secret inherited from her grandfather. Alice herself describes her literary project thus:

> I'll make it the kind of book that young or interesting people read and powerful people ignore … I'm going to include all the toys we never made, all the ideas that got scrapped, all the dreams that went wrong. That will be how I'll build up the image of PopCo … And then of course there's the other stuff. Something about a treasure map, and old puzzle … Oh, you'll see when it's done. (Thomas, 2009: 424)

The final chapter, significantly entitled 'Solution', focuses on Alice's writing of her novel, the difficulties of creating something more meaningful than an advertising campaign – that is, of creating a plot as opposed to a formula – of providing answers, and of waving the different elements into a coherent pattern. Alice summarises her authorial frustration in the following terms:

> how can I possibly think of writing a book when I don't have a proper ending? I have the PopCo story to tell (I'm pleased with that name for the company: PopCo. I think it's better than the actual name …) but what's the point of telling the Stevenson/Heath story when it has no end? Nothing about that half of my story seems to have an end. No proof for the Riemann Hypothesis. No solution for the Voynich Manuscript. And the one thing that there is an answer for, well, I know there is an answer, but I don't know it. (Thomas, 2009: 437)

As the reader of Thomas' novel has been expecting the solution to the two plots intertwined in the book, so is Alice's implied reader thought to need those very same answers. The code-breaking is not only relevant for the treasure hunt, but also for what lies under the surface of contemporary society. And, as Thomas has argued, maybe a five-hundred-page book may not, or cannot, provide 'the answer', but it may embody the writer's stance of revealing what is so concealed or so familiar that has become invisible in the readers' eyes (cited in Mondor, 2007). In the end, Alice resolves both mysteries: what pop culture hides, and the secret of the Stevenson/Heath manuscript's message. Thomas' reader is not so fortunate: the identification of the key text to resolve the mystery of the manuscript remains finally hidden. Moreover, the other codes remain unsolved as well; neither fiction nor mathematics provide all answers, sometimes they merely pose questions. In this sense, it is relevant that the fragments of code-breaking and the treasure hunt, the history of the past, are non-focalized and seemingly unnarrated. While this lack of attribution highlights the apparent objectiveness of these fragments, in Thomas' words, it is also written in a style that 'simultaneously claims authority while admitting that not much is known and all else is conjecture' (cited in Mondor, 2007).[2] The reconstruction of Alice's past, how the narrative aims to make sense of her family's experience by giving it a structure, emphasizes that loose ends – such as the text employed by Stevenson to encode his manuscript, or the fact that Alice's father disappears and never returns – are not only possible, but plausible: they are more in accordance with a reality that does not always provides the key to break its code. In this sense, in Thomas' novels, as James Scott has claimed of Barnes' seminal *Flaubert's Parrot* (1984), 'fiction, then, can only mirror conventional reality if it records the endless and rather random ramifying' by which one goes one way or another, 'without ever arriving at a meaningful end or closure' (Scott, 1990: 64).

This has an impact as well on Thomas' narrative technique. She describes *PopCo* as displaying a 'patchwork approach', a complex maze in which the reader 'could really get lost in' (cited in Mondor, 2007). The novel includes digressions on pirates, treasures, videogames, mathematics, codes, spies, recipes, vegetarianism, marketing and greed; it then 'veers from social commentary to wartime reminiscence to piratey adventure', and, more importantly, 'without straying from the author's fine target – capitalism' (Mondor, 2009). While all of these topics, then, connect to the anti-capitalist theme of the novel, they also serve a structural function. This patchwork technique or approach allows the writer to challenge the formulaic fiction of the lost and found bottle of oil, for it consists of writing 'a list of things you are remotely interested in at the moment and then the challenge is to work out a plot that connects all these things. And then another one. And again, until you get it right' (cited in Mondor, 2007). While the employment of a medley of prose genres to deconstruct the boundaries of fiction could be said to resemble some of Barnes' narrative fictions, termed 'trans-generic prose texts' rather than novels (Scott, 1990: 58), what is definitely innovative about Thomas' work is how she carries this formal experimentation to the extreme and still manages to impeccably integrate the different narrative threads into the plot, or even transforms them into the plot itself, hence challenging the conventions of prose fiction. As did other writers before her, Thomas aimed, in her own words, to 'push the novel ... as a form and see a) what it could do and b) how far I could go with it' (cited in Mondor, 2007).

The patchwork technique and the questioning of the possibility of significance and closure continue to be developed in her following novel, *The End of Mr. Y* (2006), almost unanimously considered her masterpiece. This tale's protagonist is another young woman looking for answers: Ariel Manto is a PhD student who is writing her thesis on nineteenth-century thought experiments and on a particular author, Thomas Lumas. Having found his last novel, which is said to be cursed and to have caused the death of its author, she starts a journey to follow in Lumas' footsteps and discover the terrible secret the novel seems to hide. Ingrained in her tale, Thomas now deals with Derrida, Baudrillard's simulacra, the world of academia, quantum physics, homeopathy, and culminates with a journey to the Troposphere, an alternative reality made of language, of thought, in which one may travel from mind to mind. Again, Thomas develops not only a gripping adventure, but a novel where the moments in which the characters dialogue about physics or metaphor are as essential to the story as the thrilling instances of danger.

From its start, the novel wraps itself in an air of doubt, in a description of a modern world that has been left without any certainties. Ariel reflects:

> Maybe that's where human society is now, at the beginning of the twenty-first century: not even wrong. The nineteenth-century crowd were wrong, on the whole, but we're somehow doing worse than that. We're now living with the uncertainty principle and the incompleteness theorem and philosophers who say that the world has become a simulacrum –a copy without an original. We live in a world where nothing may be real; a world of infinite closed systems and particles

that could be doing anything you like (but probably aren't). (Thomas, 2008: 43–4).

Literature, language, thought, give shape to that seemingly meaningless reality. The logic narrative patterns in stories create order in the midst of a metaphysical chaos; words frame experience and plot conventions provide sensible outlines. In Ariel's words,

> I ... wonder if life is as simple as 'there is a book'. But again I think about stories and their logic and wonder if there can be such thing as simply 'there is a book'. Once upon a time there was a book. That makes more sense. There is a book. And then what happens? There is a book and it contains a curse and then you read it and then you die. That's a proper story. (Thomas, 2008: 59)

As Ariel loses herself in her nineteenth-century readings, she pleads to be allowed to be given the chance to become part of a book, to become 'an intertextual being', because 'things in books can't get dirty, while, real life, is ... eventually ... dust', and whereas 'even books become dust', 'thoughts are clean' (Thomas, 2008: 147). In the end Ariel is granted her wish and she becomes part of a world of pure thought. The Troposphere is an extreme metaphor of the relationship between thought and matter that Thomas has dissected throughout her novel. At one point, Lura and Burlem, two academics who have decoded the mystery of Lumas' book before Ariel, explain this connection in the following terms: 'Matter has to be coded before it can mean anything. And thought is what encodes matter. Thought decides where the electron is' (Thomas, 2008: 442). Not only does thought encode matter, it is made from matter itself, hence employing the same code and allowing Lura to state that 'consciousness is also made from the same matter, the two areas that we always think are distinct – the human mind and the world of things – started working together to create, refine and mould each other. Conscious beings started looking at things and deciding what things were and how they worked' (2008: 443).[3] These beings used language to structure that thought and hence to name matter; in logical consequence, in Thomas' novel the conclusion seems to be that 'all stories are thought experiments and all thought experiments are stories', while the 'organising principle of the world of thought is grammar' (Kaveney, 2007). Taking Derrida's assertion that there are no objects, only signs, as starting point, Thomas imagines a world 'where signs and objects are the same thing, and signs create objects' (Thomas, 2010a). The novel thus revolves around 'the connection between language and the material world, and the extend [sic] to which language traps as well as frees us' (Thomas, n.d.). According to the author, it is about the tension 'between materialism and spirituality – between a world of objects that must make sense, and a "world" or dimension beyond that is, or at least should be, unexplainable' (Thomas, 2010a). This unintelligibility is related to one of the cornerstones of the novel: its reflection on the poverty of language and how it aims to dissect things and frame them in narrative. The novel displays how 'language creates the complexity of culture, morality, and ideas of right or wrong' (Thomas, 2010a); as Ariel tells Adam: language makes it all real (Thomas, 2008: 281). However, there is also 'a kind of hell where infinity is harnessed by language, and all that exists is what can be said' (Thomas, 2010a). The end of the novel belongs to an unresolved area between a happy and a tragic ending, between the conventions of comedy and tragedy, for 'Ariel and Adam never escape language and metaphor: they don't find anything absolute at the edge of consciousness, just religious imagery' (Thomas, 2008: 506) and are hence trapped 'inside language; inside a cliché' (Thomas, 2010b). The infinite is then both reflected and entrapped in the finite system of signs, while Ariel, Adam or Lumas, aiming to reach the unattainable and enlarged by that glimpse at infinity, are also enclosed in their own finitude.

The liberating or enslaving nature of language and narrative is more thoroughly considered in Thomas' last novel so far, *Our Tragic Universe* (2010).[4] Originally intended to be entitled 'The Death of the Author', it revolves around Meg, a young author who survives writing literary reviews for a magazine and genre novels, while she attempts to pen her *serious* novel and to escape a hopeless relationship. Focusing on a young writer whose 'obsession with plot' is what keeps her from finishing her novel, Thomas' narrative proves to be the perfect stage for a metaliterary reflection on the possibility of a storyless story and, once again, on the 'unrealistic neatness of western narratives' (Fisher, 2010). Most of the plot consists of long discussions about formulas and the different systems of reference by which humans make sense of reality; that is, how science, religion, or even narrative theory, provide frames to explain the characters' own universe. In so doing, she ascribes to Chekhov's or Tolstoy's theories on the need for a compassionate approach in literature, for a real interest on the motivations which move the characters into action (Thomas, 2010b).

More than any other frame of reference, narrative theory is at the core of Thomas' novel; people are taught to live through stories and myths, and to become the characters they find in fiction. At one point, an aspiring writer states:

> I realised that when someone plays hard to get, they are making themselves into a character in a story, and they choose the story that leads to the outcome they want. If a woman puts a dragon between herself and the hero, it becomes an obstacle to be overcome ... It was like people wanted to put everything in a story because otherwise it wouldn't make any sense. (Thomas, 2010c: 316)

Women often grow up expecting to be princesses, men to be heroes, though there will be fools, maids, godmothers and villains, satisfying and unsatisfying endings. Life is explained in the recurrent *topoi* and characterization of Western narratives and readers approach fiction in all its forms expecting to find neat patterns that will offer a guide to understanding the universe. However, that is not what fiction must necessarily be. Vi, an anthropologist and the greatest advocate of the storyless story, persistently gives voice to that idea:

> Characters in storyless stories, she said, didn't worry about what they wore or said or did. They were Fools stepping over the edge of the cliff on all our behalves, so that we can also step out of the restrictive frame of contemporary Western narrative. Surely, she argued, we should have stories not to tell us how to live and turn our lives into copies of stories, but to *prevent* us from having to fictionalise ourselves ... Perhaps Tricksters, the characters you're not supposed to identify with, are in the end much more interesting role models than the princes and princesses of fairy tales, and the characters in American sitcoms

that only exist in order to make us feel that we should be perfect, like them. (Thomas, 2010c: 389)

Thomas epitomizes then the attack to conventional cultural and literary narratives she has developed throughout her previous works. Instead of *perfect* characters or plots, she creates engaging anti-princesses who are as much concerned with plucking their eyebrows as with physics, and who subvert the traditional plot of marriage and motherhood. She also develops challenging plots that reject easy solutions and that prove that the novel, even with its tightly knitted structures, need not be unoriginal. As Meg asserts:

> You can use conventional structure without letting it take over. You can still find ways of being original – not just in how you use formula, but *actually* original. You can put two new things together, or ask an important question. It's hard, but not impossible. In fact, Chekhov said that writing is all about formulating questions …
>
> The story-structure is just the container. The container might be strong and reliable and familiar, but you can put whatever you like inside it. It's the space that is important. There's no reason why you can't put something unfamiliar in a familiar container. Or lots of unfamiliar things. Or an interesting question. But you can't seal the container at the end … (Thomas, 2010c: 317)

This is precisely what Thomas does. As an author, she places several unfamiliar things in the familiar container of the novel: a mysterious beast, a suicide, a poltergeist, Zen stories, and even includes the perfect metaphor for her own style, knitting. As the novel unfolds, Meg becomes increasingly skilled at knitting, in the same way Thomas has grown as an author who can patch together many different interests in the container of a story. A container that she also refuses to close when the different threads she has created remain unresolved. Once more, Thomas constructs a perfect metaphor for her own novel: the labyrinth that is being built as the novel unfolds, and which is inaugurated at the end of the story. Again in Vi's words:

> Perhaps the Labyrinth tells us why we don't simply read the last pages of books, why we don't hurry through life looking for outcomes all the

time, however many times we are told we should, and that we should be overtaking people, and overcoming things as we go. The Labyrinth doesn't tell us how to live; it shows us how we do live. There is no drama in the centre of the Labyrinth, just a place where you come to rest for a while before you walk the path out again. Perhaps walking the Labyrinth is the path of the storyless story, or perhaps that's just my labyrinth. You will all find your own way, I'm sure, even though to an external observer who hasn't walked the path it will seem to be the same objective experience for everyone. (Thomas, 2010c: 424)

With this last address to both narratees and readers, Thomas evinces, as in her earlier narratives, that the journey is more important than the destination and that the novel can be woven as a fabric full of mystery and originality. Her following novel, provisionally entitled *The Seed Collectors*, for which Thomas has undertaken an MSc in Ethnobotany, promises a ninth work brimming with new codes and conventions to be intertwined with her previous interests ... and to be challenged.

Notes

1 It is interesting to note the similarities with Smith's *The Autograph Man*, which also displays a wide range of references to contemporary culture and which satirically reminds its readers that they are not watching television.

2 This approach to history resembles Barnes' conception of it in his relevant *The History of the World in 10 ½ Chapters* (1989) as an *impersonal* tool not to provide truth, but just to offer facts. For Thomas, the past is open to creative speculation and hence history becomes *story*, a way in which to construct reality and to explain what has happened, moulding events into a narrative structure, which very clearly links with her concern with narrative patterns throughout her whole work. Interestingly, this is also the main theme of Barnes' latest novel, *The Sense of an Ending* (2011), in which memory proves imperfect, a fallible instrument that fills in the gaps and creates a coherent narrative pattern with the fragments it retains; a narrative that can be challenged and transformed.

3 The transformative power of thought which is at the core of the novel has been recurrently pointed out by its reviewers. For instance, Roz Kaveney introduces the novel with a reflection on how 'looking at things in a certain light changes them' which is a way of doing magic, and that

when 'philosophers seek to understand the world, they end up changing it whether they meant it or not'. Kaveney then asserts that 'language as well as magic is a technology of will' (Kaveney, 2007), something Thomas reflects about in her novel. Colleen Mondor, on her part, sees the novel as a tale about 'the collective power of ideas and their ability to be transformative' (Mondor, 2009).

4 Thomas overtly states that her intention in her last novel is 'to examine narrative structures and think whether they free or trap us. Whether narrative takes the infinite and tries to make it finite, or whether it can be the other way around' (Thomas, 2010a), the same theme which is so brilliantly explored in the conclusion of her previous novel.

Works Cited

Childs, P. (2005) *Contemporary Novelists. British Fiction since 1970*. Basingstoke: Palgrave Macmillan.

Fisher, A. (2010) 'Our Tragic Universe by Scarlett Thomas', *The Observer*, May 9, http://guardian.co.uk/books/2010/may/09/our-tragic-universe-book-review (consulted July 2011).

Kaveney, R. (2007) 'The End of Mr. Y, by Scarlett Thomas', *The Independent*, July 13, http://www.independent.co.uk/arts-entertainment/books/reviews/the-end-of-mr-y-by-scarlett-thomas-456977.htlm (consulted July 2011).

Mondor, C. (2007) 'An Interview with Scarlett Thomas'. *Bookslut*, March, URL (consulted July 2011) http://www.bookslut.com/features/2007_03_010799.php

Mondor, C. (2009) 'When Pop Goes Postmodern: Scarlett Thomas'. *Jacket Copy. Books, Authors and All Things Bookish. Los Angeles Times*, June 23, http://latimesblogs.latimes.com/jacketcopy/2009/06/pop-or-postmodern-scarlett-thomas.html (consulted July 2011).

Purbright, J. (2005) 'Scarlett Fever', *3am Magazine*, http://www.3ammagazine.com/litarchives/2005/jun/interview_scarlett_thomas.html (consulted July 2011).

Scott, J.B. (1990) 'Parrots as Paradigms: Infinite Deferral of Meaning in "Flaubert's Parrot"', *Ariel* 21(3): 57–68.

Thomas, S. (n.d.). 'About Scarlett Thomas', *Scarlettthomas.co.uk.*, http://www.scarlettthomas.co.uk/about (consulted July 2011).

Thomas, S. (2003[1998]) *Dead Clever*. Boston, MA: Justin, Charles & Co.

Thomas, S. (2001) *Bright Young Things*. London: Hodder & Stoughton.

Thomas, S. (2002) *Going Out*. London: Fourth Estate.

Thomas, S. (2009[2004]) *PopCo*. Edinburgh: Canongate.

Thomas, S. (2008[2006]) *The End of Mr. Y.* Edinburgh: Canongate.

Thomas, Scarlett (2010a) 'Imagining Heaven and Hell. Talk for Swedenborg Society', *Scarlettthomas.co.uk.*, May 19, http://www.scarlettthomas.co.uk/ archive (consulted July 2011).

Thomas, S. (2010b) 'Introduction to a Reading at University of Kent', *Scarlettthomas.co.uk.*, March 23, http://www.scarlettthomas.co.uk/archive (consulted July 2011).

Thomas, S. (2010c) *Our Tragic Universe*. Edinburgh: Canongate.

CHAPTER 9

'(UN)REALITY BITES'
ENGLISHNESS IN TOBY LITT'S FICTION

Laura Monrós-Gaspar

1. Exploring Toby Litt

Born in 1968 in Ampthill, Bedforshire, Toby Litt is, as Fiona Tolan asserts, 'in many ways a very English writer' (Tolan, 2008: 83). Notwithstanding Litt's scant attention to reading during his early years (MacCrum, 2001), Litt's increasing interest in literature through science fiction in his teens brought him to graduate in English language and literature at Worcester College, Oxford. At the university, Litt experimented with poetry and while teaching English in Prague (1990–2),[1] he got the attention of publishers for three novels which never came out. However, it was only after he attended Malcom Bradbury's creative writing course at the University of East Anglia that Litt seriously turned to fiction. Litt was singled out by Bradbury as a promising young writer when he included Litt's work for the course in his collection *Class Work: The Best of Contemporary Short Fiction* (1995) together with stories by other established writers such as Ian McEwan and Kazuo Ishiguro. Litt's first book of short stories, *Adventures in Capitalism*, was published soon after, in 1996, with mixed reviews in the *Observer* (16 June 1996), the *New Statesman* (30 August 1996) and the *Independent* (29 June 1996) (Malcolm, 2005). As a result of Bradbury's encouragement to write about the present, *Adventures in Capitalism* is rife with a topicality which permeates Litt's prose and constructs his sense of Englishness; a by no means alien experience to the young writers of his generation (Fernández, 2010a: 30–4). Matt Seaton observed in the *Independent on Sunday* that 'There's no doubt that *Adventures in Capitalism* marks the arrival of a fresh satirical voice, full of brio' (Seaton, 1996). Without leaving aside the early satirical tone rehearsed in *Adventures in Capitalism*, Litt's 'brio' soon collapsed the market with *Beatniks* (1997), his first novel. From *Beatniks* to *King Death* (2010), Litt's last published novel up to now, both followers and detractors of this controversial writer have seen him mature into a staple figure of his generation.

In an interview with Fiona Tolan, Litt observed: 'I do subscribe quite a lot to Bloom's "anxiety of influence" as an explanation of how writers relate to one another, so any influences I'm happy to acknowledge are possibly not the ones that have had the biggest effect on me' (cited in Tolan, 2008: 73). Nonetheless, later in the same interview, Litt discusses his association with modernism, postmodernism and, above all, with Henry James.[2] Indeed, many a critic (Flannery, 2005; Hannah, 2007; Laird, 2002) has found echoes of James in Litt's fiction, mostly in *Exhibitionism* (2002) and *Ghost Story* (2004). Furthermore, Litt is the editor of a Penguin edition of Henry James' *The Outcry* and has written the introduction to a modern edition of James' *Notes of a Son and a Brother: Forgotten Adolescent Memoirs*. Yet other critics such as Merritt Moseley argue that Litt's association with Henry James has been amply overstated:

> For some reason (presumably the author's testimony of his dedication to James, along with his recent editorship of two reprints of James's work), the rising young novelist Toby Litt is frequently included in the James gang. Reviews declare that Litt's most recent book is a tribute to James and that he has been 'inspired by James's most popular work, *The Turn of the Screw*. His *Ghost Story* pays homage to this, perhaps the ultimate psychological thriller, although Litt has denied it

is a direct updating.' And well he might deny it ... The resemblances to *The Turn of the Screw* are slight and generic: there is doubt about the existence of supernatural evil, and the plot, skillfully managed, heightens psychological tensions. That's it. We seem to have arrived at a point when linking a book with James is a marketing move, an ironic development considering the Master's own poor record in moving his own books off the shelves. (Moseley, 2005: 300)

Notwithstanding the hostile reviews of some of Litt's works (see below), the truth is that Litt is the only writer of the New Puritans who was included in the Granta listing of 'The Best of Young British Novelists' in 2003 and that he has won himself a considerable reputation in the world of letters.

Various labels that have been attached to Litt's fiction have equally praised and 'undermine[d] the intellectual capacity of his work' (Tolan, 2008: 82–3). 'Chick-lit', 'lad-lit', 'postmodern cool', 'Brit hip-lit' and 'British Bloke Novels' (Tolan, 2008: 75, 82), they all testify to the multifarious nature of Litt's narrative (Wilson, 2006: 106). Litt gets involved in psychological or sociological fiction in *Adventures in Capitalism* (1996), in the *On the Road* genre with *Beatniks*, crime fiction in *Corpsing* (2000) and *King Death*, autobiography in *Ghost Story* and in science fiction in *Journey into Space* (2009). Science fiction is also present in *Exhibitionism*, as well as 'supernatural stories, a piece of pornography, a fable, [and] a story with elements of Gothic fiction' (Malcolm, 2005). Litt himself acknowledges how his writings 'all tend to relate to one or more genres' (cited in Tolan, 2008: 77) and also reflects upon the effects that the genre variation from book to book may have had on his readers. Litt explains that even though 'the changes are such that people that liked the previous [book] may well be put off by the next ...', he hopes that what 'readers enjoy in what I write is that they don't know, as they are going in, what they are going to get' (cited in Tolan, 2008: 78). As Leigh Wilson argues, 'for Litt, the ideal reader, the reader he wants his novels to create, is the reader possessed who cannot put the book down, whose fingers reach early for the turn of the page, who is breathless with expectation as that page turns' (Wilson, 2006: 106). And the means to achieve such uncertainty are satire, metafiction, contemporaneity and genre transgression, which are recurring features in the several genres that Litt draws on. Indeed, as Claire Squires argues:

> Litt first became known for his witty, postmodern deconstructions of modern life, replete with references to the materiality of contemporary British society. In a literary marketplace often criticized for being awash with sprawling historical novels, this contemporaneity is perhaps one of the reasons Litt has acquired such prominence and is thought of as at the vanguard of — if not a new literary movement — at least a new generation of young writers. (Squires, 2003)

Furthermore, Tolan contends that 'England and the nature of Englishness is a significant point of enquiry in Litt's work' (Tolan, 2008: 83). England provides the perfect backdrop for Litt's production: a kind of fiction which seeks to undermine contemporary perceptions of modernity, life, and reality while it pulls together the various threads of the narrative tradition in England.

Great Britain and the modern construction of the nation permeates the stories of contemporary writers such as Julian Barnes, Richard Tromans, Maggie Gee and Charles Buchan, for example, who are interested in gathering evidence about a fragmented and innovative sense of Englishness at the dawn of the millennium (Fernández, 2010a: 27–8). Litt is no exception. The following section will focus on how Toby Litt explores literature by drawing a wide spectrum of (un)reality bites based on controversial topics such as sex, capitalism, violence and social relations. As we shall see, Litt explores the concept of Englishness by deconstructing prevailing assumptions on the semiotics of geographical and national identity. One of Litt's most original contributions is his mapping of the human psyche on a constellation of symbols from icons of modern British consumerism.

2. Exploring England

'If the world would be promiscuously described ...' *Adventures in Capitalism*, Toby Litt's first published collection of short stories, opens with this quotation by Samuel Johnson which encapsulates Litt's concept of modern British fiction. Set against the well-established

tradition of the short fiction of the post-war period, Litt's first contribution to modern narrative contains eighteen stories described by
Tobias Jones as 'surreal journeys beneath the surface of our consumer
lives' through which Litt promiscuously peeps at contemporary Britain (cited in Malcolm, 2005). The stories are divided into two groups,
'Early Capitalism' (the first ten stories of the book) and 'Late Capitalism' (the remaining eight), in which a wide variety of contemporary artifacts become the aesthetic objects which weave the narrative.
'Early Capitalism' deals with the effects of consumerism in England
in the 1990s. 'It Could Have Been Me and It Was', for example, which
opens the book, narrates the life of a middle-aged man who 'in a spirit
of scientific enquiry, [decides] to spend a year and a day believing everything the ads told' him (Litt, 1996: 3). Also, Rebecca Lewellyn,
the 'Boot's Please Use a Basket girl' in the Early Capitalism section
is 'a company policy decision ... a capitalistic device' (Litt, 1996:
63–4).

Adventures in Capitalism was published before the New Labour
government came to power in 1997 and the granting of devolution
to Scotland and Wales, which sparked off a new wave of English nationalism. Within this context, Litt's struggle to repossess the concept
of Englishness in this volume juxtaposes Billy Bragg's inclusive and
cosmopolitan sense of the 'new English': a (de)construction of globalized signs which replace the green rural England of the Wordswor-
thian tradition in a celebration of natural vacuity.[3] The psychological
construction of the characters is dissociated from the educational
and moral power of the English countryside and rests, instead, on
the products of a globalized society. Without the political activism
of Bragg, Litt parodies clichés from the English modern establishment in search of a new and multi-layered England. The conceptual
treatment of objects of consumption such as 'Cadbury's *Twirl*' (Litt,
1996: 5), '*Power Gen*' and '*WeightWatchers*' (Litt, 1996: 7) recurs now
and again in other elements, such as a restaurant chain in 'After Waga-
mama but Mostly Before' (*Adventures in Capitalism*), '*The Archers*', a
radio drama included in *Beatniks*, and the widely filmed London Bor-
ough Market in *King Death* to playfully deconstruct the role of the
lives of the English in modern capitalism. Nostalgia for an idyllic, old,

white England is reflected in 'Mr. Kipling' as a form of madness that, following in the line of Litt's satirical voices, anthropomorphizes the name of the brand of baked goods as a real character: 'a High Anglican [who] takes three sugars in his robust teas, smokes a long cigar, picks apples in the orchard for his Bramley apple pies' and fears the inrush of immigration into his pastoral land (Lang, 2008: 292). Remnants from the past are also traced in cultural icons, such as 'Moriarty', and 'Mimi', from *Exhibitionism*, where D. G. Rossetti and Elizabeth Siddal open the ground for an erotic tale set in London's Highgate Cemetery.

Adventures in Capitalism paved the way for Nicolas Blincoe and Matt Thorne's 'Pledge' in the 2000 anthology *All Hail the New Puritans* which demanded from authors linguistic simplicity and a recognizable reality. Litt contributed to this anthology with 'The Puritans', a short story subsequently republished in the 'Sex' section of the collection *Exhibitionism* as 'The New Puritans'. *Exhibitionism*, Litt's second book of short stories, crackles with metalinguistic references and with an autopsy-like description of sex, modern life and psychology.[4] *Exhibitionism* is probably Litt's most deconstructive book. Narrators fluctuate from the first to the second and third person (Malcolm, 2005); genres vary from elements of gothic to science fiction and sociological texts. Furthermore, Litt's use of language becomes more playful and the titles of the stories and the discourse of the characters are thoughtfully arranged to disrupt the reader's expectations.[5] Reflections on the concept of England focus on the spatial and psychological domain. 'Map-Making Among the Middle Classes', for example, from the 'Sex' section, introduces a recurring topic in Litt's fiction: the delineation of London middle and working classes. To understand the concepts of England and Englishness since 1945, Brannigan (2007: 199) argues, is to 'chart the shift of focus in post-war English rhetoric from glorifying the "extended family" of empire to "blaming the coloured invasion" for England's natural decline'. Litt's awareness of this shift is evident in the range of characters who colour the tapestry of London's white-collar life in his novels and short stories (e.g. Fumiko: Japanese by birth, Californian by upbringing, 'Map-Making…'; Kumiko, from Osaka and Pavel Smid from the Czech Republic, *King Death*).

Life and death, gender relations and allusions to contemporary and easily recognizable referents merge against the backdrop of the city of London in a detection novel which is one of Litt's literary successes: *King Death*. Litt combines his previous efforts to modernize English fiction with the most commercial conventions of crime fiction in this mature and reflexive novel which has not gone unnoticed by the critics (Weston, 2010). Every ingredient, which had been previously rehearsed in earlier works is encompassed in a deep but fluid narrative which keeps the reader in suspense up to its very last pages. Two improvised detectives, Skelton and Kumiko, a couple who split up at the beginning of the novel, lead two parallel investigations on a murder which has allegedly taken place in St Guy's Hospital, London. The two narrative voices develop the plot of the crime while their romance appears as a subplot delineated with considerable structural acumen. The forty chapters of the novel alternate between the two first-person narrators and provide a twofold perspective rife with blank spaces to be filled by the reader. The city of London is the third main character in the novel. Referents from the English middle class ethos, which provide a cultural atlas of modern London are abundant in *King Death*. Furthermore, Litt maps the social landscape of the city with a multiracial set of characters that appear in previous works such as *Hospital* (2007) and *I Play the Drums in a Band Called okay* (2008). The urban setting was earlier evoked in *Corpsing*, Litt's second novel and first foray into crime fiction.[6] Litt's *Corpsing* explores the city of London as the kind of contemporary environment already displayed in *Adventures in Capitalism* and prefigures the cultural geographies of England portrayed in *King Death*. *King Death* is yet another example of Litt's success in moulding a particular concept of Englishness, which provides a new departure for investigating modern identities. Nonetheless, the cultural colours of postmodern England are nowhere more evident than in *Hospital*, where Christian beliefs merge with Vodoo rituals.

Hospital: A Dream Vision is a phantasmagorical and highly satirical novel diametrically opposed to the introspective prose of its predecessor, *Ghost Story*, and even to the highly topical *Adventures in Capitalism, Beatniks* and *deadkidsongs* (2001). Tolan (2008: 85) contends that, 'beginning as a hospital romance and ending as an observation of a world devoid of consequences, *Hospital* moves beyond simple genre subversion and enters a space of pure narrative excess'. Such an excess, as Malcolm explains, was not well received by reviewers; and Baker, from the *Spectator*, argued that,

> At no stage in Hospital does Toby Litt allow you to forget you are reading a novel. Every means by which you might gain access to comfortable narrative territory is blocked. The impossible happens, the hospital is never given a setting, and the dialogue is often (again, one assumes intentionally) oratorical and not the sort of thing a real person would say. (Baker, 2007)

Yet the oratory of the novel is also a satirical struggle between the kaleidoscopic England of the twenty-first century and the violent rural country depicted by Philip Larkin and Ted Hughes. Following in the line of Francis Bacon's obsessive and haunting portrayal of the human body, Litt observes the rawest side of mankind set against the suffocating scenario of present-day England. Men and women are surrounded by a foggy landscape of uncertainty which epitomizes the insularity of the country. The only way out is through the metaphorical obliteration of the building (of England) through the powerful symbol of a tree which serves as a cross-cultural representation of the (re)construction of the universe. Nicola Allen examines Toby Litt's fiction through the lens of Bataille's perception of literature as a cultural mechanism which 'functions as a kind of safety valve for releasing some of the forces repressed by culture' (Allen, 2008: 11). Allen claims that Bataille's perception of a literature of transgression finds an echo in Toby Litt's narrative in the sense that it merges 'intermittent realism in detailed descriptions of place, motivation and authorial concepts' with fantasy and the grotesque (Allen, 2008: 58). Allen's case study is Litt's *deadkidsongs*, however, such an amalgamation is nowhere more evident than in *Hospital*.

Litt's reflections upon religion, life and death are more effectively expressed, however, within the science fiction of *Journey into Space* than with the ludicrous satire in *Hospital*. *Journey into Space* and *King Death* are Litt's best forays into the genres of science and crime fiction. Even though for some reviewers *Journey into Space* does not bring anything new to the genre (Zushi, 2008), the unity of plot and Litt's efforts to bring alienation into both a distorting and poetic language result in a well-written, successful novel. In a narrative replete with expected Orwellian voyeurism, Litt's imagination is more realistic than ever in this scrutiny of the human psyche and the construction of England. Journeying, whether geographical, psychological or both, is a recurring theme in Litt's narrative (see for example *Beatniks, Ghost Story* and *I Play the Drums in a Band Called okay*). More often than not, both Litt's journeys and their results and destinations bring about open questions on the meaning of the lives of the protagonists of his novels, and eventually of mankind. *Journey into Space* is Litt's ultimate approach to the disillusionment, apathy and also renewing vitality which are expressed in his narrative of exploration and discovery.

Journey into Space reimagines the imperial discourse of colonizing Britain to demonstrate that Englishness is not unified but constructed. Using the (pre)texts of travelling and utopias Litt undermines canonical narratives of conquest. Litt adopts Benedict Anderson's concept of *imagined communities* and reflects upon the crippling effects of the construction of Englishness based on the grounds of a longed-for yet unknown past (Easthorpe, 1999: 8–13; Ingelbien, 2004). Concepts such as *belonging, cultural identity* and *emblems of nation-ness* are (de)constructed when we learn about England through the cultural objects preserved by the crew of the *Armenia,* and through Celeste and August's longing descriptions of an unknown yet eulogized motherland. Thus, stylized allusions to the Lake District (Litt, 2009: 24), and also to the Eiffel Tower (Litt, 2009: 120) and the Alhambra (Litt, 2009: 123), for example, come to be extolled allusions to a non-existent Arcadia as befits any account of a nostalgic past.

Another recurring setting in Litt's narrative is the fictionalized version of rural England manifested in *Beatniks, deadkidsongs,* and *Ghost Story. Beatniks* is Litt's first published novel and second book after *Adventures in Capitalism.* The book received mixed reviews: whereas critics such as Isobel Montgomery (*Guardian*) and Alex O'Connell (*The Times*) considered it a classic from the outset, others such as

Christina Patterson (*Guardian*) 'felt it to be "at best mildly amusing and at worst, irritating in extreme"' (cited in Squires, 2003). The topical references in the book involve two geographical spaces that coincide with two cultural geographies: the American Beat generation of the 1960s and the English neo-beatniks of the 1990s. According to Litt: '*Beatniks* is a version of James's "international theme" in reverse: the British innocents go to America, with some idea of an American culture they want to be part of, and then meet with disillusionment when they get there' (cited in Tolan, 2008: 73). The novel is also a reworking of Jack Kerouac's *On the Road* (1957) in the improbable setting of 1990s Ampthill, Litt's hometown. Three characters, Jack, Neal and Mary suffer the effects of nostalgia for an episode of the history of America they never experienced. Their sense of both geographical and chronological displacement is made evident by a playful language that becomes a key feature which characterizes Litt's style throughout. Jack and Neal's Beat pantheon, for example, includes Dylan, Kerouac, Ginsberg, Dean and a choice of words emulating the spirit of the 1960s, like 'chick' (Litt, 1997: 19) or being 'hip' (1997: 48).

Displacement is also a major topic in *Journey into Space*, where the crew in the UNSS *Armenia* speculate upon the future of mankind in a homeland that seems to no longer exist. As one of the characters of *Journey into Space* states: 'The question which keeps returning, in one form or another, is this: *What is the meaning of something which is utterly gone?*' (Litt, 2009: 116). This question permeates other works by the author such as *Beatniks*, 'Map-Making among the Middle-Classes' (from *Exhibitionism*), and *Ghost Story*, which manifest, to a greater or lesser extent, the growing disillusionment of various generations of the English middle classes that Litt portrays. Neal, a main character in *Beatniks*, expresses his feeling of constraint as follows: 'England is such a small island. You drive to the edge, then all you can do is stop. There's nowhere else to go. Unless you keep driving. Unless you go over the edge—off the road—into the sea' (Litt, 1997: 136).

Beatniks reflects and challenges symbolic objects that construct the concept of Englishness as a notional and cultural label during the mid-1990s, where questions of national identity were high on the political agenda.[7] Mary's traditional white nuclear family, which

was forged during the late years of Thatcherism, provides the perfect
backdrop for the quintessential Englishness challenged by the various
others in the novel: the USA in the 1960s, in the 1990s, and a whole
generation of disenchanted youngsters who would soon echo the lyr-
ics of 'Stand Down Margaret' by *The English Beat*.

In an in-depth analysis of the concept of Englishness, Q. D. Leavis
(1983: 307) emphasizes the English interest in people from Chau-
cer to eighteenth-century character writers, William Hogarth and the
Victorian industrial novel. Litt participates in such an enquiry into
the human condition as his narrative abounds with the struggles of
individuals who confront prevailing notions of English society. In
deadkidsongs, for example, Litt moves from the cosmopolitan sophistication of *Corpsing* and returns to the rural England depicted in
Beatniks to examine violence in the 'dark heart of boyhood' (Frehilly,
2001: 55). The novel is set in Midfordshire, in a fictionalized version
of Litt's hometown, Ampthill, in the 1970s, and narrates the story of
a sadistic band of young boys (Andrew, Matthew, Peter and Paul),
which recalls William Golding's *The Lord of The Flies* (1954) without
the isolation of the island (Tolan, 2008: 80). *deadkidsongs* is an experiment with Nature, with social behaviour, violence and tensions
between generations and genders (Squires, 2003), but it is also a narratological experiment. As in *Adventures in Capitalism* and later *Finding Myself* (2003), Litt plays with typography and with the narrative
voice, which in this case is apparently split into the boys' four voices.
Furthermore, the novel excels for providing alternative endings and a
wide range of linguistic registers such as 'elegiac, tourist-brochure descriptions of the English countryside in which Litt treats the pastoral
with both sensitivity and irony' and maps *his* own perception of rural
England (Squires, 2003).

Following *Finding Myself*, Litt continues exploring the English
psyche in *Ghost Story*, a novel about gain and loss, about haunting
and healing.[8] Prefaced with an autobiographical section called 'Story',
'Ghost Story', the second part of the book narrates the process of grief
of a modern young couple who have lost their second baby during the
last stages of pregnancy. The book is dedicated to Leigh Wilson, Toby
Litt's partner at the time who is referred to throughout the first part of

the book, 'Story'. 'Story' is a narration of Litt and Wilson's experience of miscarriage set against the backdrop of English nostalgias, many of which are not their own. Litt's (2005: xxi) metaphorical confrontation with a hare testifies to the sheer weight of the haunting past that is attached to the lives of the couple. Litt approaches that past by mapping symbolic objects of the nation (the weather, the geography, etc.) which serve as the objective correlative of the psychological development of the couple. With regard to the biographical elements of the book, Litt acknowledges that:

> There was a casual link, but it seems to me that link is a much more troubled one than the biographical explanation would have it. Agatha's predicament is very different to the one that was mine. As she appears in the book, there are things that link us, or that interrelate us. But I wanted to give readers the tools to understand that interrelation, and to realize how much mutual haunting was going on. (cited in Tolan, 2008: 81)

Wilson (2006: 112) analyzes her experience of haunting from the perspective of the novel's rhetoric of possession and the reader's responses to it, drawing from her personal attachment to the narrative: 'Toby Litt is my partner. We have a son, Henry, who was born in November 2004. In 2002 I had three miscarriages. In October 2004 Litt published a novel, *Ghost Story*, which was a response to, and an explicit memorializing of, these three lost pregnancies' (Wilson, 2006: 110).

A final trope which deserves attention in an exploration of Litt's concept of Englishness is music. Music is the umbrella under which Litt analyzes the consciousness of the main characters in *Beatniks* and 'HMV', from *Adventures in Capitalism* Neal's breakdown in *Beatniks*, for example, comes when he realizes the impossibility of recreating the 'hip' life of the American 'beats' after 1966, when Bob Dylan had a motorcycle crash. After the crash, Neal claims, 'neither Bob Dylan nor the 1960s will ever be quite the same again' (Litt, 1997: 9). 'HMV' provides the setting for a profound analysis of human relations based on betrayal and isolation. Music is also a main feature in the portrayal of Skelton in *King Death*. In *I Play the Drums in a Band*

Called okay, music is the narrative thread that pulls together the life of Clap, a drummer in a popular Canadian band, *okay*.[9] Furthermore, Litt himself acknowledges the powerful influence of music in his early years as an example of the major cultural impact that bands such as *The Smiths* had on the disillusionment of the younger generations of Thatcherism (Navarro Romero, 2011):

> Me and rock biopics go back a long way. And, right from the beginning, our history has been chequered ... At the age of 12, I wanted nothing more than to be a rock star. The recurrent fantasy was that Dave Gilmour would be taken ill, RSI perhaps, and that I'd be asked to join Pink Floyd. Never mind that I couldn't play a single one of his solos. The show must go on! For me, as for many people, rock biopics are a way of vicariously living out unfulfilled dreams of musical megastardom. Luckily, I found another outlet for these when, ten years ago, I started writing about a fictional Canadian indie band. (Litt, 2007b)

As the narrative unfolds, Litt's playfulness with language and topical references subvert rock-band mythologies and immerse the reader in the rather mundane worries of a middle-aged man, which relates the text to Agatha and Paddy, the main characters in *Ghost Story* and *King Death* (Zushi, 2008).

In a conference held at the Universidad de Almería (Spain) in 2010, Litt argued that 'there are no shortcuts to the sublime; the sublime is the thing that is reached without shortcuts' (Litt, 2011: 46). Indeed, scrutinizing Litt's construction of Englishness under this notion of the sublime means to discover a meticulous and deeply thought-through process of writing which seeks to find a place of its own by struggling against a long-entrenched tradition. Nevertheless, the narrative resulting from that process fluctuates between conservatism and modernity, a dichotomy which has produced a mixed reception of Litt's fiction. The critics who extol Litt's postmodernism stress the various forms in which he transgresses genre boundaries. Indeed, neither Litt's followers nor his detractors have remained impassive to Litt's deconstruction of dominant narrative-plots. Yet a question which remains is the impact of Litt's construction of the notion of Englishness in the fields of sociology and cultural studies. Following in the line of many of his contemporaries (Fernández, 2010b: 43–90), Litt scrutinizes the cultural patterns of late twentieth- and early twenty-first-century England and their response to historical referent points which have coloured the recent social landscape of the country. Without a clear political commitment (Navarro Romero, 2011), Litt mirrors the hidden and grotesque lives of the English in order to unveil their hopes and fears through a set of objective correlatives from everyday consumerism. Mapping out Litt's characters and settings means mapping out the shades of a country which relentlessly pursues its own quest for self-definition.

Acknowledgements

The research carried out for this chapter was funded by project FFI2009-12687-C02-01 of the Ministerio de Ciencia y Tecnología in Spain. I am grateful to Dr. José Francisco Fernández and Dr. Paul Derrick for their insightful comments and suggestions.

Notes

1 Cf. http://www.guardian.co.uk/lifeandstyle/2010/may/23/toby-litt-prague-english-teacher and also http://www.tobylitt.com/translations for a list of translations by Toby Litt of Czech authors.

2 With regard to Henry James, Litt sees the Jamesian element not only in *Ghost Story* (2004) but also in *Beatniks* (1997), 'HMV' and 'The Sunflower', both from *Adventures in Capitalism* (1996), which were submitted to his writing class as 'Two Jamesians' (Tolan, 2008: 73).

3 See Reichl (2004) for a full account of the semiotics of English national identity. See also Álvarez (1997).

4 The sixteen stories in the book are divided into two interspersed sections, 'Sex' and 'And Other Subjects', with eight stories each. *Exhibitionism* includes versions of previously published stories and new ones.

5 E.g.: '"Legends of Porn" (Polly Morphus) Final Shooting Script'; 'Mimi (Both of Her) and Me (Hardly There at All)'; 'Story to be Translated from English into French and then Translated Back (without Reference to the Original)'; and 'Alphabed'. See Doyle (1989) on the use of the English language as a means to construct an English national identity.

6 Scathing reviews on the book focused on two of Litt's characteristic features: topical references and postmodern fragmentation. As Krist argues:

'In a now-familiar postmodern ploy, Litt provides us with a collection of interpolated documents loosely related to the narrative, including Conrad's hospital admissions report, a tabloid news clipping about the shooting and even some specious ad copy from the makers of the crime weapon ... These are supplemented with italicized sections minutely describing the trajectories and anatomical consequences of all six rounds fired ... Faced with such gratuitous embellishments, one can't help thinking of Elmore Leonard's supremely sensible advice to writers: to "leave out the part that readers tend to skip." (Krist, 2002: 8).

7 The novel is set in 1995, when the *New Statesman* published the special supplement *England whose England?* after the riots of a friendly football match between England and Ireland. See Cloonan (1997: 5) for a full account of the concept of Englishness in the pop music of 1995.

8 The book received positive reviews such as Barnacle's (2004).

9 *I Play the Drums in a Band Called okay*, published in 2008 is intertextually linked to *Exhibitionism*, Litt's second book of short stories. Two of the pieces collected in the 'And Other Subjects' section of *Exhibitionism*, 'tourbursting' and 'tourbursting 2', are reintroduced in *I Play...* as two chapters: 'Dog # 1' and 'Lindsay'. As Litt acknowledges, 'Roots' was published as 'tourbursting 3' in *The Talk of the Town* and *Independent*, 'LA' as 'tourbursting 4' in *The Stinging Fly*, 'Yoyo' as 'tourbursting 5' in *Ambit* and *Inculte*, 'Lydia' as 'tourbursting 6' in *Stand*, '333' as 'Girl 333' in *3:AM* and *VLNA*, 'Forest' as 'Tree/Forest' in *Hype Magazine* (Litt, 2008: *Acknowledgements*).

Works Cited

Allen, N. (2008) *Marginality in the Contemporary British Novel*. London: Continuum.

Álvarez, M. A. (1997) 'Alternativas al concepto clásico de *Englishness* en la literatura contemporánea', *EPOS* XIII: 315–327.

Anderson, B. (2006) *Imagined Communities*. London and New York: Verso.

Baker, S. (2007) 'Voodoo, Rape and an Apple Tree', *Spectator,* http://www.spectator.co.uk/books/29022/voodoo-rape-and-an-apple-tree.thtml (consulted May 2011).

Barnacle, H. (2004) 'A Hard Grind', *New Statesman,* http://www.newstatesman.com/200411010048 (consulted May 2011).

Brannigan, J. (2007) *Orwell to the Present: Literature in England, 1945–2000*. Basingstoke and New York: Palgrave Macmillan.

Cloonan, M. (1997) 'State of the Nation: "Englishness", Pop, and Politics in the Mid 1990s', *Popular Music and Society* 21(2): 47–70.

Crumey, A. (2002/3) 'Dot. Com Lite', *Irish Pages* 1(2): 241–5.

Doyle, B. (1989) *English and Englishness*. London: Routledge.

Easthorpe, A. (1999) *Englishness and National Culture*. London: Routledge.

Fernández, J. F. (2010a) 'La narrativa breve en Gran Bretaña', in B. Cantizano, J. F. Fernández, J. R. Ibáñez, E. Jaime and M. Ramírez (eds) *Distancias cortas: el relato breve en Gran Bretaña, Irlanda y Estados Unidos (1995–2005)*, pp. 17–42. Oviedo: Septem Ediciones.

Fernández, J. F. (2010b) 'Panorama del relato corto británico: autores y obras', in B. Cantizano, J. F. Fernández, J. R. Ibáñez, E. Jaime and M. Ramírez (eds) *Distancias cortas: el relato breve en Gran Bretaña, Irlanda y Estados Unidos (1995–2005)*, pp. 49–93. Oviedo: Septem Ediciones.

Flannery, D. (2005) 'The Powers of Apostrophe and the Boundaries of Mourning: Henry James, Alan Hollinghurst, and Toby Litt', *Henry James Review* 26(3): 293–305.

Frehilly, G. (2001) 'Novel of the Week', *New Statesman* 130: 55.

Hannah, D. K. (2007) 'The Private Life, the Public Stage: Henry James in Recent Fiction', *Journal of Modern Literature* 30(3): 70–94.

Holden, W. (2003) 'Hard-Boiled Chick Lit.', *New Statesman*, http://www.newstatesman.com/200306090041 (consulted May 2011).

Ingelbien, R. (2004) 'Imagined Communities/Imagined Solitudes: Versions of Englishness in Postwar Literature', *European Journal of English Studies* 8(2): 159–71.

Krist, G. (2002) 'Dinner, Interrupted: In this Thriller, a Young Londoner Tries to Figure out Who Shot Him and His Ex-Girlfriend', *The New York Times Book Review*, http://www.nytimes.com/2002/01/27/books/dinnerinterrupted.html?pagewanted=all&src=pm (consulted April 2011).

Laird, N. (2002) 'Review of *Exhibitionism*', *Times Literary Supplement* (1 March): 22.

Lang, J.M. (2008) 'Redefining Englishness: British Short Fiction from 1945 to the Present', in C. A. Malcolm and D. Malcolm (eds) *A Companion to the British and Irish Short Story*, pp. 279–93. Oxford: Blackwell Publishing.

Leavis, Q. D. (1983) *Collected Essays: The Englishness of the English Novel*. Cambridge: Cambridge University Press.

Litt, T. (1996) *Adventures in Capitalism*. London: Secker and Warburg.

Litt, T. (1997) *Beatniks. An English Road Movie*. London: Vintage.

Litt, T. (2000) *Corpsing*. London: Hamish Hamilton.

Litt, T. (2001) *deadkidsongs*. London: Hamilton.

Litt, T. (2003[2002]) *Exhibitionism*. London: Penguin.

Litt, T. (2003) *Finding Myself*. London: Hamish Hamilton.

Litt, T. (2005[2004]) *Ghost Story*. London: Penguin.

Litt, T. (2007a) *Hospital. A Dream Vision*. London: Hamish Hamilton.

Litt, T. (2007b) 'Star Gazing: Toby Litt Has Been Obsessed with Rock Biopics since Childhood, But Only this Year Has His Devotion to the Genre Been Rewarded', *New Statesman*, http://www.newstatesman.com/music/2007/12/rock-biopics-review-dylan-film (consulted April 2011).

Litt, T. (2008) *I Play the Drums in a Band Called okay. A Novel in Short Stories*. London: Hamish Hamilton.

Litt, T. (2009) *Journey into Space*. London: Penguin.

Litt, T. (2010) *King Death*. London: Penguin.

Litt, T. (2011) 'The Curse of the Cursor', in J. R. Ibáñez and J. F. Fernández (eds) *A View from the South: Contemporary English and American Studies*, pp. 45–6. Almería: Servicio de Publicaciones de la Universidad de Almería.

Malcolm, D. (2005) 'Toby Litt', in C. A. Malcolm and D. Malcolm (eds.) *British and Irish Short-Fiction Writers, 1945–2000. Dictionary of Literary Biography, Vol. 319*. Literature Resource Center, Detroit: Gale, http://go.galegroup.com/ps/i.do?&id=GALE%7CH1200012690&v=2.1&u=bib_nal&it=r&p=LitRC&sw=w (consulted April 2011).

MacCrum, R. (2001) 'It's a Boy Book', *The Observer*, http://www.guardian.co.uk/books/2001/feb/11/crimebooks.fiction (consulted April 2011).

Moseley, M. (2005) 'Henry James and Novelistic Impersonation', *The Sewanee Review*, 113: 298–308.

Navarro Romero, B. (2011) 'Coming to Terms with 21st Century British Politics: An Interview with Toby Litt', *Journal of English Studies (JES)* 9: 277–86.

Reichl, S. (2004) 'Flying the Flag: the Intricate Semiotics of National Identity', *European Journal of English Studies* 8(2): 205–17.

Seaton, M. (1996) 'Degree Show. *Adventures in Capitalism*', *Independent on Sunday*, http://www.independent.co.uk/arts-entertainment/books/degree-show-1338464.html (consulted April 2011).

Squires, C. (2003) 'Toby Litt', in M. R. Molino (ed.) *Twenty-First-Century British and Irish Novelists. Dictionary of Literary Biography Vol. 267*. Literature Resource Center, Detroit: Gale,http://go.galegroup.com/ps/i.do?&id=GALE%7CH1200010984&v=2.1&u=bib_nal&it=r&p=LitRC&sw=w (consulted April 2011).

Squires, C. (2009) *Marketing Literature. The Making of Contemporary Writing in Britain*. Basingstoke: Palgrave Macmillan.

Tolan, F. (2008) 'Toby Litt', in Ph. Tew, F. Tolan and L. Wilson (eds) *Writers Talk. Conversations with Contemporary British Novelists*, pp. 72–87. London: Continuum.

Weston, G. (2010) 'King Death by Toby Litt', *Guardian,* http://www.guardian.co.uk/books/2010/jun/05/king-death-toby-litt (consulted August 2011).

Wilson, L. (2006) 'Possessing Toby Litt's *Ghost Story*', in Ph. Tew and R. Mengham (eds) *British Fiction Today*, pp. 105–16. London: Continuum.

Zushi, Y. (2008) 'Rock'n'roll dreams', *New Statesman,* http://www.newstatesman.com/books/2008/04/litt-band-clap-okay-play (consulted May 2011).

CHAPTER 10

AFTERWORD

David James

Disruptive, irreverent, internally inconsistent, certainly resistant to critical assimilation – writers of the New Puritan generation were and remain instigators of their own unfinished argument about what New Puritanism itself could be. Shrewdly shunning the privilege of critical retrospection that tempts us to impress coherence on movements appraised in hindsight, this book is the first of its kind to do justice to a group of writers who defy the usual protocols of generic grouping, and who are 'significant', as Paul March-Russell observes in this volume, precisely because they compel us to 'question how literary history is periodized through the use of group identities' (p. 30). In tracing not only the genesis but also legacies of New Puritanism, the essays here testify both to the initial significance of Blincoe and Thorne's intervention in contemporary British scene and to the enduring relevance of their catalogue of commitments. In what follows, I contemplate the very vocabulary we might use to address the nature of that endurance, thereby registering some of the metacritical implications of the insights yielded by this volume as it points to the contradictions and consequences of the New Puritan ethos.

Declarations of newness, of course, often turn out to be more performative than substantive. Such was the case where the original 'New Puritan Manifesto' was concerned, as the epithet of novelty seemed to be one of many tactical gambits played by the editors in the interests of advertising their own contentiousness. As the preceding chapters here rightly imply, while an important part of the New Puritan sensibility seemed premised on its own dissociation from literary heritage, in practice the writing fashioned under its banner actually 'imagined the possibility', as José Francisco Fernández notes, 'of new forms being born of past traditions' (p. 94). Far from being a fatal contradiction, the not-so-new dimensions of New Puritanism may in fact be the reason why we can still legitimately apply it to such figures as Toby Litt and Geoff Dyer, who continue to engage with emblematic moments in the development of postwar fiction – such as those represented by J. G. Ballard and John Berger, to name but two of key 'precursors' with whom Litt and Dyer, respectively, have remained in artistic dialogue. But the affinities of New Puritan values with other twentieth-century precedents extend beyond simple matters of influence; aspects of the movement's anteriority, so to speak, also resonate at a compositional level with an earlier generation, insofar as they echo views of more established writers about the affective, involving capacity of fiction – and, crucially, about the adequacy of current critical discourse for apprehending and accounting for that capacity in terms that do not simply aspire to neutralize its challenges and enchantments.

Consider Toni Morrison (2008: 59), for instance, whose recurrent aim has been 'to have the reader work *with* the author in the construction of the book'.[1] This objective shares Thorne's endorsement of the 'pact' between reader and writer (Blincoe and Thorne, 2000: xv), as well as his accompanying praise of the demands readers face in grasping what is so emotionally compelling about writers who '[s]trip their fiction down to the basics' (Blincoe and Thorne, 2000: vii). Likewise, just as the New Puritan manifesto concluded with the implication that new modes of narrative innovation are best detected by the challenges they pose to reading, so Morrison admits that the reason she aims 'to bring the reader in as co-author or a complicitous person re-

ally stems from my desire to be engaged as a reader myself' (cited in
The World, 2008: 46). That form of intense engagement is defended
and theorized at length in Leigh Wilson's moving meditation on her
partner's novel, *Ghost Story* (2004). For Wilson, Litt's writing not
only invites but also necessitates our involvement and all-consuming
immersion. In so doing, Litt compels us to rethink the interpretive
discourses with which we disseminate the experience of such readerly encounters, without diluting the salience of those encounters
with the sanitised terms of systematic analysis. It is a tendency briefly,
yet pointedly, glossed in *Ghost Story* itself, when we are told that Agatha's first-class degree in English 'had taken away from her, or forced
her to suppress and disguise, any language of passion – which meant
any passion in the language read and any passion in the language she
was allowed to use to discuss it' (Litt, 2005: 78). As Wilson observes,
Litt's work suggests that we should conceptualize how our visceral
interactions with fiction are generated by aspects of form and not
merely by the emotional economy of diegetic events. As such, Litt
requires us to read affectively at the level of articulation and construction, not only at the level of content alone, for works like *Ghost Story*
reveal themselves to be 'possessed by possession beyond character
and theme'. For Wilson, modal conventions also play a key role, as
'familiar gestures and idiosyncrasies of genre seduce the reader', and
in turn 'the use of ends-directed plot (revenge, love story, whodunit)
privileges possession over cognition in the reading experience' (Wilson, 2006: 105–6).

But aside from these generic and structural catalysts for the en-
thralment and immersion of the reader, what is it about narrative
expression itself – that is, at the somewhat different level of register
and idiom – which solicits such involvement? One quality, certainly shared by Garland and exemplified in 'Monaco', is what Bianca
Leggett calls that 'forensic eye for detail' (p. 111). In the case of *Ghost
Story*, descriptive forensics might also be seen as an integral part of
that wider New Puritan goal, as Fernández puts it, to address 'the
quotidian in a prosaic way' (p. 10), to evoke the everyday in a minimalist manner that in itself offers a stylistic correlative to the bare or
seemingly unexceptional domestic surroundings described. Litt's mi-

croscopic yet sympathetic mode of scrutinizing the mundane makes his portrayal of Agatha's agoraphobic depression all the more arresting and poignant – so dramatically unsettling yet at the same time syntactically taut:

> Agatha sat straight-backed in the middle of the sofa, affirming her enthronedness within her own life. She queened it over the world for whole half-hours at a time: it was a good feeling, regality, almost unique, *since*, and what was most marvellous – though she did not marvel, because that would have ended the effect – was that she did not instinctively interrupt herself with guilt.
>
> It was during one of the nights early in this week that Agatha first noticed something unusual about the sound of the waves. When she had been trying to go to sleep at the same time as Paddy, Agatha had often used to lull herself by listening to the very quiet and very distant sound of the soft waves on the pebbly beach. She longed – part of her longed – to go down to the sea itself, but she remembered that even when she had been at its edge in times before, had sat for an hour and stared out across it, or dipped her hand in up to the wrist, or – in summer – swum out beyond the breakers (she was a strong swimmer), even then she had not felt intimate enough with the differing element. (Litt, 2005: 80–81)

To track across these two paragraphs is to move panoramically between two scenes that are not only temporally and spatially different for their own sake, are not only juxtaposed for the purposes of nostalgic reminiscence; rather their nimble contrast reaffirms the pathos of the distinction between the kind of everyday freedoms Agatha used to enjoy and the self-confinement she cannot altogether help herself now from policing. By the same stroke, there is an affective continuity sustained between these scenes – one that arcs over the paragraph break and underpins the episode's modulation between present immobility and the sensual abandonment of 'times before' – a continuity of focalising consciousness achieved by the intensity of Litt's manipulation of narrative perspective. Indeed, although Wilson (2006: 115) attributes the implied voice of *Ghost Story* to an 'omniscient, seemingly detached narrator', one could argue that episodes concerned with Agatha, as here, showcase Litt's nimble use of free indirect style to align us with an unnerving perspective of self-incarceration. Which is to say, it is precisely because Litt refuses the ostensible detachment of a heterodiegetic narrator that our participation in Agatha's situation is so compelling. The presence of free indirect discourse at work is revealed, especially in the first paragraph, by several telltale signs that Agatha is inflecting the diction itself, when neologized adjectives ('enthronedness') and their complementary verbs ('queened') aptly lend verbal form to the mental picture she paints of herself savouring these stately vigils. The second paragraph offers a shift in location and memory, the prolonged recollection of visiting the surf staging a scrutiny of the sea that the reader surmises is partly also a scrutiny of the 'differing element' that has now become her volatile selfhood. Such sequences, at once visually luminous and affectively disconcerting, contribute to Laura Monrós-Gaspar's broader contention about the remapping of identity in Litt's work, since the process of charting his 'characters and settings means mapping out the shades of a country which relentlessly pursues its own quest for self-definition' (p. 178).

With its arresting simulation of psychologically precarious states in everyday environments, *Ghost Story* extends the idiomatically modernist impulse to engage readers in the interior flux of extraordinary minds in seemingly ordinary contexts. In this respect, while Litt's fiction offers an all-consuming reading experience, complementing Blincoe and Thorne's injunction that 'the most subtle and innovative form available to prose writers is always going to be a plot-line' (Blincoe and Thorne, 2000: viii), he also justifies their suggestion that truly 'great fiction recreates the immediacy and rhythm of life itself' (Blincoe and Thorne, 2000: x) – a conjuring act that is played out across the scene from *Ghost Story* we have just read and that is redolent of the modernist attraction to capturing in the very texture of narrative discourse sudden and poignant 'moments of being'. As readers of Woolf's *To the Lighthouse* or *Mrs Dalloway* will recall, such moments give priority to perception over plot, thus seeming – in Litt's case, at least, as an inheritor of this kind of perspectival evocation of interiority – to contradict the New Puritan commitment to 'plot-line'. Discrepancies of this kind do not need noting and rehearsing as critics have done in relation to the New Puritan 'pledges', for it is more productive to observe how vitally and imaginatively figures like Litt have subsequently reconciled such aesthetic contradictions without then giving us reason to dismiss the original manifesto as having no significant bearing on the style or sensibility of fiction written in its wake.

But if such internal tensions between New Puritanism's intentions are there to be embraced – as contributors to this book have done – what does it mean to pinpoint a more coherent and tangible legacy in the work of writers from the generation Blincoe and Thorne originally marshalled, who have since dispersed and diverged from the manifesto's foundational beliefs about the renovation of contemporary fiction? One answer is offered by the recent work of the original volume's most established contributor: Geoff Dyer. Without suggesting that Dyer is still riding the crest of the New Puritan wave, I want to turn to his 2009 novel *Jeff in Venice, Death in Varanasi* as a text that demonstrates what a matured version of New Puritanism might look like. This composite narrative invites us to gauge the prescience of Blincoe and Thorne's (2000: vii) prediction that New Puritanism could mark the 'beginning of a new wave' of literary innovation, '[a] chance to blow the Dinosaurs out of the water'.

Jeff in Venice, Death in Varanasi showcases Dyer's idiosyncratic inventiveness on a number of levels, but first and foremost in its promiscuous use of genre, as the narrative shifts between travelogue, art criticism, and a satirical engagement with masculine desire. The text could thus be aligned with the tactics of Scarlett Thomas who, as Miriam Borham-Puyal neatly summarizes in her chapter, 'places several unfamiliar things in the familiar container of the novel' (p. 160). Dyer's generic plurality in this respect contrasts his style, where things seem more consistent. Rhetorical acrobatics do modulate the register, as we shall see in a moment. When taken as a whole, though, the novel is inflected throughout by what David Mitchell beautifully describes in his cover endorsement as 'Dyer's derelict luminosity'. With such iridescent dereliction, though, comes the potential for bathos, and Dyer deftly presents us with a self-immolating character in a mode of free indirect discourse that appears to know full well when it is taking itself too seriously. With this conceit at work, the novel's manner forever teeters on the threshold of relinquishing its own lyrical introspection – or else alerting us, at least, to the costs of that relinquishment.

One upshot of this self-reflexivity comes in the form of an invitation to the reader to become absorbed in the execution of verbal play – a rather different version of the kind of immersive possession Wilson identified in Litt's work – as Dyer constructs whole scenes through the repetition of nouns or clusters of nouns. As innovations go, this is hardly new. We need only recall Lawrence's recursive adjectives, pronouns and deictics. Such prevalent use of repetition has been 'often misunderstood', as James Wood points out, when in fact it offers 'a good test-case of how D. H. Lawrence tries to capture the trembling stream of existence' (Wood, 2007). In Dyer's novel, the existence in question belongs to the rather world-weary journalist, Jeff, who we follow to Venice for the opening of the Biennale. The scene of prestige and posturing he encounters there in the sweltering heat is both spectacular and predictable. Beneath that beguiling atmosphere for which Venice is so often romanticized, the convention that is the art-world party has a routine of consumption as rigid as a feeding-time at the zoo. Conveying Jeff's awareness of this custom of mass-imbibing, while exploiting its satiric potential, Dyer takes the basic premise of the crowd's anticipation of a long-awaited serving of complimentary risotto and turns it into a motif. In the following sequence, that motif recapitulates and punctuates Jeff's unfolding perception of the scene in ways that are worth quoting at length, revealing how deceptive the simplicity of Dyer's fugue-like arrangement of repetition actually is:

> By the time he arrived there must have been a thousand people stuffed into the garden and hundreds more – the great uninvited – trying to get in. It was as if the government of Venice had fallen and the last helicopters were about to take off from the Guggenheim before the victorious armies of Florence or Rome occupied the city. Invite in hand, he was ushered through the gates by the scrupulously polite security. Inside, everyone was belting back bellinis as usual. The waiters were struggling to cope with the insatiable demand for bellinis. There was barely room to move and around the drinks tables it was mayhem. Jeff had got it into his head that risotto had been promised. He assumed he'd got this idea from the invite, but there was no mention of it there

and, at present, no risotto was in evidence. In view of the numbers, producing risotto was an absurdly ambitious and labour-intensive undertaking, but it seemed that Jeff was not alone in expecting risotto. The risotto and its potential non-appearance was, in fact, the chief topic of conversation in the garden. People were counting on risotto to line their stomachs; a lack of risotto would have a significant impact of their ability to belt back bellinis. (Dyer, 2009: 78)

The verbal waltz here between 'risotto' and 'bellinis' is played out in the idiom of argumentation in its most classical sense. Argumentation involves the systematic reasoning of an idea or, as here, the prospect of an expected outcome. And Dyer mimics that kind of systematicity by aligning repetition with reasoning, allowing Jeff's observations of a scene of growing appetites to be couched in the language of formal logic. With this parody of argumentation, Dyer's clipped narration becomes reminiscent of what Beckett described as his 'syntax of weakness', whose 'incongruities and defections from linguistic propriety', as Laura Salisbury (2005: 83) notes, 'are as amusing, comic, pleasurable – like the tremors and quivers that announce the imminent release of a sneeze – as they are paradoxically troubling'.

The novel's implicit homage to Beckett is manifested in Dyer comic use of linguistic recursion and inversion as Jeff's quest for the risotto reaches its finale. The hubbub of the expectant crowd is temporarily interrupted as an American attaché enters to introduce the Pop Art icon, Ed Ruscha. Yet, the audience, from Jeff's perspective, remain more enticed by rice than Ruscha, and with the US dignitary's speech out of the way, we are told that 'then the doors to the gallery itself opened' (Dyer, 2009: 79), and Dyer's rhetorical fugue resumes: 'This was it! The risotto, obviously, was now being served. There was an amazing stampede as people seized on the idea that the risotto moment was imminent' (Dyer, 2009: 79). However, once 'in the galleries', Jeff finds himself,

> confronted not by vats of creamy risotto but art, paintings and sculptures from the glorious heyday of modernism – Duchamp, Max Ernst, Picasso, Brancusi – when it was impossible to believe that there would come a time when all people cared about was free risotto to mop up

all the free bellinis they'd been swilling in the garden. (Dyer, 2009: 79)

Entertaining though such moments of aesthetic inattentiveness here and elsewhere in the text can be, there is a cautionary tale of distraction that seems all the more pointed in light of Dyer's own art-historical criticism on John Berger and, more recently, on photography in *The Ongoing Moment*. In that later study, he defends a mode of close looking that tries to 'see if *style* could be identified in and by – if it inhered in – content' (Dyer, 2005: 7), a mode of seeing that has a low survival-rate in *Jeff in Venice, Death in Varanasi*, where absentmindedness takes precedence over an sort of aesthetic judgment or reflection.

That tale of inattentiveness may be cautionary, but it is not altogether condemning. And it takes on a more pathetic hue later in the novel, when Jeff's passionate affair with the Californian Laura, whom he met at the first social gathering in Venice, is cut short when she leaves for her pre-planned trip to India. Here Dyer abides by what was 'Rule 8' of the New Puritan manifesto, namely, to 'avoid all improbable or unknowable speculation about the past or the future': this pledge, says Thorne (in an surprising turn of phrase), is 'like a *comforting* pact between the writer and the reader', one that 'stops the writer weighting the odds' and that 'gives the characters a dignity that can be robbed by an omniscient narrator' (Blincoe and Thorne, 2000: xv, emphasis added). The ramifications of 'Rule 8' can be observed in the following sequence that tracks Jeff's self-reflective resignation. Though Dyer's linguistic playfulness is once again in evidence, there is an emotional gravity to the episode that supersedes any stylistic gamesmanship. Indeed, it is the refusal of an omniscient perspective – with its insinuation of authorial diagnosis and indictment – that enables Dyer to preserve the integrity of character, as Jeff's melancholic admissions are focalized by him alone rather than by some external, pathologizing point of view:

> He'd noticed this lately, about drinking and drug-taking. Doing either was like shining a UV light into his brain, illuminating its burned-out circuitry. Over the years great stretches of cognitive processing had been ruined, laid waste. Under normal conditions the full extent of

the damage was hidden from view, but it took only a bit of bingeing to reveal the inner disintegration. A few years from now his brain would be like damaged coral, like brain coral, in fact, brain-damaged coral, lifeless, colourless, dead. Hair you could fix, dye, but the brain ... At the very least he was going to have to start taking supplements: memory stimulants, serotonin boosters, neuron steroids. In the meantime, spying an approaching waiter, he held out his glass, his begging bowl. The act of doing so enabled him to regard his brain troubles in a new, less troubling, more optimistic light. (Dyer, 2009: 146)

Extending the fugue-like elaboration of adjectives, Dyer generates poignancy without having Jeff descend into self-pity. This effect is cultivated not so much semantically (where the diction is straightforward and largely denotative) but by the syntactic compression of one studied reflection giving way to the next:

> When he was young he had prided himself on *being clever*. Walking down the street, not even thinking anything, just walking along like every other moron, he'd had a distinct sense of how *clever* he was. He'd never done anything with that cleverness except write stupid articles and make occasionally clever remarks, most of them not even clever. He just *felt* clever, and it was a good feeling, feeling clever. Now he felt, with equal conviction (and rather more evidence), that he was entering the stupid years. The stupid years complemented the vague years. They went together. The vague years and the stupid years were the same years and they had already started. Well, bring them on. Forgetting everyone's names – as those adverts in the newspapers were always reminding you – was embarrassing, but apart from that, being stupid was fine, like a premonition of enlightenment. (Dyer, 2009: 146, emphasis in original)

The staccato accumulation of Jeff's pithy insights builds toward the distillation of the uncompromising acknowledgment that his sharp years are behind him, if indeed they were ever really his to squander in the first place. Culminating in a tone of crystalline forthrightness, the concision of Dyer's free indirect style preserves for this portrait of Jeff's self-scrutiny the kind of 'dignity' that, for Thorne, was the New Puritan 'rule' he 'like[d] best' (Blincoe and Thorne, 2000: xv).

What does *Jeff in Venice, Death in Varanasi* ultimately amount to, then, as a legatee of New Puritanism? And what might that persistence – if New Puritan commitments *do* recognisably persist in this novel – contribute to our understanding of what novelistic experiment might now mean, not just to Dyer but also to those other similarly polymathic and multi-generic writers of his generation whose work has been explored in this collection? I would suggest that there are two distinct implications arising, one to do with narrative discourse, the other concerning the act of interpretation itself. The former, narratological consequence points beyond the confines of the New Puritan manifesto and the debate about its uneven legacy in twenty-first-century fiction, because Dyer's aim to ensure integrity in depiction and thereby to conserve the dignity of character may be affiliated with a much broader – we might even say, paradigm-shifting – emergence of *sincerity*. As Adam Kelly has detected in writers like David Foster Wallace and Benjamin Kunkel, this new preoccupation with sincerity reveals the refusal by a younger generation of novelists through the 1990s of metafictional self-consciousness, exemplifying as they do the effort to write their way out of postmodernism's indulgence in the parodic examination of representation for its own sake (see Kelly, 2010).

The second, interpretive upshot of Dyer's 'New Puritan' affiliation is best summarized by Nicolas Blincoe himself. Drawing the manifesto to a close, he claims that because 'the stories in this collection are so obviously both new and fantastic, I think it presents a real challenge to the critic to explain just why they work so well' (Blincoe and Thorne, 2000: xvii). This was a credible prophecy. For while Blincoe's assertion sounds presumptuous, perhaps it is New Puritanism's capacity to contradict our critical expectations and vocabularies that remains its most valuable bequest to readers today. As *Jeff in Venice, Death in Varanasi* suggests, the 'pact between the writer and the reader' that New Puritans strive for shouldn't be understood as a 'comforting' one, in Thorne's definition, so much as an active, participatory relationship thanks to which our preconceptions are undermined and our attention is drawn, in turn, to the ethical implications of that representational strive for sincerity. At a time when, in the wake of high theory, scholars are reflecting on the adequacy and possibilities of our own critical lexicon – when they are wondering, as Catherine Belsey (2011: 55) does, whether 'a criticism that continues to privilege realism risks obscuring other genres, imposing arbitrary limits on the recognition of what art can do' – New Puritanism's lasting potential becomes clear. For it aggravates stock responses and compels us instead to find new words for describing why fiction stripped back to its essential ingredients might elicit such enchantment and suspense – the potential, in short, to be the kind of moment in fiction's development that squares up to the very critical models imposed upon it. The generation of onetime New Puritans may have dispersed. But the example they set for investing in a collaborative creative process that can trigger the advent of an alternative critical practice is what turns their intervention from a one-off incident in the history of contemporary fiction into the premise for debating how we apprehend writerly collectives and shared aesthetic values in an age of artistic individuation and celebratory authorship.

Notes

1 Ultimately a coincidence more than a valid comparison, perhaps, but it is nevertheless worth noting the match here between Morrison's modelling of novelistic innovation on the figure of the jazz musician 'who practices and practices and practices in order to invent and to make his art look effortless and graceful' (cited in Schappell, 2008: 81), and Litt's argument that 'Writing as the performed self can best be explained by analogy with music, it is writing-as-jazz. The genius of improvisation is dependent upon the years of hours of practice' (Litt, 2003: 46).

Works Cited

Belsey, C. (2011) *A Future for Criticism*. Oxford: Wiley-Blackwell.

Blincoe, N., and M. Thorne (2000) 'Introduction: The Pledge', in N. Blincoe and M. Thorne (eds) *All Hail the New Puritans*, pp. vii–xvii. London: Fourth Estate.

Dyer, G. (2005) *The Ongoing Moment*. London: Little, Brown.

Dyer, G. (2009) *Jeff in Venice, Death in Varanasi*. Edinburgh: Canongate.

Kelly, Adam (2010) 'David Foster Wallace and the New Sincerity in American Fiction', in David Hering (ed.) *Consider David Foster Wallace: Critical Essays*, pp. 129–44. Austin, TX: SSMG Press.

Litt, T. (2003) 'Writing', *Poetry Review* 93(3): 42–48.

Litt, T. (2005[2004]) *Ghost Story*. London: Penguin.

Morrison, T. (2008[1984]) 'Rootedness: The Ancestor as Foundation', in C. C. Denard (ed.) *What Moves at the Margin: Selected Nonfiction*, pp. 56–64. Jackson: University Press of Mississippi.

Salisbury, L. (2005) 'Beside Oneself: Beckett, Comic Tremor and Solicitude', *Parallax* 11(4): 81–92.

Schappell, E. (2008[2002]) 'Toni Morrison: The Art of Fiction', in C. C. Denard (ed.) *Toni Morrison: Conversations*, pp. 62–90. Jackson: University Press of Mississippi.

Wilson, L. (2006) 'Possessing Toby Litt's *Ghost Story*', in P. Tew and R. Mengham (eds) *British Fiction Today*, pp. 105–116. London: Continuum.

Wood, J. (2007) 'Heavenly Creatures', *Guardian, Review*, 10 March, http://www.guardian.co.uk/books/2007/mar/10/fiction.dhlawrence (consulted January 2012).

World, The (2008[1988]) 'A Bench by the Road: *Beloved*, by Toni Morrison', in C. C. Denard (ed.) *Toni Morrison: Conversations*, pp. 44–50. Jackson: University Press of Mississippi.

INDEX

Index